Eyes and Ears

This essential primary-source reader brings together documents collected over decades of research into security agency tradecraft and Chinese Cold War-era human intelligence. Michael Schoenhals' expert translation of the texts teases out meanings from memoranda, decodes marginal notes from senior officers, and unpacks the hastily scribbled communications of covert assets. Together, these sources trace the resilience of covert human intelligence as an institution, even when faced with revelations of major misconduct and calls for its reform. With editorial introductions providing valuable context, this collection offers an informed interpretation of the domestic recruitment and running of agents that sheds critical new light on Chinese security agencies' intelligence gathering operations and capacity building during the Cold War.

Michael Schoenhals is Professor Emeritus of Chinese at the Centre for Languages and Literature, Lund University. He is the author of *Doing Things with Words in Chinese Politics* (1992), *Mao's Last Revolution* (with Roderick MacFarquhar) (2006), and *Spying for the People: Mao's Secret Agents, 1949–1967* (2013).

Eyes and Ears
Secret Agent Work in Cold War China

Michael Schoenhals
Lund University

Shaftesbury Road, Cambridge CB2 8EA, United Kingdom

One Liberty Plaza, 20th Floor, New York, NY 10006, USA

477 Williamstown Road, Port Melbourne, VIC 3207, Australia

314–321, 3rd Floor, Plot 3, Splendor Forum, Jasola District Centre, New Delhi – 110025, India

103 Penang Road, #05–06/07, Visioncrest Commercial, Singapore 238467

Cambridge University Press is part of Cambridge University Press & Assessment, a department of the University of Cambridge.

We share the University's mission to contribute to society through the pursuit of education, learning and research at the highest international levels of excellence.

www.cambridge.org
Information on this title: www.cambridge.org/9781009604413

DOI: 10.1017/9781009604420

© Michael Schoenhals 2026

This publication is in copyright. Subject to statutory exception and to the provisions of relevant collective licensing agreements, no reproduction of any part may take place without the written permission of Cambridge University Press & Assessment.

When citing this work, please include a reference to the DOI 10.1017/9781009604420

First published 2026

Cover image: Sergey Ryumin / Moment / Getty Images

A catalogue record for this publication is available from the British Library

A Cataloging-in-Publication data record for this book is available from the Library of Congress

ISBN 978-1-009-60441-3 Hardback
ISBN 978-1-009-60438-3 Paperback

Cambridge University Press & Assessment has no responsibility for the persistence or accuracy of URLs for external or third-party internet websites referred to in this publication and does not guarantee that any content on such websites is, or will remain, accurate or appropriate.

For EU product safety concerns, contact us at Calle de José Abascal, 56, 1°, 28003 Madrid, Spain, or email eugpsr@cambridge.org

Contents

List of Figures	*page* viii
Preface	ix
Part I Agent Recruitment	1
Introduction	3
1 The Target's Own Story	5
Part II Capacity Building	13
Introduction	15
2 A Director of Public Security Remembers	19
3 Developing Doctrinal Terminology	31
4 Trial and Error	34
5 Big Brother Dispenses *Operativnyy* Experience	42
Part III Best Practice	61
Introduction	63
6 Agent Files: *Management and Utilisation Regulations*	67
7 Recruitment: One Template and Two Profiles	74
8 Agent Termination	83
9 Tradecraft Dos and Don'ts	90

Part IV From the Agent Work File — 95

    Introduction — 97

10 Raw Intelligence: All Quiet in the Northeast Linen Mill — 101

11 Welfaring Agent 107: 'She Now Has Misgivings …' — 108

12 Tasking Agent 371: Active Measures — 119

13 Debriefing Agent 594: Monitoring Campus Unrest — 130

Part V From the Agent Personal File — 153

    Introduction — 155

14 Operational Brief: On the Recruitment of Yang X — 159

15 Yang X's Offer of Service — 162

16 Private Correspondence Monitored — 164

17 Give and Take: Apologies and a Nanny — 169

18 Agent Validation: Professional and 'Leftist' — 172

19 Declining Performance? A Two-Day Brush-Up Course — 177

Part VI Component Chiefs: Feedback and Direction — 187

    Introduction — 189

20 On a Case Officer's Contact Reports: 'Why Never Anything Negative?' — 191

21 On Courses of Action Proposed — 201

22 Whose Collection Requirements Should Enjoy Priority? — 206

Part VII Crisis Management — 209

    Introduction — 211

23 Agent Work: Findings and Recommendations of an Inquiry — 213

24 Opponents: 'Shitting and Pissing on the Heads of the People' — 217

25 Proponents: 'An Indispensable Operational Resource' — 223

26	The Government Advocates a Return to the *Status Quo Ante*	227
27	Deconfliction: *Provisional Guidelines on Informant Capacity Building*	230
	Glossary	236
	Notes	243
	Index	254

Figures

1	Nationalist military intelligence officer's sworn declaration to serve the Communist Party (1947)	page 2
2	Agent registration form (1950)	14
3	Intelligence registration and processing record (1956)	62
4	Information shared with case officer (1950)	96
5	Drawing on special budget funds to reward an agent (1962)	154
6	A case officer's agent contact report (1963)	188
7	Marshal Ye Jianying's address to a National Public Security Conference (1973)	210

Preface

Eyes and Ears is a collection of primary sources in translation on what American law enforcement calls the development and operation of confidential human sources, British media the recruitment and running of agents, and one critical study by a Canadian academic the work of 'intelligence informers – people who secretly supply information to a domestic state security agency'.[1] It is aimed at students of history whose linguistic comfort zone does not extend beyond the Anglosphere but whose curiosity does, to what the crisp title of a book published in Washington DC some years ago called *Intelligence Elsewhere*.[2]

Public access to primary sources on the operation of sources/agents/ informers by security agencies is rarely regarded by those who control it as in the public's best interest. Consequently, historians who look upon the supremacy of *evidence* as the foundation of our discipline often find research on the subject prohibitively challenging. It invariably involves probing a praxis that includes dissemblance, deception, and concealment among its defining characteristics. State security agencies, in the words of one frustrated British scholar, 'do not exist to serve independent historians', but are themselves served by what two colleagues of his later likened to a 'special security squad of weeders and censors [that] patrols the boundaries of ... [the] official past'.[3] In the carefully censored archival records to which the public may in the end be granted access, historians encounter information preselected and packaged by the very institution we seek to understand.[4] The release of this information entails, among other things, a calculated attempt by that same institution at setting and shaping our research agendas.[5]

Students of present traces of the past troubled by epistemological and methodological concerns like these may well be surprised to discover that *Eyes and Ears* is made up of translated records (dating from 1947–1973) from China, a country not normally associated with open government or freedom of information on what there goes by the name of 'agent work' (*teqing gongzuo*).[6] An explanation is therefore in order: unlike, for example, *The Mitrokhin Archive* – that remarkable book produced by

x   Preface

Cambridge historian Christopher Andrew on the basis of illicitly copied KGB documents 'translated and carefully checked' in advance by officers of Britain's Secret Intelligence Service (SIS) and Security Service (MI5), and US intelligence agencies, and thereafter made available to him 'in an SIS office in both hard copy and on a computer database with sophisticated indexing and search software' – this is not a translation of vetted records shared with the editor behind closed doors by a 'hostile service'.[7] Nor does it stem from a Chinese state declassification initiative. It is merely the product of a determined effort by an outsider to make the most of the fact that when China's security agencies entered the digital era, the security protection they accorded more than half a century-old reams of crumbling paper files on agent work ceased to be all that stringent. With antiquarian booksellers and flea market vendors acting as their middlemen, archivists entrusted with the disposition of such files occasionally ignored the implementation of formal disposition schedules and instead entered into a curious win-win relationship with the history profession by allowing random analogue records slated for destruction to be salvaged, rather than pulped, and sold on the internet and in urban flea markets. It is here that those translated in *Eyes and Ears* have over the years been acquired.

Two Worlds

'A translation is not a direct source', the Italian semiotician Umberto Eco once observed, expanding on the conduct of research, but an instrument analogous to 'a pair of glasses ... a means by which I gain limited access to something that lies outside my range'.[8] What that 'something' amounts to here is a record not in the English language of covert human intelligence (HUMINT) activity, while *limited* access (in addition to signalling, as Eco no doubt meant it to, that some things are irretrievably lost in translation) may be read as a reminder of that record's vastness.

Paradoxically, the more readable a translation – the greater the visual acuity provided by Eco's 'pair of glasses' – the more a reader who knows only the target language may become tempted to assume semantic transparency and here incline to the identification of a common lexicon. No such lexicon exists, however, whereas what does in *Eyes and Ears* are common and therefore 'familiar' *conceptions* that have migrated effortlessly across the language barrier: they include metaphorical references to human assets as instruments and to the process of agent recruitment as cultivation, metonymical characterisations of informants as eyes and ears and of surveillance targets with the help of visual signatures ('the white worker's cap headed north at 10.40 a.m.'), synecdochic use of a part to symbolise a quality occasionally presumed inherent in both intelligence assets *and* targets ('we need to fight poison with poison'), and so on and so forth.

One conception of consequence is omnipresent in the vast record as a whole: that of bifurcation. During the Cold War, it had rendered any discussion of universals, symmetries, correspondences, or analogies on all sides of the iron and bamboo curtains suspect. The motives, purposes, ethics et cetera on that informed intelligence and security on one side were always characterised as incontestably different from what may have been the case on the opposite side. In the summer of 1955, a Soviet intelligence officer in a lecture on agent work took this bifurcation as his narrative point of departure. The fundamental distinction that had to be maintained at all times and in all contexts, he insisted, speaking through an interpreter to a Chinese audience, was that between 'the security agencies of capitalism and our own security agencies. While the purpose of operational activity in capitalist countries is to protect the interests of capitalism and consolidate capitalist rule ... its purpose in our case is to suppress all counter-revolutionary elements, protect the interests of the people and consolidate the People's Democracy.'[9] In the United States, the same bifurcation appeared as the trope of choice in public awareness campaigns and writings like J. Edgar Hoover's 'Communist "New Look": A Study in Duplicity' – the 1956 article in which the director of the FBI identified and denounced what he called the 'double-think, double-talk lexicon of communism' as an example of 'sabotage by semantics'.[10] And in 1957, the Chinese authors of the textbook *Lectures on the Subject of Agent Work* devoted an entire chapter (entitled 'The Concepts of Agent and Agent Work') to what they insisted were *differences in essence* between China's organs of People's Public Security and the intelligence and security agencies of the 'capitalist states (their vassal states included) headed by the United States'.[11]

Half a History

That intelligence officers and perception managers alike should have embraced this bifurcation is perhaps not surprising, given how it facilitates the demonisation of one's enemies. Why historians of the operation of sources/agents/informers by security agencies, on the other hand, should let the same conceptual framework shape their representations of the past is less clear, unless they happen to be former practitioners, in which case the reason may be as simple as the habits of a lifetime being hard to kick.[12] When the home of the Cold War as an organisation of knowledge shifted from political science to the domain of history, however, quite a few scholars in the Anglosphere seized upon conceptual bifurcation when prefiguring their field of study and began to ascribe paradigmatic status exclusively to the development of intelligence communities in 'democratic regimes', while reducing the pasts of their counterparts in 'authoritarian regimes' to a role comparable to that of contrast fluid.[13] This Cold War bifurcation reincarnate – presented as a finding, to advance historical research in a unipolar world – had it that only in the victorious 'West' had modern intelligence communities grown to serve 'policy needs for information', provide 'information support to the decisions of others', and ensure that 'information obtained reached the consumers in government'.[14] In the 'East' their now 'former' namesakes were said to have done nothing of the sort, but evolved 'out of an almost paranoid concern about threats to regime survival', served a purpose that had 'more to do with pursuing and suppressing dissidents and "counter-revolutionaries" than policy', and functioned as 'Soviet-style underpinning architectures of social control and political order'.[15]

By the beginning of the twenty-first century, fluid understandings articulated in this way had gelled into a quasi-coherent whole that saw academics, journalists, and former intelligence practitioners in the Anglosphere embark on an ambitious effort to revisit intelligence's recent past and consider in the present the purposes and consequences of different methodological approaches to its study. In his foreword to a seminal anthology *Journeys in Shadows* that grew out of the effort, British historian Baron Hennessy of Nympsfield insisted in 2004 – on behalf of what he called 'We intelligence scholars' – that 'Our slice of history must be carefully contextualised and fitted into the whole.'[16] How this was to be done was explained in what has since become the anthology's most frequently cited chapter, in which Christopher Andrew (in 2004 concurrent Official Historian of MI5) cautioned against the use of one and the same stock of words to represent empirical evidence in two distinct worlds, given the potential of language to obscure what he asserted was the 'fundamental asymmetry' between (1) intelligence communities in parliamentary democracies and (2) their counterpart in 'The one-party state, the most malign political innovation of the twentieth century.'[17] Seductive in its simplicity, the terminological apartheid that the distinction implicitly encouraged has since become so widely accepted in what English-language textbooks in the field of intelligence studies call 'our mainstream writing', it has lost what F. R. Ankersmit in *History and Tropology* had once called 'the property of being a proposal', and become what he instead referred to as 'a rule'.[18] The exclusions, conventions, and discursive practices involved in intelligence history's construction of the self – here including its semantic inventory – are

Preface   xiii

inseparable from the identification of an 'other', and this applies no less to forays into rarefied intelligence theory than to thick descriptions of basic HUMINT praxis like surveillance. In the latter case, the *rule of law* now provides the positive unity and cohesion within which historians chronicle the evolution of empowering outreach programmes that promote security by encouraging dutiful citizens to act as seeing/saying servants of the public good, while the *informer state* is the elsewhere in which historians situate cautionary tales of cultures of denunciation and betrayal, and the operation of secret police forces.

Troublesome Evidence

Eyes and Ears insinuates itself into all of the above recognising that historians must now and then include in our narratives, accounts of this or that event for which the facts that permit a plausible explanation of its occurrence are lacking. In the words of Hayden White, we have no choice but to 'interpret' our materials by 'filling in the gaps in [the] information on inferential or speculative grounds'.[19] But, as we proceed, our accounts – woven into a particular overarching narrative – must not only appear convincing as vehicles for the claims we advance: their power to persuade must be a function of *evidence* and not of the contemporary political issues with which we may be engaged.[20] If we simply adopt the narrative strategy of the inverted commas (like the author of one textbook discussion of national concepts and institutions who draws a distinction between 'intelligence services in open societies' and the '"intelligence" services of non-democratic societies'[21]), we run the risk of having our work dismissed even by curious readers who like to think that Eric Hobsbawm was too pessimistic when he concluded that 'historians as an occupation are the primary producers of the raw material that is turned into propaganda and mythology'.[22]

The primary sources translated in *Eyes and Ears* could be from anywhere and, as already clarified, it is only by accident that they happen to come from 'Communist China' – a country designation that the CIA Directorate of Intelligence had concluded by 2011 no longer has a contemporary referent and therefore, as explained in its *Style Manual & Writers Guide for Intelligence Publications*, 'should be used only in historical contexts'.[23] The translations may be read as examples of how one Cold War 'informer state' operated and such a reading may well add to the persuasive power of the Anglosphere's bifurcated trope. This, however, begs the question whether there really is anything uniquely 'Communist' about officers exposing what they see as serious operational irregularities and a corrupt system, or about a low-level agent's dull observations on the activities of his target ('At three o'clock in the afternoon, I saw X writing a letter. As soon as he finished writing, he placed the letter in an envelope.') as in Chapters 24 and 10 below? Or whether there is anything distinctly Chinese about a case officer explaining to his superiors that the agent he runs needs money to employ a nanny, or about an intelligence consumer struggling to decipher a handwritten contact report and asking its case officer-author to write more legibly in the future as in Chapters 17 and 20 below? In 1993, Eric Hobsbawm argued that the end of the Cold War at long last made it possible for historians to 'abandon the pattern of mutually exclusive binary opposites', but he also at the same time admitted that it was unclear which alternative to that pattern could be 'most usefully' substituted. His answer was that 'we shall have to leave it to the twenty-first century to make its own decisions'.[24] The hope of the editor of *Eyes and Ears* is that the translations will be understood generically and allow readers, in the spirit of Umberto Eco, to gain limited access to hitherto known *unknowns* in the vast *terra incognita* of primary sources outside the linguistic comfort zone of the Anglosphere.

'Historical accounts are the bedrock for our work', admitted the co-author of the widely read and influential *Intelligence in an Insecure World*.[25] But those accounts need to be created from evidence. As argued in a classic elaboration on the subject that now sadly, well over half a century later, comes across as old school: 'The writing and reconstruction of history amount to a dialogue between the historian and his materials. He supplies the intelligence and the organising ability, but he can interpret and organise only within the limits set by his evidence. And those are the limits created by a true and independent past.'[26]

If we degrade evidence and no longer perform the operation hinted at here, our historical accounts cease to be the bedrock on which we erect our theories: sinkholes will sooner or later open up and swallow our erections. Ironically, historians concerned with the limits set by evidence now face a major methodological challenge in the form of the increasingly sophisticated system of disclosure and control of intelligence/security service records developed in the liberal-democratic order, the dominance of which in the immediate post–Cold War years had been briefly compared to 'the end of history'. While history may not yet have ended, what is precipitously on the way to oblivion is the concern with evidence, for which intelligence's preferred substitute has now become information or reporting. In the CIA *Style Manual & Writers Guide* mentioned earlier (which according to the sensitivity readers who compiled it 'reflects an enduring commitment to the highest standards of care and precision'), evidence appears on a watchlist of 'possibly troublesome words'. The entry reads in full: 'EVIDENCE: is not a synonym for information or reporting. For the most part avoid the word and get on with the analysis. Such phrases as *available evidence indicates* are essentially meaningless.'[27]

*****

Eyes and Ears is composed of seven thematic sets of translated texts (Parts I–VII). Introducing each set is a contextualising summary and each translation, in turn, is preceded by a brief editorial headnote on the what, who, where, when, and why of the text. Set number one (Part I) is the only one made up of no more than a single text, a first-hand account of an agent recruitment that here doubles as an introduction to the book's subject matter. Part II documents general issues that any new government, in the wake of regime change or transition, may face as it embarks upon the process of HUMINT capacity building, while Part III exemplifies results of that process – operational guidelines, routines, best practice, and so on. In Part IV and Part V, the focus shifts from the impersonal machinery of agent running to the men and women of flesh and blood on the ground – the operational targets, the agents themselves, and their security agency recruiters and handlers. Translated here are runs of reporting in the raw and memoranda chronicling agent briefings and debriefings, followed by content sampled from files of the kind maintained to monitor performance, ensure security, and manage an agent's welfare. Part VI looks at the paper trail left behind by senior operational officers, including their observations and comments on intelligence and submissions that landed on their desks. Finally, in Part VII, the translated texts illustrate the resilience of HUMINT as an institution when faced with revelations of major misconduct and calls for its fundamental reform.

Work on this book was supported by the Société Royale des Lettres de Lund. For their assistance, I want to thank the interlibrary loans staff in the Libraries of the Lund University Joint Faculties of Humanities and Theology and Nancy Hearst, librarian of the John K. Fairbank Center for East Asian Research at Harvard University. For their deeply appreciated editorial support, a very special thanks to Lucy Rhymer and Rosa Martin at Cambridge University Press.

Part I

Agent Recruitment

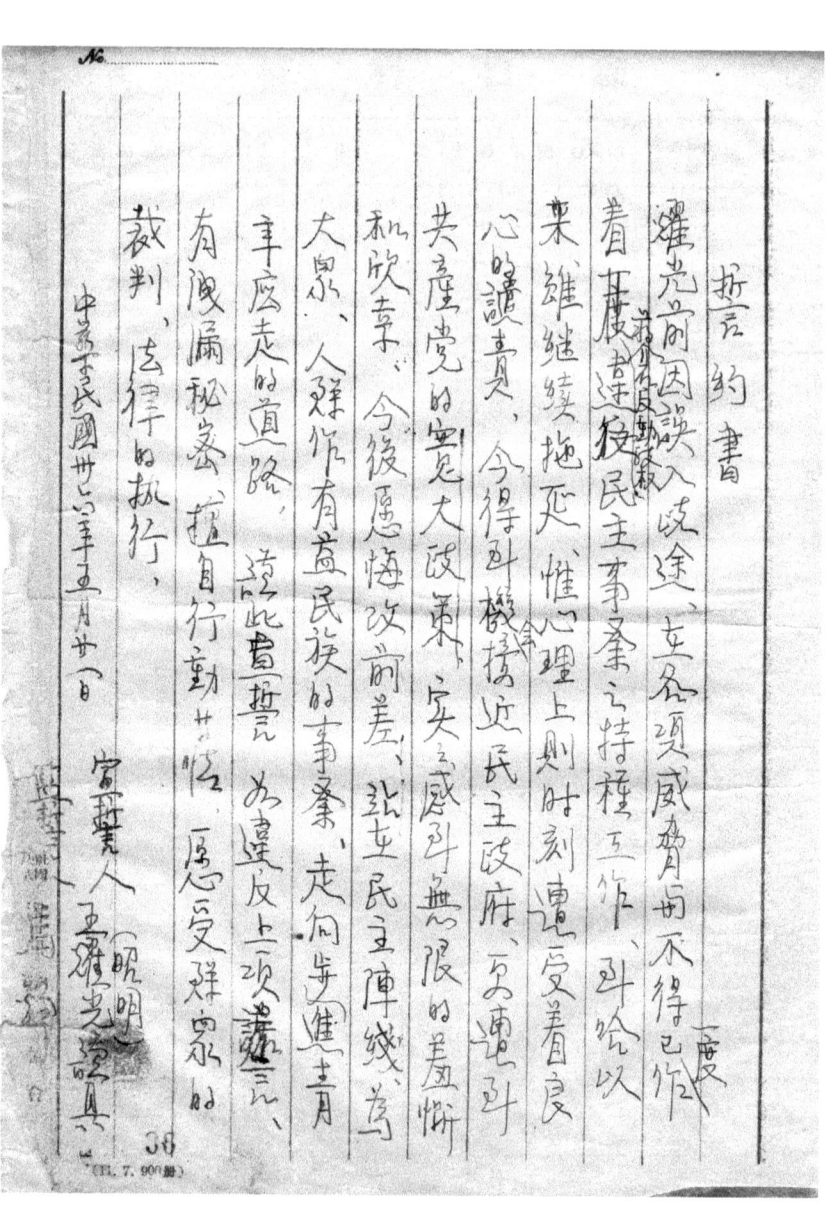

Figure 1 Nationalist military intelligence officer's sworn declaration to serve the Communist Party (1947)

Introduction

The word *agent*, so the dictionary says, 'usually names the one who does the work as distinguished from the one who wills, plans, or orders'.[28] It presumes a *motive* – be it an emotion or a desire, which operates on the will and definitely moves it to activity. In the mind of the lexicographer who merely seeks to discern and define the meanings of words, neither the meaning of agent nor that of motive is likely to trigger problematic or irksome associations. In covert human intelligence (HUMINT), however, things are different. 'He's an agent. He's a man to be handled, not known' is how a senior intelligence officer in John le Carré's novel *The Looking Glass War* replies to a junior colleague's inquiry about a man he has just been told 'is not one of us'. When the junior officer goes on to suggest that loyalty must be behind the man's readiness to act as an agent, he is told that 'I mistrust reasons. I mistrust words like loyalty. And above all ... I mistrust *motive*. We're running an agent; the arithmetic is over.'[29]

To better understand the motive or combination of motives that, in the real world, may incline a citizen to agree to secretly serve as an 'agent' of his or her national security agency, an employee of East Germany's *Ministerium für Staatssicherheit* (*MfS*) in 1967 surveyed close to a hundred active Main Informants, Secret Informants, and Secret Collaborators (as they were formally classified at the time) in the city of Potsdam and asked them to state what had motivated them to consent to do the work willed, planned, and ordered by the agency. Their replies were wide ranging and included the following:

'I couldn't explain to myself why they approached *me*. But I thought, they must have their reasons and in that case I'd better agree.'

'Although I personally do not regard such work as particularly honourable, one cannot turn a blind eye to the fact that it is, after all, necessary these days. And so, I agreed.'

'Given that it was the state that urged me to do it, I agreed to cooperate, despite my unwillingness to do political work.'

'It promises to be exciting, so yes.'

'It's a necessary and good thing, so I had but one option which was to agree.'
'I said yes, because this work is a civic necessity.'[30]

Much as the respondents will have sought to truthfully recall their own motives, their replies really only illustrate how they rationalised a decision made years, in some cases over a decade, earlier. British intelligence historian Christopher Moran has observed that oral testimony provided long after the event is often '*polluted* by what has been absorbed from subsequent experience and discourse', and the German officer who (as part of his postgraduate studies in jurisprudence) conducted the *MfS* survey also found that the passing of time had a way of impacting on agent testimony but used a different metaphor (from the same cluster as Moran's) to characterise experience as driving an observable '*purification* of motives'.[31] Personal memory is, at best, a slippery medium and researchers attempting to interpret it often find themselves assessing their respondent's own 'perceptions and sensibilities, rather than the factual accuracy' of claims regarding events that once occurred ... or perhaps did not.[32]

Historians have an obligation, writes Robert W. Winks in his delectable *The Historian as Detective*, 'not to allow their mortal subjects to acquire false reputations on the basis of misunderstood motivations'.[33] To get just that tiny bit closer to what at the time may go through the mind of an individual who finds him- or herself targeted for agent recruitment, what those of us who are biased in favour of the evidential need is a contemporaneous first-hand account, a record preferably committed to paper while events are still ongoing, their outcome uncertain, and the writer not yet in a position 'to strike out faulty judgements, or to add new and better strokes to the old picture'.[34] Furthermore, in order to contribute an optimal degree of real-world complexity and suspense of the kind that will command attention, the circumstances in which the recruitment succeeds or fails should, preferably, be perilous and volatile. No circumstance is more so than that which, once safely in the past, merits identification as regime change: even one of lesser magnitude than a war or civil war never leaves a security agency's HUMINT relationships unscathed, and the loyalty that may have sustained an agent's relationship with the *ancien régime* may or may not prove transferable to a new master. Regime change is the recruitment setting in which the prospective agent is unable to trust that, tomorrow unlike today, he or she will still be recognised as a patriotic citizen serving his or her national government rather than be accused of treachery!

The primary source in Chapter 1 is just such a firsthand account, intended here to serve as an introduction to the subject matter of this book.

1 The Target's Own Story

This account from 1947, when much of China was in the throes of civil war, of an attempt by Chinese Communist Party (CCP) counterintelligence to recruit the author as an agent, was written by Wang Yaoguang, a member of the Songjiang Group of the Republic of China's Military Intelligence North Manchuria Station. The story it tells unfolds in the city of Harbin, which, following the departure of the Soviet Red Army that had liberated North Manchuria from the Japanese, had been under the control of the CCP for over a year. Wang is at the time of writing in administrative detention, his recruitment having been aborted. His account is not explicitly addressed to anyone in particular and survives among miscellaneous records in a thin police file on him. He is unaware of the fact that the Songjiang Group had been compromised early on and that two of his junior colleagues had all along been briefing CCP counterintelligence on its activities.[35] An official history of public security in Harbin refers to Wang by name, and cites the neutralisation of the Songjiang Group as an early example of what in 1950 would become the official long-term policy of China's security agencies, of 'taking a long-term view and making operational use of penetration agents'.[36]

Translated Text

At nightfall on 20 May [1947], I had just left the site where we maintained our radio communications equipment and was on my way home when two comrades suddenly appeared and seized me as I passed the entrance to this building. They said: 'You walk past here every day. Today we would like you to come in for a chat.' Since we were close to a sentry point and they had already seized me, resistance seemed pointless, so I entered the building with them. By coincidence, our equipment had malfunctioned that day and I had not been able to send or receive any messages, so when they frisked me, they did not find any incriminating papers on me.

Untitled handwritten record deposited in a file opened by the Harbin Public Security Bureau on 5 May 1947. Closed file weeded out from the bureau archive on an unknown date.

I was then taken to another room and told to wait. The sudden and unforeseen turn of events had made me panic and tremble, and my heart beat like mad, but I now got a moment's respite and did my best to calm down. Worrying whether the terror I felt would be obvious, I sought to compose myself. I also thought about how best to deal with the impending interrogation.

While my mind struggled to return to normal, I was taken to see Mr Ma, who began a conversation with me.[37] At first, I had hoped to be able to keep my identity [as our group's radio communications officer] secret and to deceive him with a set of identification papers from Mudanjiang that I was carrying. But when Mr Ma addressed me by my first name as 'Yaoguang' (I wondered how he knew it, since my real name did not appear anywhere on my papers!), I realised that I would not be able to pull the wool over his eyes. All I could do was improvise. As I started to feel that the situation was increasingly hopeless, I realised I would just have to wait and see.

Given that there was little I could do to keep it secret, I began by admitting the kind of work I did. Giving voice to a just cause, Mr Ma then enlightened me by explaining the Communist Party's policy of leniency to me: 'We are always willing to rescue young people who have lost their way, in particular those who have lost their way due to external circumstances.' I only half believed what he was saying, so when he gave me a piece of paper and told me to describe the inner workings of our group and how we communicated by radio, I held back and wrote down things that were either only half-true or incomplete. The only current radio communication call signs and transmission times that I gave him in full were those of the Shenyang [Radio Communications] Desk, which had already been silent for some time. But even in this case, I intentionally provided transmission times that were off by one hour, since, I thought to myself, if you're already listening in, you'll know that transmission times tend to fluctuate, and won't be able to hold me responsible. In the case of the Changchun Desk, I wrote down an old call sign no longer in use.

I did not think the Communist Party would be lenient with me, much less believe me or ask me to work for it. Until then, I had never been in touch with or talked to any of their people. What latent sympathy for the Communist Party I may have had (or any other nod in that direction), I had never shared with a soul. So why should they be prepared to trust me? I felt it would have been strange if they did, and feared something altogether different was in the offing. I therefore asked Mr Ma for assurances, which I received.[38] In my mind, I was entertaining the idea of leaving things to chance, but thought that, no matter what, I first of all have to make sure I get out of here alive. What happens after that would depend on the circumstances. At the time, I was still leaning towards the

1 The Target's Own Story

other [Guomindang] side. Throughout our entire conversation, Mr Ma remained very cordial, and I was very moved by his concern for my personal well-being and by the fact that he gave me some medicine. This was the first time in ages that someone seemed to really care about me. Although I had worked myself to the bone for the others and had fallen ill as a result, they had not even agreed to cover my medical bills. Our conversation drew to a close as dawn approached. Mr Ma's timing suggested that he was prepared to trust me. Otherwise, if they'd seen me 'walk past here' several times every day, why would they have picked nightfall to make their move? When the first rays of the morning sun appeared, I walked together with Mr Ma back to where I lived.

After that night-long conversation, I was all giddy. Returning home with a bad headache, I collapsed on my bed. I had to calm down, but no matter how hard I tried, I was unable to fall asleep. Twisting and turning as I lay there, I thought about last night's sudden twist of fate, about Liu Xingya, about my work as of now, and not the least about Zhao Minqiang and the others.[39] In the end, I made up my mind not to tell anyone, but to wait and see what would happen. My mind, in short, was one big mess, about to burst from the contradictions and conflict. Meanwhile, the silent pain in my lungs returned with a vengeance. In a daze, I finally managed to fall asleep, and I slept all the way until noon when Zhao Minqiang came to inquire why I had failed to turn up at the home of Wu Guodong that morning.[40] I made up some story about having enjoyed a night out in Daoli district and becoming sick due to having had far too much to drink, and therefore slow to get out of bed.

I had agreed to meet Mr Ma again on 23 May to report on the activities of other members of our group and to share the contents of incoming and outgoing messages with him. I spent the next two days preparing this information, picking up the contents of selected decrypts from Zhao Minqiang's office and compiling a factual report on the activities of the other members of our group based on my own observations.[41] Meanwhile, as I moved about in the city, I discovered that I was being followed, which was highly unsettling as I began to fear yet another unexpected turn of events. At some point, on 22 or 23 May, I reminded the others in our group to be circumspect in their movements. We had often cautioned one another in the past, but this time I was doing so most of all to lessen my own responsibility and to reduce my sense of guilt. I was, on the one hand, unable to share the recent turn of events with them, as I was still planning to wait and see how much this [Communist Party] side was really going to put its trust in me and then decide which way to lean. On the other hand, I was also very much torn by the feelings of camaraderie that had developed over time among the members of our group. Under these circumstances, I could do no more than hint at the importance of caution. But I dare say that nothing in my behaviour at the time would have triggered suspicion on their part. The way we had been going about our business, day in and day out for so long, told me that no one was paying much attention to such details.

When I met Mr Ma on 23 May, I handed over what he had asked me to write down and added some explanations. He, in turn, issued certain operational instructions and instructed me to surrender our group's Desk Cipher at our next meeting which, we agreed, would take place on 25 May.[42] At that moment, I was afraid that once he had obtained our Desk Cipher and was able to decode and inspect our messages, the fact that I had lied about some of their content would come to light. In the hope of being able to ward off this possibility, I eventually opted to surrender no more than one set of expired encryption keys. I do not know what possessed me at the time. It wasn't that I was still completely leaning to the other [Guomindang] side, since, after all, I had not told them [the Guomindang] what had happened to me, nor had I sent a message alerting the North Manchuria Station or made any kind of plans to run away or hide. Then again, to say that I was leaning this way was contradicted by my continued double-dealing and deception. I was thinking perhaps I should wait to see how much this side really put its trust in me, and test the waters for a while. In any case, this turned out to be the beginning of my real troubles.

At our meeting on 25 May, I handed over the transmission encryption keys to Mr Ma and gave him an update on recent developments that was as close as could be to the truth. I then returned to the Wu residence where I ran into Zhao Minqiang. When he showed me an already completed travel permit that would allow him to leave for Changchun, I was overwhelmed by an intense feeling of distress. All emotional, I told him what had happened to me and I urged him not to leave Harbin for the time being, but wait and see. I explained that I had intentionally held back from saying anything earlier for fear of causing him distress and panic. He heard me out and did not inquire further. We agreed to meet again that evening at the Wu residence to confer, whereupon he left. I have not seen or heard from him since. At the time, I thought if I notify this side, Zhao will surely be arrested before he can leave for Changchun, which I could not bear. At the same time, I also asked myself if Zhao is arrested, will my own work still be able to continue? Concerns like these were what led me to make what proved to be a major mistake. To be honest, I was most of all swayed by my emotions, and my thinking at the time was still very unsettled.

The next day, when neither Zhao Minqiang nor any of the others showed up, I panicked. I tried unsuccessfully to reach Zhou Yunting on

1 The Target's Own Story

the phone to find out what was going on.[43] When I realised I would not be able to speak to him on the phone, I went in person to the Daowai district, hoping to find him in his office, only to discover that he too appeared to be avoiding me. I left a note for him and the others, telling them not to misunderstand but get in touch as soon as possible so we could talk through various scenarios. By that point, I was filled with deep anguish, knowing that this side would hold me responsible for the disappearance of Zhao Minqiang and the others, not to mention everything else, such as my vacillation, my betrayal of their confidence, and my failing of their test. Furthermore, once they lost confidence in me, even if I were to switch my allegiance altogether, what would be the use?! Meanwhile, did the silence and disappearance of Zhao and the others not already suggest that they no longer had any trust in me and believed that I had already quietly changed sides?

Wu Guodong and I now both tried to locate Zhao Minqiang. Meanwhile, I maintained a perfunctory attitude towards this side, hoping that a solution might be found once Zhao had returned. When I met with Mr Ma on 28 May, however, he subjected me to a most intense cross-examination after having discovered that most of the information I had surrendered up to that point had been spurious. Given that Zhao Minqiang had not been seen for days and appeared to have escaped, Mr Ma questioned me in depth about whether I had revealed any details to him. I had no way of denying it, so I decided to use the opportunity to come clean about all my double-dealing up to that point and about my attempts to stall. I also promised to surrender my transceiver and book of codes/ciphers as well as my gun, and to amend and correct falsehoods in my earlier information. But I still did not admit to having told Zhao Minqiang about what had happened to me because I was afraid I would then be held responsible for his disappearance. I was still hoping to be able to locate Zhao. During our conversation, Mr Ma enlightened me on a number of points. Once it dawned on me that Zhao Minqiang had no trust in me and no sympathy for my predicament, I became very upset.

On 29 May, I surrendered my transceiver and book of codes/ciphers, and on 30 May I also handed over my gun. During our conversation on that same day, Mr Ma inquired repeatedly about Zhao Minqiang. He told me what happens to those who are discovered to have concealed facts, but he also explained to me how to make amends. Certain pre-emptive measures, if adopted, would allow me to retain the initiative, he said. I became very interested in and much intrigued by the technical issues involved. When I then came clear about the Zhao Minqiang matter, Mr Ma instructed me to continue searching for him while also preparing to handle radio communications with the station in a perfunctory way. From then on, I felt as if I had finally been relieved of all the heavy emotional and physical burdens I had been carrying, and I abandoned all my earlier plans and ideas of putting my trust in fortitude. I began leaning unreservedly to this side, doing all the work it was asking me to do. At the same time, I also considered myself lucky for not having rashly notified the station, since if I had done so, the work I was about to do [for the Communist Party] from then on would from the outset have been bound to fail altogether. I also felt unlimited gratitude to the Communist Party for having on a number of occasions already treated me leniently. Even after I failed to locate Zhao Minqiang and the others, this side still did not put any greater pressure on me. As a consequence, I became more calmly focused on my work, and I was eager to produce results as a way of making up for my past faults.

On 2 June, as our transmissions drew to a close, a junior colleague of Mr Ma's instructed me to remain where I was until Mr Ma returned. He later told me to sleep over rather than to return to my home for the night. The next day, given the overall situation, Mr Ma urged me to remain in hiding on site for a few days. I did not think much of it at the time, since a few days earlier Mr Ma had already asked me what I thought about going incommunicado for a few days, as this would facilitate his attempts to locate Zhao Minqiang and the others.[44] At first, I remained calm, reading some books while not on the air. I learnt a lot of new things from the books and they made me realise how I had been deceived by the despicable doings and ruses of the Guomindang 'government'. I also made some comparisons between the situation where I had been after V-J Day and what I now had a chance to read in the book *Unvarnished Accounts of the Territory Controlled by Chiang Kai-shek*. I discovered just how much Guomindang accounts had been full of rumour and falsehood, and to what extent the Guomindang side was characterised by corruption and filth. However, when one is immersed in that environment without any point of reference, it becomes a challenge to fully comprehend the full situation.

After nearly a fortnight had passed, the constraints imposed by my environment began to make me feel anxious. I made repeated requests to be permitted to go out as long as my work would not be affected. To be honest, for anyone accustomed to moving about freely outside, prolonged confinement is very difficult to bear. I was then ordered to write an autobiography. While I spent my spare time immersed in my writing, I was able to bring my impetuousness under control. I made every effort to recall events and to put them down on paper. In the end, I was able to produce a truthful autobiography. It took quite a long time, but I am rather pleased with the result – in my whole life, I have never written

1 The Target's Own Story

anything so frank and honest. Finally, I also amended my account, explaining some things about which I had previously not gone into detail. In the end, after having kept it secret and fretted over it in my mind for too long, I came clean about the group running the Qiqihar Desk. I dare say that I have by now managed, without any reservations, to say all that I know. Moreover, after having put everything down on paper, I feel immensely relieved and at ease. It is as if I have completely unburdened myself of everything that has being weighing me down for so long.

One day in mid-June, acting on orders, I transmitted a prepared message informing the other side about what I claimed were the developments at this end, and I suggested times and means of secret communication. A few days later, the station replied. Expressing concern for me, it instructed me to keep the lines of communication open and so forth. I was delighted by this reply because I believed the establishment of a secret line of communication would count as a meritorious achievement of mine. As I set out to compose a new message, I did everything I could do to make it come across as genuine in all respects. I also made a number of proposals to this [Communist] side in the hope of henceforth seeing my work stabilise and develop. On the day – the twenty-something – that I sent my second message, I settled with an officer (by the name of Li) at the other end on a means of secret communication, but for two days after that, at the agreed-upon time of six o'clock in the morning, there was no incoming signal from the other side. This, in turn, led this side to begin to distrust me. When on one occasion after that I failed to get on the air with a sufficiently strong signal because my external antenna refused to connect properly, the distrust grew even stronger.

As a matter of fact, because of the sheer number of individuals involved on the other side – not all of them necessarily properly briefed and including a fair number of inexperienced hands like the operator of theirs who not only sent the secret call sign backwards but also got the transmission time wrong – it was easy to see just how chaotic and confused the handling of the agreed-upon secret contact must have been at the other end. The external antenna was not the problem. I had tested and managed without one in the past and I would not have been that stupid, to insist on going on the air at an unscheduled time when I knew no one was expecting a transmission. Anyway, as far as I am concerned, I was never making any secret plans to contact the station. By this time, after the change in ideological circumstances that I had been through, would I at this crucial juncture (when my work was showing signs of progress) really have sought to surreptitiously liaise with the other side? I had no way of explaining myself when all this happened, and I never got a chance to attempt a second transmission. The pain of this injustice has remained in my heart ever since.

. . . . . .

On 3 July, I was suddenly detained without anyone explaining the reason to me. I was overcome by fear and went over every possibility in my mind. If it was due to my earlier offences, then it was the punishment I deserved, but if it was for reasons that had to do with my final radio transmission, then my imprisonment, I felt, was really unfair. But whatever it is, a punishment like this one always has a wherefore that one day will be unveiled.

In custody, I fell ill due to the combined pressures of mental strains and the physical environment. At the beginning, I merely felt a pain in my chest and coughed up some blood. But later I was diagnosed with pleurisy compounded with the flu and ended up painfully emaciated and miserable. Gradually, I settled down and during long and uneventful days, I had time to reflect on what had happened and also to think about what the future might bring. I became very sad, considering that I had just discovered the right path, yet recklessly lost my way. Then again, I trust the Communist Party will not just cast a young person aside as long as he is not a reactionary beyond redemption. Therefore, I keep on hoping that I shall be saved and given a chance at a new life, become an upright person under the democratic government and leadership of the Communist Party, and be able to serve the people to make up for my past errors.

Yue Guang[45]
16 September 1947

Part II

Capacity Building

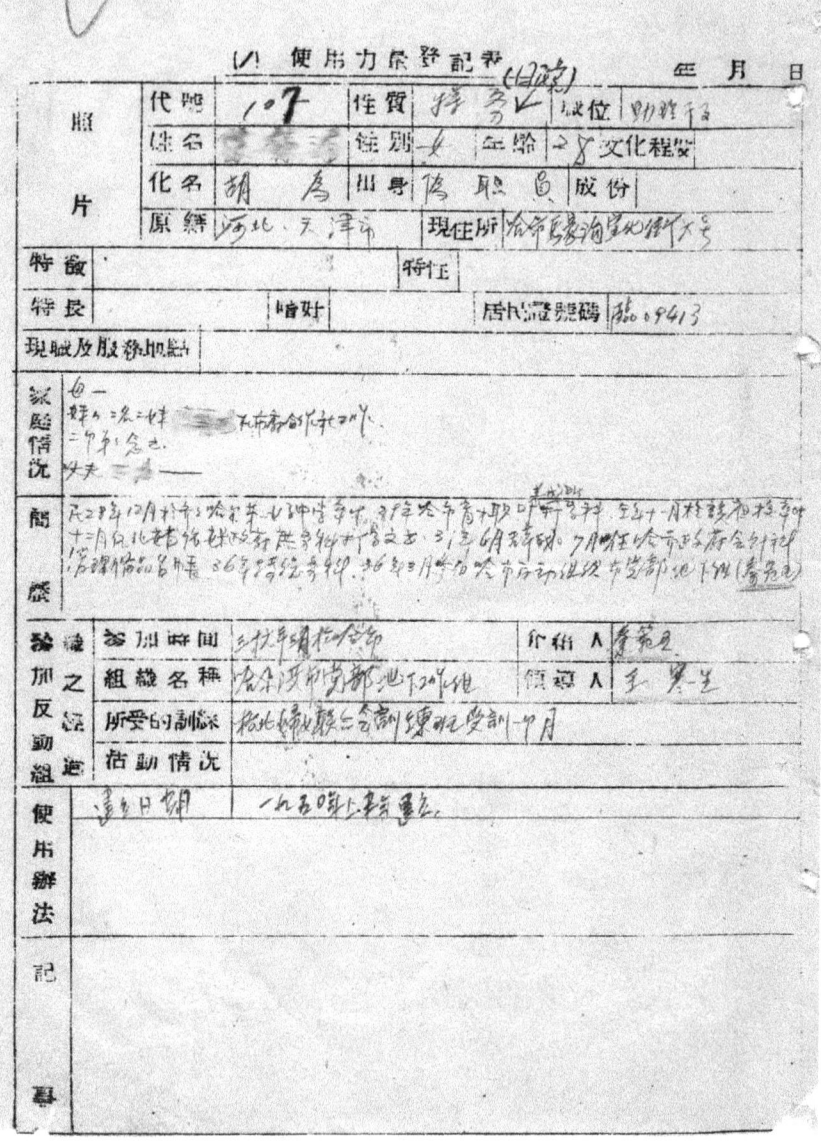

Figure 2 Agent registration form (1950)

Introduction

The early Cold War period witnessed an expansion of security agency mandates and resources as national governments declared threat levels elevated and public opinion in turn demanded forceful responses. To counter, contain, and disrupt activities that bore the suspicious hallmarks of subversion – 'political-ideological diversion' in East Berlin, 'disruption of the constitutional order' in Bonn – or foreign espionage, HUMINT capacity building called for little in terms of investment in expensive infrastructure. The optimum towards which governments quietly strove by way of appeals to a higher loyalty (J. Edgar Hoover spoke of 'an obligation of citizenship') was a vigilant citizenry, its members mobilised to serve as the eyes and ears of the state.[46] In Europe, one retired security agency chief boasted when the Cold War was over about the nationwide web of agents that his men and women had been able to call on when a job demanded it. A medley of contemporaneous and reminiscent matter, his memoirs describe how they approached 'people who are able to serve as sources. Each section of the Security Police actively maintains its own web made up of altogether thousands of local politicians, union officials, business leaders, regional government civil servants, and residents close to military installations. Composed of the pillars of society, the web is a powerful resource.' He concluded with the following observation: 'The web of agents is *not* a typically Swedish *modus operandi*. This was also the way in which the other side worked, not the least the Soviet and East German security and intelligence agencies. It was the spirit of the times.'[47]

A first sense of how the 'spirit of the times' fuelled HUMINT capacity building may be gained from reading the in-house histories since produced by some security agencies. As secondary sources on agent operations, written to preserve institutional memory, rather than for the market or as public relations exercises, those that have been declassified reveal fascinating details based on original records and input from the men and women involved. Needless to say, even the most informative ones (Chapter 2) are still no substitute for public access to the sources themselves.[48]

16   II Capacity Building

Rarely raised by agencies in their own accounts is the development of doctrinal terminology, including words given classified meanings to safeguard assumptions and sensitive information. In 1955, the 'father figure of CIA research and analysis', Yale-trained historian Sherman Kent, had reminded his colleagues that absent rigorous definitions of terms 'we are likely to find ourselves talking at cross purposes', but the role played by agency terminologists and glossary developers goes well beyond the mundane one to which he drew attention.[49] As Murray Edelman put it in *The Politics of Misinformation*, language is 'a creator of the realities in which we live and move: It is a framer of worlds with particular features'.[50] Today, historians with disciplinary backgrounds in linguistics and cultural studies seek to transcend the limitations imposed by yesterday's doctrinal terminologies and refuse to pose questions about HUMINT on the basis of what with hindsight appears to many as but another *déformation professionelle* of the Cold War's duly indoctrinated agent runners.[51] But, as we exploit the primary sources they have left behind, this does not absolve us from the duty to acquire a firm command of what their language meant to them and how agencies everywhere created (Chapter 3) their own 'worlds with particular features' framing how officers 'lived and moved'.

When it involved codification and oversight, HUMINT capacity building was a process of trial and error, even where security agencies could draw on a rich pre–World War II *Verwaltungskultur*. Professionalisation was gradual: most countries, in the words of two American intelligence historians, 'struggled to keep up with the times and reorganised their way forward'.[52] To understand just *how* that reorganisation unfolded calls for time-consuming detective work on the part of historians who must be willing to embark on 'slow research' and self-immerse in the widely scattered document streams in which agencies up-dated their officers on agent work progress, or lack thereof, in localities X, Y, and Z, and circulated descriptions of how agent-running components A, B, and C struggled to meet expectations (Chapter 4).

Particular caution is merited when assessing the impact and quality of input from foreign services. In the early 1950s, the CIA had maintained that the 'guidance' it was giving the still nascent West German intelligence community – in the form of 'training material and techniques specially adapted to the preparation of agents for USSR operations, i.e. tradecraft, "Sovietization" lectures, etc.' – resulted in a 'substantial enhancement in operational competence on the part of the Germans'.[53] Claims like these, when they come to light in archival records kept by the party *giving* the input, sometimes have a way of acquiring greater evidential weight than they deserve. Each agency had reason to maintain its own record, and a description by the *receiving* party of what transpired may well point historians in a somewhat different direction. Few instances of capacity building lacked an international dimension altogether, but even where primary source transcripts survive of what officers heard colleagues from a sister service say in, for example, lectures on tradecraft (Chapter 5), historians must not, bar the presence of additional authenticating evidence, jump to conclusions about inter-agency influence, emulation, or replication.

2   A Director of Public Security Remembers

This is a retrospective on HUMINT capacity building in the city of Shenyang during the transition of political power on the Chinese mainland from the Nationalist Party of Chiang Kai-shek, ruling in the name of the Republic of China, to the Communist Party, governing under the name of the People's Republic of China (PRC). Its author, He Xia, served as municipal director of public security in Shenyang in 1948–1952, and his account is one chapter in a longer classified history of well over 300 pages written with generous institutional backing. It touches on numerous tradecraft-related specifics, from agent profiling and direction to the management of handler-agent liaisons and monetary rewards. The author also comments on the usefulness of agents in general and the importance of avoiding cultivation clashes and recruitment duplication, and he shares some personal insights into agent psychology. Today's readers need to firmly keep in mind that he employs the word agent in a way consistent with how it was used in early PRC public security records to refer *exclusively* to assets who were 'alien class elements' and *not*, for example, to those who 'came from the grey masses, or belonged to the basic masses'. As will be seen in Chapter 3, it was not until 1952 that agent (*teqing*) became the umbrella term by which Chinese public security officers would henceforth refer to *all* of their human intelligence assets.

Translated Text

In the wake of the big round-up that we carried out after entering Shenyang in 1948, we proceeded to intensify agent work capacity building while stepping up efforts to combat collaborators and root out enemy operatives. Agent work required tailoring the approach to, and the management of, each target individually and the setting of priorities with respect to the target's exploitation, cultivation, training, and utilisation. As a general policy, furthermore, it entailed painstaking operation and prolonged utilisation in order to allow agents to successfully infiltrate or

---

He Xia, 'Yewu jianshe' (Professional Capacity Building), in *Jiefang chuqi Shenyang gongan gongzuo huigu* (Retrospective on Public Security Work in Shenyang during the Early Post-Liberation Period) (Shenyang: Shenyang shi gonganju, November 1993), pp. 186–197.

approach and strike at the enemy and to perform their vital role in combatting collaborators and rooting out enemy operatives.

Prior to the liberation of Shenyang, we had managed forty-seven underground agent contacts and we later continued to draw on twelve of them. The total number grew to sixty-four once an additional fifty-two contacts were transferred in from Dalian. Two-thirds were underground contacts, among whom more than one-half were elements about whom there were doubts in the Liberated Areas at the time, but who, nonetheless, had played a definite role in the liberation of Shenyang. After the big round-up, not only did the enemy change significantly from operating in the open or half-openly to operating covertly; the individuals who had previously been our own covert underground contacts also changed and started to go public. Some insisted we resolve their financial situation or provide them with jobs, and they were unwilling to keep their links to us concealed, which in turn meant that we had to suspend any further use of them as undeclared assets. In addition, there were signs of suspicious behaviour among some individuals, including instances of fraud and blackmail. All this called for thorough analysis and examination, followed by appropriate action. As far as the individuals in question were concerned, to judge them solely on the basis of the role they may have at one time played would now have been as much of an error as to treat all of them as suspect.

As part of our intensified agent capacity building, in the spring of 1949 we initiated a validation review of our old assets while also beginning the process of developing new ones. The standards of validation for old assets were as follows:

1. Those who had performed quite well or who had maintained qualifications that remained open to utilisation, and to whom a specific practical role could be assigned, would be kept on as trial-use assets. Eventually, if what they achieved over an extended period of time proved their loyalty to the People, their utilisation, direction, and management would be consolidated.
2. Those who had performed quite well but for whom a more specific practical role could no longer be found were to be retained as casual social investigation assets.
3. Those who had performed quite well but who ended up in environments unsuited to continued operational work were to be transferred to other departments and contact with them limited to casual social-investigation purposes.
4. Those who had performed poorly, whose contacts with us were surrounded with ambiguity, and whose past work had given rise on occasion to problems, were to be purged and disowned.

5. Those who had broken the law and, as a result, had been subject to legal sanctions were to be cleared out.

The outcome of the validation review was that after some were transferred to other departments and others were disowned, purged, sanctioned, or cleared out, altogether thirty-two individuals remained. Some twenty-four newly developed individuals were added, resulting in a total of fifty-six agents.

By the spring of 1950, in the course of the deepening of the covert struggle, the number of our agent contacts had grown to 355 individuals. Among these, the Shenyang Public Security Bureau's Investigation Section managed 215, its Government Organs Protection Section managed 32, and its municipal district branches managed 108.

Almost all of these people were enemy operatives recently [detained and] released from custody. They did not represent the main direction of our operational capacity building, but for a period of time, prior to our thorough disruption of the various components of the enemy's *tewu* apparatus, they allowed us to continuously and closely manage and degrade some specific components and, to some extent, in concert with the overall imposition of a People's Democratic Dictatorship, successfully familiarise ourselves with, manage, and establish control over the membership of the enemy's *tewu* apparatus up to that point.[54] As we combatted collaborators in newly reclaimed cities, the special instrument represented by the agents proved indispensable.

In a whole string of our central tasks – such as attacking covert action *tewu*, digging deep for Central Statistics Bureau *tewu*, compelling members of reactionary political parties and organisations to register with the authorities, striking at reactionary secret societies (and, later, at imperialist elements in the Catholic Church), and suppressing counter-revolution – our glowing achievements are inseparably tied to how, on the basis of mobilising the masses, we managed to deliberately, purposefully, and vigilantly make controlled use of agent elements inside specific components of the enemy's *tewu* apparatus.[55] Discussed below are selected aspects of our work:

The Usefulness of Agents

After the liberation of Shenyang and after more than a year of agent work, we summed up some of the experiences gained in the course of our utilisation of agents. By the autumn of 1949, those experiences more or less covered the following aspects.

First, among the assets whom we managed – who were either (a) alien class elements (i.e., agents), (b) came from the grey masses, or (c) belonged to the basic masses – it was the agents who had the best access to the enemy and were able to play the most important roles. For example, among our six penetration assets, it was the agents who had 100 per cent access to the enemy and were able to provide us with constant updates on the enemy's circumstances.

Second, among the agents who were either members of reactionary political parties and organisations or *tewu*, the more important role was by comparison played by those who held middle-ranking or senior positions. Half of our six penetration assets were middle-ranking or senior members of reactionary political parties and organisations, while among an additional twenty-three assets providing us with updates on threats, thirteen (or 55 per cent) were middle-ranking or senior members of reactionary political parties and organisations.

Third, elements whose reactionary histories were relatively brief, whose family backgrounds were not well-to-do, and who within the enemy ranks felt sidelined and, as a result, could easily be swayed or converted were also able to play comparatively important roles. The opposite was true of individuals who were related to or who had close and friendly relations with enemy operatives. It often proved difficult to make controlled use of them. Senior Guomindang *tewu*, because of their elevated social status and their stubborn reactionary thinking, also proved difficult to control and, because of their senior positions, difficult to operate.

Agent Handling

In order to be successful, a case officer must have a firm political stand, be able to clearly distinguish between friend and foe, and employ flexible tactics. To recruit and handle agents calls, in practical terms, for the 'flexible application of firm rules', boldness, and an ability to solve problems with an open mind and a proactive attitude.

In our handling of agents, we followed a three-in-one policy that fused managing (*guan*), training (*jiao*), and tasking (*shi*). When utilising agents (alien class elements), case officers had to identify, target, and subject their weak spots to carefully calculated blows, and then they had to follow up with training. Managing, training, and tasking have to be closely linked through the entire agent utilisation process: in isolation, the effectiveness of any one of the three is either significantly reduced or completely absent. If the agent is not managed at all, or if the agent is mismanaged, slip-ups are bound to occur. For example, in his self-examination, agent Zhao X eventually stated that an important reason for the mistakes he had made was that, in dealing with him during the early post-Liberation period, we had been overly preferential and he, as a result, got all carried away. The lesson we learnt from this was that the mistake of our case officer had been to merely utilise and not train the agent. In scenarios involving managing without simultaneous training, agents would hesitate to approach us or they would develop a sense of dread as soon as they saw us, which similarly reduced their usefulness.

Management entails controlling and possessing *kompromat* on agents, setting rules and ensuring their compliance and performance as intended. Training is meant to raise their appreciation [of the situation in which they find themselves], alert them to the consequences of non-cooperation, make them see their own present and future clearly, and gradually have them put their trust in us. Tasking includes testing the performance of agents in the course of their work for us. As in the case of both training and managing, when setting tasks case officers must be both strict and open-minded – generous and firm at the same time – since only then will the agents comply and willingly seek to improve their performance.

Long-term calculation and painstaking operation. When it comes to the utilisation of agents, case officers need to engage in long-term calculation and must expect painstaking operation. They also should be ready to solve problems with initiative, creativity, and an open mind. Agent achievements should be rewarded and transgressions punished: to merely issue demands and expect results is not the right way to proceed.

The running of an agent should be assigned as a specific responsibility to a particular officer who then assumes responsibility for the handling of all matters – superficial or in-depth, general or concrete – involving the agent in question. Agents should be assigned tasks that take into account their level of awareness, trustworthiness, and competence, whether weak or strong. When in contact with their agents, case officers should evaluate their circumstances, review their performance, and provide briefings – in other words, task them and monitor their work. The officer, furthermore, should take the initiative to resolve any difficulties in the agent's work or difficulties that have arisen as a result of private circumstances.

Agent tasking and briefing must take into account the past positions and spheres of activity of the agents. If they are given merely vague or sweeping orders to obtain and report information, or, alternatively, if they are given tasks they simply cannot execute successfully, both sides in due course will grow dispirited and give up.

The utilisation of an agent must have a beginning and an end. One should not decide to retain or to terminate an agent simply on the basis of how well he executes a single task or how he performs on a single occasion. The decision should be based on repeated tests and assessments. A good agent may be given a more sophisticated task, whereas a bad agent may, at some suitable moment, be terminated. Both retention and termination should involve certain formalities and routines. If continued use is desirable, formal endorsement must be obtained from a specific level within the [public security] organisation. Additional required formalities and routines may involve the *kompromat* one has on the agent and the setting of rules (different in the case of members of the grey masses or Communist Party and Youth League members). A decision to terminate an agent must be preceded by a clarification of merits and demerits. The reason for termination must be explained to him and he should be instructed to respect confidentiality and to abide by the law.

Officers' Mental Blocks

As we proceeded to develop agents, we encountered the following circumstances.

One was a fear on the part of some officers that in the end a prospective agent would prove to be useless. When selecting a target for cultivation and when contemplating whether or not it would ultimately be of use, some officers put excessive stress on the qualifications, histories, social connections, proficiencies, and so forth that the agent, in their view, had to possess. They therefore hesitated to boldly cultivate elements they believed might 'not necessarily be up to the job'.

Another circumstance was a fear on the part of case officers whose public security roles remained undisclosed (such as the members of our Social Investigation Group) of compromising clandestinity in the course of their cultivation attempts. They worried that once they got to the point at which they had to hint at what they expected the target to do, if the target expressed an unwillingness or showed false willingness accompanied by much reluctance, not only would the recruitment end in failure but their own cover would have been blown. As a result, they hesitated to boldly cultivate targets. Case officers were, of course, right to consider whether upon cultivation a target would make a useful agent. Both the limitations of the individual and the limitations imposed by the operational environment ensure that there will be differences in this respect, be they small or large. When selecting cultivation targets, one should naturally identify and select those who are potentially capable of playing a significant role. But this is only one aspect of the problem, since limited qualifications on the part of an agent are never absolute, and the key is how well we manage and employ the agent. The quality of management and training may directly affect the ability of an individual to be useful. Moreover, we should not demand the same of every agent. Clearly, during the initial stages of a recruitment attempt it is wrong to worry excessively about a target's future utility and as a result not to proceed boldly in cultivating it.

Whether clandestinity can be maintained during cultivation should also be of concern. But it is permissible, as well as entirely possible, to resolve this matter with the help of control and training measures. One solution involves having open and secret work operate in concert and letting the public security officer assign the running of the agent to a proxy. In this way, the officer's own role need not be compromised and clandestinity can be maintained.

The Scope of Agent Profiling

The old agents upon whom we continued to draw [after our 1949 validation review] as well as our new and recently developed agents had all been vetted on the basis of information already in our bureau files. When profiling for suitable recruitment candidates, we were limited in our ability to prioritise particular components of the enemy's *tewu* apparatus or to target specific locations, professions, social strata, and so on. This was a shortcoming illustrated by the twelve agents recruited by our Beiguan Municipal District Branch. Eleven of them were members of the enemy's armed forces, only one was a *tewu*, and not a single one was an element representing a reactionary political party or organisation. Very clearly, our agent recruitment base remained narrow in its scope and was not yet very broad.

The scope, whether narrow or broad, of our profiling efforts had a direct impact on how finely meshed an operational net we would in the end be able to cast. In order to remedy the flaws we had identified, we initiated profiling efforts among both recently released scoundrels as well as among those still in custody while continuing to look for prospects in Public Security Bureau files. We also decided to involve agents who had already proven themselves in the identification of new prospects. We sought to cover all components of the enemy's *tewu* apparatus as well as the different physical locations and social strata. It was by way of this carefully considered expansion of our profiling efforts that we were able to embark on a significant scaling-up of our operational work.

Managing the Direction of the Agent

Agent work is by no means simply a matter of locating people capable of providing information, but rather it also involves highly complex and fine-grained work, from profiling and running background checks to arduous study, analysis, and training of the recruited individual. The way we went about this was to have the Work Team (later the Station) of our Investigation Section put three or four staff officers in charge of managing the ordinary agents, while the senior comrades on the Section/Team (or Station) managed those elements whose reactionary positions were senior and activities by comparison wide-ranging, and who therefore were more difficult to handle, as well as our penetration agents in ongoing cases. Our agent direction and management praxis was one of 'concentration above, dispersal below', and as such it entailed individual case officer responsibility under collective [Public Security Bureau] Party Group leadership.

Agent Allowances

Experience shows that unless an agent is given a relatively fixed allowance (material rewards), long-term calculation and painstaking operation leading to optimisation of the agent's utility will be impossible.

The psychology of the ordinary agent invariably involves the attainment of financial security. In actuality, all people are the same in this respect. If they cannot make ends meet, they will not be able to concentrate on their work. On this point, we initially failed to act with sufficient initiative and speed, and the problems that arose as a result were not appropriately resolved. Take, for example, our disowned contact XX. From the outset, he asked us repeatedly to help him make ends meet, but we kept procrastinating and failed to respond. In the end, he went on to choose his own way of making a living, and in a letter he left behind for us he wrote that our 'organisation has all along declined to give me a firm answer. In order to survive financially, even though I do not want to relinquish it, I cannot afford to manage my assignment and my regular work at the same time!' This was a profound lesson for us.

To show that we cared about our agents, we also did things such as helping them acquire jobs, putting up funds so they could operate small peddler stalls, or present them with a one-off subsidy. Later, regular fixed-amount subsidies were given to those agents who did not have a job or who were in dire financial straits. This worked quite well. Once a long-term solution to their financial problems was found, they settled down and became more motivated.

Liaison and Rendezvous Sites

Liaison and rendezvous with agents should either be conducted on premises set up specifically for that purpose or, when the circumstances call for it, by creatively exploiting suitable sites in the wider community.

Initially, for the most part we could rendezvous with our agents inside government organs (case officers serving in the municipal branches of the Public Security Bureau often met with their agents on the branch premises or at a local police station) or in the living quarters of our operational officers. Both these types of sites were not really well-suited for this, however, since in the former case the identity of the agent was easily compromised, while in the latter case [the assignments of] our officers were easily compromised. Specifically, meeting in operational officers' living quarters should be avoided at all costs.

In order to be able to liaise regularly without jeopardising clandestinity, we set up separate dedicated premises in suitable locations in each municipal district to rendezvous with our agents. In addition, we also cleverly and creatively exploited additional sites and ran a variety of liaison premises.

Avoiding Recruitment Clashes

As they proceeded to develop agent work, the operational components of the Shenyang Public Security Bureau and the bureau's municipal district branches had to maintain close contact in order to avoid clashes.

Initially, both the municipal bureau and its branches simultaneously sought to develop large numbers of agents, and the way they went about selecting their targets was invariably by consulting bureau files. Because the bureau and its branches maintained insufficient contacts, it then easily happened that the same person was cultivated and approached by both.

In order to avoid this, the following practice was adopted: For the agents who had already been recruited, the branches completed a special form that was filed with the municipal bureau for future reference; for the agents they anticipated recruiting, the branches also would complete and submit a form, but would put off the recruitment until the municipal bureau could ensure that there would be no clash [with efforts by its own operational components] (and, in important cases, until formal endorsement had been received). Whenever the municipal bureau itself expected to conduct a recruitment, it would inform the relevant district branch. By proceeding in this way, contacts were streamlined and the duplication of efforts avoided.

Insights

The insights I gained from my years of agent work were that certain principles had to be respected in order to successfully develop and manage an agent. A first prerequisite was to understand the agent's state of mind. [After 1949,] as I was to discover, the following complex states of mind existed among agents:

1. Anticipating and imagining that the enemy would return, hence only going through the motions. Some agents imagined that the Chiang Kai-shek gang would stage a comeback and they longed for a quick outbreak of a third world war. As a result, in dealing with the tasks we gave them, they would stall and respond in a perfunctory manner.
2. Regarding agent work as merely an alternative form of probation. Some agents maintained that asking them to work for us was no different (other than the venue) from the kind of probational control that demanded they show up regularly at the local police station or municipal district branch to 'report back'. In their minds, they found this hard to endure.
3. Accepting the work but alarmed by the remaining element of control. Some agents had become resentful and depressed while on probation and hoped that by agreeing to work for us control would either be reduced or suspended altogether.
4. Looking for a way out financially. Many agents, because of their stained pasts, had difficulties finding work and could not make ends meet. They tried to cope by working for us or they hoped to use their work for us as a springboard to regular employment.
5. Worrying about not having any achievements to point at. Because the primary concern of many agents was to resolve their personal problems, they were particularly eager to have something to deliver. What they feared most was to be seen as dispensable.
6. Worrying about hurting people's feelings. As almost invariably they reported on relatives, close friends, or colleagues at work, they felt that what they were doing was 'digging up dirt'. At the same time, they really did not want to offend anyone. They were afraid of confrontation if what they were doing was to become public knowledge, and they feared a dramatic falling out among friends. Therefore, they did only the minimum expected of them.
7. Afraid of becoming implicated. They did not really want to approach elements from reactionary political parties and organisations as they feared the government would think they were being roped in.
8. The [ethnic] Koreans loved to work for the government, while the Japanese looked down on the Chinese. Because they had been oppressed for a long time, the Koreans developed warm patriotic sentiments, and as agents, they provided our government with plenty of information on sabotage and leads. The attitude of the Japanese

towards the Chinese and Koreans remained hostile, and as agents, whatever they reported had to be double-checked and authenticated more than once.

The characteristic states of mind listed above were those that we had to identify and manage as we cultivated and utilised agents. In dealing with them, our remedies, calling for much patient persuasion and education, had to match the symptoms. It was out of the question to treat our agents the way we treated members of the special demographic subject to probational control. It was necessary to avoid confrontation, and clandestinity had to be ensured. Agent achievements had to be given due credit and rewarded when appropriate, while errors that agents may have committed required rectification. The agents had to be encouraged and weaned of their misgivings.

A second prerequisite was the need to establish respect. The management, utilisation, and direction of an agent will only be successful if the organisation commands due respect in the eyes of the agent. The establishment of such respect begins with matters of attitude, trust, problem-solving, and so on.[56]

When interacting with an agent, the attitude of the case officer, if he is to command respect and recognition from the agent, must be serious as well as amicable and sincere. Assuming no unforeseen circumstances, agreed-upon rendezvous times must be respected so agents do not lose confidence. When agents raise issues involving their work or their financial situations, they must be given a sympathetic ear and the issues must be handled conscientiously. Only then will our public security organs command respect and will our agents know they can count on and place their trust in us.

The balance between 'carrots' and 'sticks', furthermore, must be properly handled. In the context of agent recruitment, whether one should begin with 'carrots' or with 'sticks' should depend on the circumstances.

When handling ordinary elements who had come clean in the course of registering with the authorities, who had ceased to be active, and who showed a good attitude, it was fine to first employ 'carrots' and then, after identifying their weak spots and developing a sense of how these could be exploited as *kompromat* proceed to 'sticks'. Later, this same procedure could be reversed, and the emphasis again could be put on 'carrots'. In the case of individuals on whose pasts we had reliable intelligence, who had not yet registered with the authorities, or whose registration had been perfunctory and whose weak spots were known to us and on whom we had *kompromat* (involving, for example, rumour-mongering or holding back information), it was fine to begin by wielding 'sticks', even in the absence of current activities on their part, and then later to proceed to the use of carrots.

Regardless of whether one opts for 'sticks first' or for 'sticks later', the goal should be to improve utilisation of the agent. To meet that goal, one must optimise the timing and force of one's blows.

A final prerequisite is that agents, whether newly cultivated or not, must complete certain formalities. Some officers worry that it will impact negatively on the agent's state of mind if an agent who has already concluded a trial use period or has been active for quite some time suddenly is asked to fill out a form, swear an oath, or formally commit to abide by [agent] rules. Practice proves that not only does this not have a negative impact but, on the contrary, it allows the agent to put his mind at ease and conclude that 'I have now been accepted as a professional, both permanently and properly.' Completion of the formalities merely strengthens the agent's commitment and readiness to put his trust in the organisation. It is not counterproductive.

3 Developing Doctrinal Terminology

In this excerpt from a conference report that became compulsory reading for public security officers in 1953, China's Minister of Public Security Luo Ruiqing elaborates on the term 'agent'. He argues that it would be politically as well as professionally appropriate for public security officers in New China to use the term to speak of *all* of their assets, irrespective of their political backgrounds or their status. As a feature of the operational world in which they would henceforth live and move, Luo wanted officers to refrain from professionally labelling 'bad guys' differently from 'good guys' as long as they were all 'our guys'. At the time, his proposal was a novel one, and a term with such a broad referent had yet to become part of doctrinal terminology. What Luo had to say illustrated a problematic general trend at the time. An investigation conducted by the Beijing Public Security Bureau in 1951 noted that 'the categories used by one unit do not match those used by another' and 'when statistics are compiled', this mismatch 'is not explained in detail, and hence errors and mistakes are the result'.[57] Luo's aim was to reduce, as part of HUMINT capacity building, the degree to which communications practices prevailing among officers on the ground clashed with the conceptual rigour mandated by rational management and impeded the development of accurate estimates and reliable interpretations of intelligence reporting.

Translated Text

I will refrain from raising things I have already discussed on numerous occasions, but I want to further clarify a matter that has to do with agents.

In the past, we used to think of the term 'agent' as designating only (or mainly) turned elements from the antagonistic classes. It was not all-inclusive. We knew from firsthand operational experience that, in actual struggle, agents constituted covert assets employable in routine surveillance

---

Luo Ruiqing, 'Teqing wenti' (Agent Matters), excerpt from a report to the Second All-Army Conference on Protection Work, 29 November 1952, reprinted in *Jingji baowei gongzuo huiji* (Collected Economic Protection Work), Vol. 5 (July 1953), pp. 1–3.

as well as in case-related operational activity. While we now allow ourselves to continue to recruit such assets from among the elements of the antagonistic classes, we should also, in the same way, proceed to recruit them from among the masses and the activists – or even from among Communist Party and Youth League members – as long as they possess the necessary qualifications. To assume that our agents may *only* be recruited from among the elements of the antagonistic classes, not from among our own base of masses and activists, or to maintain that only individuals from the antagonistic classes serving operational needs may be spoken of as agents (while individuals recruited from among our own base of masses and activists serving operational needs may not) is to have an incomplete understanding. It is, as a result, incorrect or not entirely correct.

If we fail to make use of elements from the antagonistic classes to strike at the enemy, we are admittedly not clever. But if we do not, at the same time, also employ politically reliable members of our own base of masses and activists to serve as covert assets directly engaging the enemy in combat – as the backbone and leading core of our agent work – not only will we find ourselves weak and powerless but also in a very precarious situation. Therefore, our practice of rigidly dividing all our assets into the three categories of confidential guardians, agents, and informants is no longer entirely appropriate and should be reassessed.

My view is that we cannot expect the agents whom we recruit to possess identical political qualifications any more than we can expect them all to be equally qualified when it comes to ability. Take their political qualifications: It should be the case that some of them can be fully trusted politically, that some of them can on the whole be trusted but not entirely, while yet others are altogether untrustworthy and must be controlled by way of special, coercive means. Some individuals cannot be trusted today but may change in the course of being tested in struggle. As far as abilities are concerned, there are people who manage to carry out very sophisticated high-level missions, including long-term penetration operations, and then there are people who manage to do little more than engage in routine information gathering. There are also individuals who start out unable to carry out high-level missions or to serve as penetration assets but who, after training, tempering, and due preparation, may turn out to have, or to have acquired, what it takes.

I believe it would be more appropriate and more clear-cut for us to apply this realisation to the recruitment and enrolment of agents. We should let our analyses and categorisations rest on these criteria in the case of all people whom we enrol rather than rigidly dividing them into confidential guardians, agents, and informants. Some comrades do not like the sound of the word 'agent' and still have to be persuaded. Our revolution is about striking at the counter-revolutionaries, so why hesitate to become an agent in the battle against counter-revolution?

To make a long story short, this is what we do. Our business is what is known as 'giving somebody a taste of his own medicine'. The issue is not one of labels but of differing political standpoints. Even when we exploit elements who have broken with the antagonistic classes, we should not disregard the differences prevailing among them. Some of them are not honest with us, and they force us to be on our guard. Some superficially back us, but in their heart of hearts really back our enemies. When they are exposed, they must be severely punished. Then there are those who used to be our enemies, but who are now attacking the enemy. After having passed the test, they still cannot be regarded entirely as our own, but they should nonetheless not be treated indiscriminately as enemies. While remaining vigilant, we should also make efforts to win them over and to train them. In the past, we used to stress the element of vigilance because it was often in short supply. We now need to adopt a more overarching principle.

In our agent work we also need to pay attention to protecting secrets. Agent work is top secret work that cannot be conducted without complete secrecy. Some comrades running agents frequently reveal to the agent the entire operation as well as our operational aim; other comrades are very careless in how they handle the rendezvous with their agents and frequently compromise the identity of the agent. These are all violations of the principles of agent work, and as such have to be rectified. They must not under any circumstances be allowed to persist.

4 Trial and Error

The records from 1953–1954 excerpted below draw attention to some of the issues that public security organs in the early PRC had to grapple with in the course of HUMINT capacity building. These excerpts are merely grainy snapshots, but together they provide a glimpse into how agencies 'reorganised their way forward.' In the first excerpt, the Shenyang Municipal Public Security Bureau discusses the organisation and division of responsibilities among operational components. In the second excerpt, frustrated Public Security Bureau leaders in Xinjiang province (today the Xinjiang Uighur Autonomous Region) draw attention to miscommunications and other operational irregularities. The third excerpt quotes a report circulated nationwide for reference by the Ministry of Public Security, documenting the degree to which profiling, training, and utilisation of agents in enterprises and infrastructure in Jiangxi province had, until recently, been marred by 'flaws and errors'. In the fourth and final excerpt, a senior public security officer from Hebei province draws on accumulated local experience of agent recruitment and operations to highlight some positive findings and model practices that, in his opinion, merit wider emulation.

Translated Text

'How Should We Proceed?'

How should we proceed in merging what [in Shenyang's economic protection sector] are currently agents, informants, and confidential guardians and in designating all of them agents?

The creation of a single uniform designation calls for identifying the specific utility of each agent, carrying out individual validations, and deciding on the level at which the agent is to be run. (*Note*: below, informants and confidential guardians are all referred to as agents.[58])

Excerpt from 'Guanyu gongchang qiye neibu teqing gongzuo jiancha qingkuang baogao' (Report on an Investigation into the Status of Agent Work in Factories and Enterprises), 29 July 1953. Mimeographed 12-page original, weeded out from the archive of a state-run enterprise in Shenyang on an unknown date.

4 Trial and Error

Agents about whom we already have a pretty good idea are to be examined in detail; agents about whom we still really do not have a good idea must be scrutinised in depth and exhaustively, and their recent records as well as their documented pasts must be appraised repeatedly. In the end, we must produce conclusive validation reviews to determine our decisions about whether to retain or to terminate.

. . . . . .

How are the operational line sections of Public Security Bureau divisions and the protection sections (sub-sections) of district branches, large enterprises, etc. to divide up the running of agents among themselves? In practical terms, they are to abide by a division of labour based on the following principles:

1. According to the principles spelled out in the instructions issued by Minister Luo [Ruiqing], agents tasked with following up on leads as part of case-related operational activity are, without exception, to be run directly by operational line sections, while agents tasked with guarding critical assets and production processes may be run by the protection sections.
2. Based on the current professional status of the agent, important technical personnel (above the level of assistant engineer or technician) and senior employees, and administrators (above the rank of section chief) are to be run by operational line sections, whereas the remainder are to be run by the protection sections (sub-sections).
3. Based on the agent's past reactionary professional status, former members of reactionary political parties and organisations who used to hold positions equal to or higher than those of district party department secretaries or team leaders; former field officers, or higher, in Chiang Kai-shek's bogus army; former section chiefs, or higher, in the enemy's bogus government; former warrant officers, or higher, in the enemy's bogus police force and gendarmerie; former professional Central Statistics Bureau or Military Statistics Bureau *tewu*;[59] and Yiguandao initiators or higher are all to be run by operational line sections.[60] The rest may be run by the protection sections (sub-sections).

Of the above three principles, the first one enjoys precedence. For example, if the agent meets the criteria under 1, and even if he happens to be a member of our Party or Youth League or an ordinary worker, he is to be run by an operational line section. However, if he only meets the criteria under 1 or under 2, he may in some cases also be run by a protection section (sub-section). The three principles must, under no circumstances, be separated from one another, with only one of them in isolation being cited in support of a particular agent running arrangement. The principles are integrated and applicable as a single whole.

'Your Understanding Is Muddled!'

1. Your understanding of the two concepts 'agent' and 'social intelligence' [provider] is blurred, and you confuse two fundamentally different issues.

In his *Summary Report to the Second All-Army Conference on Protection Work* Minister Luo [Ruiqing] explained that 'agents' are 'covert human assets employable in routine surveillance as well as in case-related operational activity'. In the past, depending on the utility and social background of the individual, we mechanically divided our human assets into three different categories – confidential guardians, agents, and informants – but this was not entirely appropriate, and, as of now, they may all be spoken of as 'agents'. When the time comes to recruit and enrol agents, one may analyse or categorise them based on their political qualifications and abilities, but there is no need to impose any further rigid 'terminological' (*'mingci' shang*) distinction. (The new explanation of the concept of agent is detailed in issue No. 60 of *Public Security Construction* that the localities are encouraged to study.)

'Social intelligence', in contrast, involves gathering information on how different social strata are responding to our Party's various policies and major domestic and international events.[61] While agents are covert human assets in the struggle against the enemy, social intelligence entails providing information for reference on developments in society and the community to support the Party's setting of short- and long-term policies. The two concepts differ in nature as well as in their uses, and they must be strictly distinguished from each other.

2. The development of agents among resident foreigners. It was ruled early on that this could only take place with permission of the Centre, but as of yet your recruitment of a number of new agents from among Pakistani expatriates has not been handled in accordance with the set procedures. This is not right, and we hope you will promptly produce the relevant documentation and submit it to the provincial Public Security Bureau to process a supplementary examination and approval.

Excerpt from Xinjiang Public Security Bureau comments on the Kashgar Public Security Division, 'Qingli zhuan'an shencha teqing zhengdun judian baogao' (Report on Cutting Back on Case-Related Operational Activity, Examining Agents, and Consolidating Secret Premises), 9 May 1953. Reprinted in *Xinjiang gongan* (Xinjiang Public Security), No. 4 (1953), pp. 10–11.

4 Trial and Error   37

3. In the past, we failed to pay sufficient attention to the training and cultivation of the agents whom we utilised, and we were inclined almost entirely to use coercive methods, which resulted in phenomena such as agents providing false intelligence, framing innocent people, and deceiving us. Officers utilising agents must now be trained to avoid this. Agents must not only be subject to strict controls but our own officers must also remain extremely vigilant and, whenever called for, they should be prepared to either punish the agents or subject them to ideological education in order to ensure that they serve us loyally.

'Reclaiming Wasteland'

Agent work and case-related operational activity in Jiangxi's economic protection sector during this past year may be compared to 'reclaiming wasteland'. Prior to July of last year [1952], no more than a handful of units were operating agents and the domain as a whole was in poor shape. It was only in the wake of the Third National Conference on Economic Protection Work in August, as part of a new long-term policy of transformation, that [operational] components were set up and properly staffed, work was gradually initiated, and a tentative foundation was established. At this point, the number of problems that we must properly resolve is still very large. Below is a brief report on the unfolding situation.

In the economic protection sector of our province as a whole, there are currently *nn* agents, *nnn* confidential guardians, and *nnn* informants (to use their original designations). Among these, a majority were opened up in the course of validations, accident investigations, and systematic investigation and research after the Third National Conference on Economic Protection Work.[62] Meanwhile, our original contingent of agents and informants has undergone a thorough sorting out (based on their qualifications and utility) that began with an examination of each individual's political circumstances, ideological track record, and work attitude, followed by study of records, research, analysis, investigation, and fact-finding in combination with interviews. This has allowed us to achieve clarity and to finally decide, in each instance, whether to retain or to terminate the agent. We have also produced a critical summary of past techniques and methods of control and training.

Excerpt from Jiangxi Public Security Bureau, 'Yinianlai jingji baowei fangmian de teqing gongzuo he zhuan'an zhencha jinxing qingkuang baogao' (Progress Report on Agent Work and Predicated Case Investigation in the Economic Protection Sector during the Past Year), October 1953. Reprinted in *Jingji baowei gongzuo huiji*, Vol. 6 (December 1953), pp. 12–18.

The agents and informants who have been let go were all recruited in the course of past movements, and most of them were no longer serving much of a function. The main reason for this is that their profiling, training, and utilisation were marred from the outset by a lack of care and discretion, not to mention flaws and errors. In some instances, all that happened was that a person would report something and once the information was recorded, he was counted as an agent (or informant). He sometimes might have even remained on the books as an agent even though no one could remember his name. Nothing was done that deserves to be called probing the person's political mien, ideological circumstances, or qualifications and utility. For example, in the Tianhe Coal Mine, a *tewu* was recruited as an agent even though he had not yet come clean about his own problems and he was known to want to avenge the execution of his own father. In the case of an agent in the Pingxiang Mines, recruitment began with the execution of his brother on day one and then, on day two, he was forced to swear an oath in front of Chairman Mao's portrait. In the Dajishan Tungsten Mines, one agent was told over the phone to report, while another agent, when the head of his workshop asked where he was going, announced loudly that 'I am on my way to the Protection Section to report', thereby committing the error of revealing his role as an agent. In Ganzhou, after having failed to come up with any *kompromat*, a protection section officer who had ordered that his agent show up in person, slammed his fist down on the desk, angrily glaring at the agent and giving him a dressing down that lasted the better part of an evening. The officer later described this as an effort to display both kindness and authority in order to command respect and to exercise ideological control. The outcome was that the agent in question went into hiding and thereafter no longer wanted to meet the officer face to face.

Failure to assign the running and training of an agent to a specific officer was even more widespread. All that some officers did was demand intelligence, while others, after having recruited an agent never again got in touch with him. So, for example, in Factory XXX, there was an agent who had been transferred elsewhere months before the officer meant to run him had become aware of this. In short, we still face very many problems when it comes to the recruitment of agents. Officers are ideologically ambivalent about the whole thing, and the way in which recruitments are conducted is all very chaotic – to the point where errors of a principled nature persist and the utility of agents remains limited.

4 Trial and Error

'I Wish to Highlight the Following'

Based on the state of agent work in our province, I wish to highlight the following matters of principle:

A. Basic Principles of Agent Work:

1. Agent work must proceed in accordance with 'necessity and capability'. What is meant by 'necessity' here is the necessity of countering the enemy. There are two sides to this – that of offence and that of defence. In offence, in order to achieve pre-emption, the necessity is in case-related operational activity to task the agent with establishing operational control of the enemy's *tewu* organisation and its activities. In defence, it is mainly to employ agents to guard critical assets and production, as well as to position agents in the social strata or in places where the enemy may be lurking in order to attain full informational control and flexibility in handling him. 'Capability', in contrast, means to consider whether among our prospective agents the people willing to serve us are up to the task and whether our own capability will allow us to run them.
2. One can essentially divide agents into three categories based on their political backgrounds: members of the revolutionary masses, representatives of the backward masses, and antagonistic class and *tewu* elements. Depending on what is called for in each instance, recruitment may involve profiling targets belonging to any one of these categories. Regardless of the required agent qualifications, one must firmly adhere to the principle of one-to-one recruitment.
3. Categorising agents based on their assigned tasks. First, there are case agents, then secret investigation agents, and finally agents guarding critical assets and production. The agents in the former two categories must be directed on their own by operational line departments. It is absolutely forbidden, for instance, to have one such agent recruit a second agent, or for agents in these categories to be run as a group. Members of the working class who are either Communist Party or Youth League members or activists, and who have been recruited solely for the purpose of guarding a critical asset may, however, with permission, be directed in groups. For now, the localities have been permitted to do this on a trial basis in one or two factories or mines to gain experience. The purpose of opening up this kind of agent group is

Excerpt from Zhang Minghe, 'Zai disanci quansheng gongan huiyishang de zongjie baogao' (Concluding Summary Report at the Third All-Province Public Security Conference). Published in *Gongan jianshe* (Public Security Construction), No. 99 (30 September 1954), pp. 29–46.

to meet special challenges and to facilitate the management and training of agents, but aside from meeting separately with the head of the group, the agents in the group are not to maintain any lateral contacts among themselves.[63]

B.   When Recruiting and Enrolling Agents, One Must:

1. Establish clear aims and demands. Agents are to be employed in case-related operational activity and to guard critical assets in order to uncover and get to know the enemy, and then on the basis of this knowledge they are to attack the enemy. If the opening up of an agent is done without a clear target of attack or without a target to be protected, the result inevitably will be deviation in the form of blind and chaotic recruitment.
2. Proceed by way of investigation and research to profile and get to know prospective recruitment targets and agents. If operational officers fail to investigate and probe society and the masses in depth, they will not be able to spot and profile targets who have true potential. In the case of agents already recruited, unless they are carefully cultivated and operated, they simply will not be able to play their intended roles.
3. There are basically two ways of recruiting an agent: one way is to win him over by education and persuasion and then to see him work for us on the basis of his political consciousness. The other way is to exploit *kompromat* and then proceed from a coercive recruitment to a genuine readiness to work for us. In this context, *kompromat* may refer to either political crimes or simple criminal conduct, but coercion is not to be employed when attempting to recruit ordinary members of reactionary political parties and organisations or persons who merely nurse grievances against us. Stains on a person's private life should not be exploited as *kompromat*. Naked force as a means of agent control, and the crash approach as a recruitment technique, are extraordinary strategies not meant to be employed by county-level operational line departments. When prefectural- or municipal-level operational line departments need to employ them, they may only do so with the permission of the provincial Public Security Bureau.

C.   When Directing and Handling Agents, Officers Must:

1. Abide by the principle of 'common soldiers approaching other common soldiers, and generals approaching other generals', and a specific officer must be assigned to the management of each agent. Case agents and agents from the ranks of senior technicians tasked with guarding critical assets and production processes are to be controlled by the relevant public security organ's operational line department (exemptions apply

in factories and mines that have been granted operational powers). Protection units in factories and mines are to assist in agent profiling and in controlling and directing ordinary agents.
2. Diligently provide training and conduct regular agent validations, including an assessment once every six months or, in the case of important agents, once every three months.
3. Establish ground rules and explain routines, spelling out strict punishments and rewards.
4. 'Clearly distinguish between inside and outside, between the enemy and ourselves.' Means used to deal with antagonistic class elements may not be used to handle agents who belong to our Party or Youth League or who are members of the ordinary masses. In the same way, some of the means used and called for when dealing with our Party or Youth League members do not apply to the handling of agents who come from the ranks of the enemy.
5. Create a card catalogue of documented threats.

5 Big Brother Dispenses *Operativnyy* Experience

In the following, an anonymous Soviet officer shares with Chinese colleagues his KGB expertise on general agent tactics, categories, recruitment, and handling, as well as on female agents, undeclared cadres, safe houses, and more. In the 1950s, officers like the speaker were valued by their PRC counterparts because of their resources. Selective digestion of what they had to say helped shape curricula in Chinese public security academies. As the speaker makes explicit, he neither wanted nor expected his audience to merely 'mechanically copy the methods developed in the Soviet Union', and it is important to note that only relatively few of the points he elaborates upon in terms of 'What this means is ... ' left traces in Chinese doctrine as such. A Ministry of Public Security interpreter later remarked that although KGB experts had indeed provided his officer colleagues with much operational advice, 'much of the time their proposals were inappropriate, at times even laughable', and unsuited to Chinese surroundings.[64] Equally noteworthy, in the case of this particular speaker, is that some of the narrowly tradecraft-related points he deals with in terms of 'This is how x is done ... ' would be repeated almost verbatim in the textbook *Lectures on the Subject of Agent Work*, produced under the auspices of China's Ministry of Public Security in 1957.[65] The source of the text translated into English here is a rough transcript by a brachygrapher in the speaker's audience, of the translation from Russian into Chinese provided by the speaker's interpreter.

Translated Text

While their class natures (class essences) are fundamentally different, our agent work and the *tewu* work of capitalist countries differ in other principal respects as well, such as agent tactics. The roles of our security agencies differ from those of the security agencies of capitalism. While

---

Handwritten entries, 'Zhuanjia tan teqing gongzuo' (Expert Discusses Agent Work) (13 July 1955) and 'Zhuanjia jieda teqing wenti' (Expert Elaborates on Agent-Related Questions) (27 July 1955) in notebook maintained from 1955 to 1959 by an officer in the First Office, Second Group of the Dean's Department (further details uncertain).

the purpose of operational activity in capitalist countries is to protect the interests of capitalism and consolidate capitalist rule (and for that purpose to employ all available means to suppress progressive figures, workers, labouring people, revolutionary elements, and all progressive organisations), the purpose in our case is to suppress all counter-revolutionary elements, protect the interests of the people, and consolidate the People's Democracy. Our agent work, in other words, has a different essence with respect to its operational aims and tactics.

Not only do the agent tactics differ but so too does the composition of our agent contingent. An absolute majority of our agents are patriotic elements; only a minority consists of disloyal, hostile elements who require post-recruitment education and conversion in order to foster loyalty to us. The absolute majority of our agents are patriotic elements who are loyal in terms of their thinking and, on the basis of ideology and awareness, are prepared to voluntarily aid the state in going after counter-revolutionary elements and in building the motherland.

The agents of capitalist countries are morally degenerate elements, including swindlers greedy for money, self-seeking careerists, liars and swindlers, and elements who [*illegible*]. Some have been recruited from bourgeois strata, others from backward strata and from among the jobless, etc. They include people who sow discord using trumped-up charges, such as Harvey Matusow, who started out as a member of the Communist Party USA and then became an FBI informant who fabricated evidence about the Communist Party leadership, resulting in the arrest of its members. Eventually, Matusow changed his evidence and admitted that it had been fabricated, proving that American agents are swindlers and morally degenerate.[66] Or take American Trotskyite element Louis Budenz who had wormed his way into the Communist Party USA but later was expelled; he agreed to testify when the American reactionary government arrested and interrogated progressive elements.[67]

In his 1928 characterisation of capitalism, Mikhail Kalinin made the observation that, given that it opposes the People, 'no person of integrity will ever voluntarily serve the security agency of a capitalist country'. As we have seen, agents in capitalist countries are indeed morally degenerate elements.

Agent Tactics

The code of conduct for agents in capitalist countries includes threats and intimidation, provocation (as a counter-operational tactic) and blackmail, fabricating charges and framing people. In our case, we make people agree to work for us out of their own free will, by way of persuasion and education. Only a tiny handful of antagonistic class elements are coercively recruited with the help of *kompromat* and then educated and converted.

In capitalist countries, agent work involves the use of provocation, slander, intimidation, and so on. We, in contrast, objectively analyse every circumstance and reject the bag of tricks employed in capitalist countries. We always educate our agents to be loyal and honest, and urge them to always provide us with truthful information on our operational targets. Provocation is totally impermissible, as is fabrication of charges and framing of people.

The agents of capitalist countries have been bought with money and, as a result, they show no loyalty. Instead, they serve whoever pays them the most. Agents like that will collect bogus intelligence and sell it for money. Whoever will give them money can have their intelligence. In other words, if they have intelligence, the agents of capitalist countries will receive money, whereas if they have no intelligence, they will not receive any money. Our agents, in contrast, as long as they remain ideologically loyal to us and continue to work willingly for us, [*illegible*] cannot be bought.

Bourgeois agents will employ counter-operational tactics when it permits them to present a false picture of success to their handlers. They will fabricate things and provoke people, and then, once they have succeeded, they will ask for money. We must eschew agent tactics such as these.

Categories

How our agents are to be categorised [by social background] has been explained in detail more than once by Minister Luo [Ruiqing]. The categories we employ today match our present circumstances. If those circumstances were to change in the future, the categories will need to be revised accordingly. The Soviet Union recognises only two categories, namely, patriotic elements and antagonistic class elements, but in China, given the actual circumstances, one may continue to recognise the current number of categories.

When it comes to foreigners, one must distinguish between the resident expatriates (that is to say, the elements with foreign nationalities who live in China) and foreign officials, trade representatives, embassy and consular staff, military attachés, and so on. Most foreign representatives and diplomats (from the capitalist countries) are *tewu* and they know we keep them under surveillance. They will attempt to recruit as their agents elements who are hostile to us, loyal to them, and [*illegible*].

5 Big Brother Dispenses *Operativnyy* Experience

It is part of our mission to subject each and every one of the foreign officials to prolonged and careful scrutiny, using physical surveillance, agents, and other operational instruments to expand our knowledge about them. We must research and study their individual weaknesses and hobbies, whether they like to party, sing, enjoy a drink, pick up women, and so on. Our aim is to understand them in specific detail and, especially, to gather compromising material and determine if they have ever broken the law, either in their own country or in China, and to establish whether they have any conflicts with their consulate.

For example, if they have committed a currency crime by exchanging US dollars for Chinese currency, or if they have disrupted the financial order by trading on the black market, we may be able to secretly detain them and attempt a crash recruitment by taking advantage of their vulnerability. In a different scenario, if they have been selling opium, we may be able to exploit that. If we know that a certain foreigner finds it difficult to make ends meet – if either his woman or he himself needs money – then that too may be something we can exploit. Let's say a certain embassy employee has lost a confidential document which has ended up in our hands. If we publicise the identity of this element, he will be disciplined. This means we may be able to target him for a crash approach and convince him to work for us. In short, in our work we must excel at exploiting our enemies' vulnerabilities.

Foreign consulates and embassies often employ nannies, chauffeurs, and other local service staff. We can arrange for our agents to engage in such work or we can recruit the people already doing such work, and then through them we will be able to discern the vulnerabilities of the foreigners, such that during their tenures in China we may attempt to turn them into our own assets. Their service staff will allow us to develop a sense of their regular activities and to discover their vulnerabilities such that we may be able to mount a crash recruitment.

Female household staff and nannies are particularly useful as agents because through them we can determine the regular comings and goings [of embassy and consulate staff] as well where documents are kept. In the latter case, once we know this, we can secretly access and photograph the documents. We may be able to use them as *kompromat*, or with the help of our agents, determine, for example, who is selling opium and then mount a crash recruitment. The work of convincing foreigners to serve as our agents is difficult but important. Prior to any recruitment attempt, one must already have substantive and sufficient information at one's disposal so that the target will be unable to take any evasive actions. Comrades in this line of work must be experienced; if they bungle it, our government will be presented with a diplomatic note and this will have negative repercussions.

Working on ordinary Indonesian, Thai, or Malayan expatriates who have lived here for over two decades is relatively easy, since one can use the threat of expulsion to get at them. By comparison, they are easier to recruit and handle than people from [Western] capitalist countries.

When planning an agent recruitment in religious or democratic party circles, we must profile our targets meticulously and look for information that will increase our chances of success. People in these circles include those who are loyal to our regime, and therefore, by way of persuasion, can be convinced to work for us. In the case of certain ideologically backward elements and others who hate the Americans but at the same time resent the momentous steps taken by our Party, we may use ordinary arguments involving our desire for peace and our opposition to American imperialism to educate them and to convince them to work for us. Many of them have been deceived and developed views that are different from ours, but they nonetheless oppose occupation and war, and they support peace. We can exploit their peace-loving stance to make them do work for us. *Kompromat* may be used, if it will achieve the desired results, as we do not [in the case of believers] in each and every instance need to wait for the target to express absolute loyalty to us. For instance, in the case of [*illegible*] and Protestants, we merely need to carefully study their weak spots and then exploit any *kompromat* that we may find. If as believers they have broken the commandments or have violated the teachings of their religion (like Muslims who consume pork, for example), then this may be exploited.

Here is another example. In the case of religions that require clerical celibacy, if we discover that a cleric is maintaining an illicit sexual relationship with a married believer, we can raise this with him and talk about what might happen if his breach of the religious commandments were to become public knowledge. What would happen, for example, if the woman's husband, or other members of his congregation, were to find out? This is something we can use to coerce the individual into becoming our agent.

Agent Recruitment

In preparation for actual recruitment, first of all, one must develop a clear understanding of the target's past as well as of his personal background. One must first control and develop all available information about him. Only then will it be possible to make an informed decision about whether, when, where, and how to attempt a recruitment. The necessary information may be obtained through physical surveillance or through other overt means.

After having studied the information, and based on the concrete circumstances, one must decide *when* and *where* to mount the recruitment attempt. If, for example, our investigation has allowed us to ascertain at what time the target tends to be at home alone, then that might be a good time and place. If research has allowed us to determine where the target works, then we might go through the employer's cadre or personnel section to make contact. If he works in a factory where there has been an accident, then an investigation into the accident may be a good excuse to engage the target in conversation and to raise the issue of [secret collaboration]. Officers in the protection departments of the transportation sector may attempt to recruit during accident-related conversations.

When deciding on when and where to conduct the recruitment interview, it is crucially important to ensure clandestinity. The interview must not draw people's attention. This is a point that must be respected by all operational officers who, in order to be successful, need to be able to creatively develop and exploit alternative agent recruitment strategies. Officers must also keep in mind that to enrol or operate agents inside the institutions of [Communist] Party committees is not permitted. Such institutions are Party organisations, not agent recruitment sites. In the same way, our public security organs also operate under the leadership of the Party. Given that we are all united as one vis-à-vis the outside, agents should not be used inside Party committee institutions.

The recruitment of an agent may not occur inside the offices of our public security organs. The use of public security premises for agent recruitment purposes will compromise secrecy. If they discover that he has visited those premises, the superiors of the target for recruitment will become suspicious. In special circumstances, however, one may nonetheless bring the target to the public security premises. For example, if one has *kompromat* on the target and he has refused to show up for meetings elsewhere, one may opt to take him into custody and move him to a public security facility to take appropriate measures and to work on him there. This was the tactic opted for in the case of Wu Shuyun who, after having rejected a recruitment opportunity offered at the local tax office, was taken under guard to the Public Security Bureau to be coercively recruited. When dealing with people like that, one has to ensure secrecy. By having their arrest take place inside the Public Security Bureau, people on the outside will be prevented from finding out.

No matter *how* one conducts the actual recruitment interview with the target, and regardless of which social stratum the target represents, one should always be polite and calm. It is only to be expected that questions will arise. As we set out to be persuasive, we should explain to the target that we want his help in pursuing counter-revolutionary elements and enemies. If we hope to get him to work for us, we must absolutely refrain from swearing or threatening him. It will not be helpful if we display such attitudes when attempting to recruit him. As much as possible, we should employ the tactic of persuasion, since it makes the task of agent recruitment consolidation that much easier. Even when the target is an antagonistic class element, one must exercise restraint and pose one's questions politely and logically, and one must not right away make coarse or crude threats, such as 'You're a counter-revolutionary element! Do as you are told or we will throw you in jail or have you shot!' One must be good at making the target appreciate the options he faces and, in that way, make it all but impossible for him to reject the offer to work for us. When dealing with a philandering cleric, for example, one should not simply curse him (which may actually exacerbate his resentment), but instead we should explain what he stands to lose. In this way, we shall be able to convince him to work for us.

One may begin by selecting a light-hearted topic that will facilitate the opening of the conversation, proceed to some fairly innocuous questions, and then watch what happens and take it from there.[68] If we determine that the target is prepared to work for us, we can then turn to concrete matters and deepen the conversation. But while still talking about general matters (such as helping the public security organs pursue counter-revolutionary elements, etc.), we must refrain from stating explicitly that we are interested in having the agent provide information on a certain somebody or something. At that point, the identity of the operational target must not yet be divulged, since the recruitment still must be consolidated and the agent's loyalty must be ascertained. The identity of the operational target may, in due course, be mentioned during a subsequent contact with the potential agent. Only once he has been duly vetted is the agent to be told who he is meant to work on.

Recruitment needs to be preceded by meticulous research and an understanding of the target, so that one does not discover after a few days that he cannot be used as intended and should not have been recruited in the first place. This will have compromised secrecy, created problems, and rendered the entire effort meaningless.

As for the way in which to carry out the recruitment, there is also what in the Soviet Union is known as the tactic of 'gradual recruitment' that involves having one of our officers, under the cover of a journalist or a united-front cadre, over a period of time cultivate a contact, get to know him, engage him in conversation, and develop a rapport prior to raising the matter of his working for us. The gradual recruitment tactic is a good option when one has information on a target but is unable to mount a more direct recruitment effort.[69] This is often the case when the target – typically a member of the intelligentsia, a technician, engineer, professor, doctor, scientist, and so on – is not a revolutionary or may refuse to work for us if approached directly. In such a case, by befriending him we may still manage to enrol him. When it comes to representatives of the bourgeois democratic parties, they may initially not be willing to work for us since many of them think the public security organs are engaged in inglorious *tewu* activity. But once we have befriended them and have been able to change their minds, we may still be able to successfully recruit them. By then, the target will have already shared, in a friendly conversation, information that will make a difference, and when we propose that he work for us, it will no longer be possible for him to dodge the matter.

Agent Running

The running of an agent is an integrated process that includes direction, education, and utilisation. Our aim is to nurture the capabilities of the agent in order to see him develop a high degree of ideological sophistication, become proficient in his craft, and capable of swiftly detecting the criminal plots of the enemy. The direction and education of the agent must not proceed in a simplistic and ad-hoc fashion. Rather, it should be consistent, systematic, and meticulous.

An agent should not be directed or trained by way of a single rigid formula. Rather, he should be guided or instructed creatively and variably depending on the kind (category) of agent, his educational level, political beliefs, length of time in our service, and so on. Every agent has a different educational background, and while some may be from the revolutionary ranks, others may be hostile elements. Some will have already been working for us for a long time, while others may have been working for us for only a very short period of time. This is why there are differences in how agents are run. The following principles must be respected when directing and training the agent:

1. Providing Ideological and Political Education Every agent must be given an ideological and political education in order to develop his loyalty to the Motherland, the [Communist] Party, and the People and to ensure his constant readiness to carry out his operational assignments. The agent should arrive at an understanding that completion of his assignments is his professional duty as a patriot. This is only possible by way of a patriotic education. Therefore, when in contact with an agent, every operational officer must provide an ideological and political education touching on current domestic and international events, while also noting, and if necessary explaining, the required attitude of the agent towards our Party's policies and actions

The agent must receive an ideological and political education regardless of his religious faith or political status. How such an education is to be conducted, however, must take into account both the individual and the context. For example, we should not talk to agents from religious circles about Marxism-Leninism Mao Zedong Thought. Instead, we should take the international situation as our point of departure and make the point that unlike the war-mongering American imperialists, we oppose war and strive for peace. Such an education will arouse the agent's patriotic sentiments and help ensure that he will work for us. The same goes for members of the bourgeoisie who may be somewhat disgruntled with our Party's policies, but who nonetheless may be convinced to work for us by arousing their fervent patriotism. The education process must be tailored to the individual, and it can be modified depending on the agent's political status and religious faith.

The ideological and political education of agents who have infiltrated the enemy's inner circles is particularly important. One has to ensure that they remain loyal to us and that the enemy does not turn them into enemy assets and traitors of the People.

2.   *Improving Professional Performance*   In the process of utilising the agent, we need to pay attention to improving his professional performance. This is mainly done by giving him concrete operational assignments and explaining to him how they should be carried out. When briefing him on an assignment, it is not a matter of pointing out where he will be in relation to the target or whether or not the target is a *tewu*, but rather it is a matter of hinting how, in executing his operational assignment, he will find certain concrete means and tactics particularly useful. When debriefing the agent after completion of his operational assignment, the aim is to understand how he went about completing the assignment and to discuss with him specifically what he did right and what might have gone wrong. One should also point out how he can avoid errors in the future.

While operating the agent, one should also improve the agent's powers of observation about what the enemy is doing. In that context, one should hint at how to gain access to the enemy and how, in the heat of battle, get information from the enemy without raising suspicions or jeopardising clandestinity. The agent has to be cautioned against the use of counter-operational tactics. He must report with factual accuracy what he discovers through his operational assignment about the enemy's activities. If it is found that he is being dishonest in this respect, he must be warned.

3. *Safeguarding Operational Clandestinity and Respect for the Rules Regarding Operational Activities* While confronting a hail of bullets, the agent must learn to abide by the rules regarding operational activities and to safeguard operational clandestinity. At home, the agent must never reveal his secret status to anyone. He must never make illicit use of his power as an agent or use his status as an agent to threaten other people. The agent must learn to strictly safeguard secrecy and to abide by the rules for operational activities. He must learn how to behave in the presence of the enemy in such a way that he will never trigger suspicion. He must also learn how to pose questions as part of his assignment in a way that always safeguards clandestinity. When maintaining his liaison with us, after any rendezvous, he must have a prepared excuse for his absence so as not to arouse the suspicion of family or friends. In order to safeguard clandestinity, our liaison with him must be arranged in such a way that it matches his ordinary patterns of behaviour.

It is particularly important to educate the agent about how to abide by the rules for operational activities. For example, he must show up on time for his meetings or be prepared to explain why he is late. In addition, when he is given an operational assignment, he must execute it. If he fails to execute it successfully, he must report to us and provide the reason.

4. *Maintaining Correct Relationships between Officers and Their Agents*
As part of his work, the operational officer must establish a correct relationship with his agent. The officer should serve as a role model for the agent as far as his own behaviour – his regular interactions with the agent – is concerned. He must act with great conviction and ideological determination and be polite, knowledgeable, and easily approachable. In all these respects, he must be someone whom the agent can look up to.

Consequently, the operational officer must outmatch the agent in terms of capacity and professional skills. The officer is only allowed to interact with the agent on a professional level, and he must not exploit the agent for his own personal needs or make use of the agent for private purposes. Proper relations must be maintained. Relations between officers and agents must be appropriate, which is to say they must be professional and not become like those of friends or social acquaintances who enjoy eating, drinking, and having a good time together. They must not be garrulously vulgar.

5.   *Caring for the Agent* When working with an agent, the operational officer must show consideration and care. The officer must remember that the agent is carrying out an assignment given by the state to uncover hidden enemies, and he must not look with prejudice or bias on the agent or think of himself as somehow of superior status, elevated far above that of the agent. He must always consider the agent's needs and do his utmost to provide him with help if, for example, the agent finds it difficult to make ends meet. In this way, the operational officer will be showing consideration for the agent. Now and then, the operational officer must also reward the agent. (A topic already covered in the *Agent Work Manual* and therefore not further discussed here.)[70]

At no time should the operational officer forget his solemn promise, that he will have given the agent, to stand by his word. Failure in this respect will diminish his standing in the eyes of the agent. For example, if the agent falls ill and the officer has promised to check him into a hospital, then the officer must not make up any excuses or attempt to shift responsibility to someone else. If the agent asks for help with a sick child, the officer must not make any immediate promise that ultimately he might not be able to fulfil, and instead he should promise to look into the issue and get back to the agent. If the officer immediately agrees to take the child to the hospital the following day but in the end is unable to do so, his standing in the eyes of the agent will have diminished.

6.   *Monitoring and Checking on the Performance of the Agent* The operational officer must constantly monitor and check on the performance of the agent. Monitoring and checking allow us to timely identify any flaws or errors in the agent's performance, to determine how active the agent is in safeguarding clandestinity, and to discover if the agent may be double-dealing or deceiving us in any way. It also lets us identify signals of a possible betrayal. In the same way that trust and checking feature in the context of the activities performed by the agent, questions of trust, monitoring, and examination also feature in the case of individual agents irrespective of their backgrounds.

Procedures:

– Analyse and assess the information provided by the agent to determine whether it contains any fraudulent, untrue items.
– Verify matters by talking directly with the agent.
– Compare the agent's information to that obtained from other agents to determine whether there is a match. In this way, one agent can be utilised to monitor and check the performance of another agent.

5 Big Brother Dispenses *Operativnyy* Experience

- Place the agent under surveillance. For example, tell him to go to X to do Y, and then check to see whether or not he has done so.
- Inspect his correspondence to determine whether he may be disgruntled with us or whether he may be revealing any secrets to relatives or friends.

7. *Assign Direction of the Agent to a Specific Officer on a Permanent Basis* It is not good for operations to change the officer directing the agent too often. The good thing about using the same officer for a longer period of time is that he can then routinely study and get to know the agent, educate the agent, and become aware of the agent's traits, both his strengths and his weaknesses. This will facilitate direction of the agent. Also, the agent himself will then be better acquainted with the officer in question. Of additional and particular importance is that this will facilitate safeguarding clandestinity since the fewer people who are aware of the agent's identity, the less the likelihood of compromise.

Female Agents

In our operations, we must also use female agents in the battle against counter-revolution. What has just been said with regard to general principles applies equally to the direction, tasking, and education of female agents.

Female agents are generally used to keep foreign officials, consular staff, resident expatriates, sailors, and so on under surveillance and to put foreign youth and student delegations or bourgeois youth groups under surveillance. Female agents also operate in religious circles, dealing with the many female believers. They may be tasked with keeping foreigners under surveillance because it is relatively easier for them to approach bourgeois foreigners. Young and attractive female agents, in particular, will find foreigners particularly accessible. As a rule, the recruitment of women who have many children is to be avoided. Because they must care for their children, they rarely have the necessary time to perform well as agents.

The following are some of the requirements for an officer handling a female agent:

When briefing the agent on her operational assignment, the tactics that will permit her to succeed in carrying it out must be spelled out in concrete terms. This is particularly the case when a female agent is assigned to place a foreigner under surveillance. Her performance must also be rigorously monitored, with particular attention paid to her ideological and political education, because the foreigner under surveillance may well exert a negative influence on her. In the absence of such an education, the female agent risks being talked around or corrupted by enemy *tewu* and, with the help of small favours, or an affair, incited to defect. Therefore, the operational officer handling a female agent must remain particularly vigilant, strengthen ideological and political education, establish a proper and correct relationship, and maintain only a professional liaison with her. Intimate relationships must be discouraged because love affairs and the like all impact negatively on one's work. During their meetings, the officer must keep in mind what makes a female agent special, maintain a serious tone in their conversations, and allow the female agent to use her unique qualities to close in on the operational target.

With respect to former social butterflies, taxi girls, delinquents, and other once very frivolous women, one should not be too damning or scornful of their pasts. They remain in contact with a lot of people and to ensure their effective cooperation with us, we should strengthen their ideological education rather than end up in ideological conflict with them. For example, it is important not to discriminate against female agents who are prostitutes since this will only make them hostile, which does our work no good. Today, what needs to be done is mainly to strengthen the education and direction of such people. Counter-revolutionary elements from the old society, reactionary military officers, drug dealers, thieves, and common criminals are the people most likely to spend the night with prostitutes, and therefore the use of agents who are prostitutes is a good way for us to close in on and nab such people.

The briefing of the female agent should be kept simple and concrete. When suggesting to her how to tactically carry out her operational assignment, the operational officer should use a soft approach, so that she will find it easier to agree to work for us.

When utilising a female agent, clandestinity is of paramount importance. This is the case, in particular, if she has small children and a husband, or if she is single but has a boyfriend. In such cases, the rendezvous with her must be carefully timed so that she is able to return home at a regular hour. Otherwise, the husband or boyfriend may well start to think that she is having an affair. If the officer and the agent end up on bad terms, clandestinity will easily be compromised.

Undeclared Cadres

The [Communist] Party may assign a cadre to operate inside a democratic party, as an undeclared [Communist] Party member to gather intelligence. Such cadres are on a secret and special mission. They are not agents. Rather, they are cadres executing a special Party mission. A [Communist] Party member may, for example, be assigned to join a democratic party organisation, and it will be as a member of that organisation that henceforth he will appear in public, even though in actuality he is operating inside the organisation [as an undeclared member of the Communist Party]. The democratic party organisation is his cover. The identity of the undeclared cadre is known only to the superior [Communist Party] leadership that draws upon him. There is no need to share his identity with any members [of the democratic party], since, given the high level of required secrecy, that would serve no useful purpose.

Matters involving undeclared cadres differ from matters involving the use of agents, and they merit a separate discussion.

In addition, we [the public security organs] may send cadres from operations (*zhen'gan*) to serve inside one of the democratic parties or inside the Association of Industry and Commerce as a secretary, etc. They will remain there [*illegible*] going grey and they will not declare their [Communist] Party membership. They are not agents; rather, they are operational cadres (*zhengong ganbu*).

Clandestine Agent Contact Points

How should contacts with an agent be arranged? The direction and education of an agent calls for face-to-face contacts. It is during such contacts that the agent will be directed and educated. To manage the agent contact well, its clandestinity must be ensured. The best way to do this is to establish clandestine premises and secret rendezvous premises. However, there are times when meetings may take place in hotels or other places, but absolute secrecy must always be maintained.

A clandestine premise is normally a permanent site located within a building that belongs to the public security organs. An operational officer will have been installed there as the tenant and the keeper of the clandestine premise where operational work and agent contacts may then take place. There must be no public connection between the site and the public security organs. Nor should there be anything that will lead people to suspect that it is serving as a clandestine premise. Only the mayor will have been told that we are occupying the premises in question. When clandestine premises are set up, they must meet our needs and be given a suitable cover. If their clandestine use may easily be compromised, we should refrain from using them. A considerable sum of money has to be spent on the operation of the clandestine premises, so their cover must be [*illegible*] and must hold water. For them to be able to function as intended calls for far more than merely budgeting and generous funding.

A secret rendezvous premise is a premise used for a limited period of time only, such as a private residence secretly used one evening per week for a specified length of time. The keeper of the premise obviously must be reliable. For example, he may be one of our own agents, a so-called 'landlord agent'. A secret rendezvous premise is operated only temporarily, not for an extended period, and it will be selected on the basis of its specific location and because its use can be kept secret. Utilisation of official premises [not connected to the public security organs] may occasionally also be considered, for example, after hours when the regular office staff has left for the day so they will remain unaware of such utilisation. It is also possible to arrange a secret rendezvous with an agent in a club, theatre, and so on, but in such cases the manager (who must be reliable) of the property must be told in advance that a room will be needed between certain hours. There is, however, no need to tell him the purpose.

When contemplating how best to arrange contacts with an agent, the concrete circumstances prevailing in China must be kept in mind. So, for instance in Beijing, there are shops, medical clinics, photography studios, and so on that can be used. One can always temporarily borrow the office of the manager of a state-operated department store or, under suitable cover, a state-owned photography studio. In the latter case, there must be a separate room that no outsider can enter, and the manager of the studio must be reliable and sworn to secrecy. In Beijing, there are also public parks and places like the Cultural Palace where the management may be told that a room will be borrowed for regular use on such-and-such weekday between certain hours. There is also the option of temporarily renting a room in a hotel.

In the countryside, one can use market days or the evening hours to arrange contacts. If the meeting takes place on a market day, some disguise may be called for. If clandestinity can be safeguarded, the contact may also take place while the agent is on a work-related errand, arranged specifically for such a purpose. Depending on the setting, one can arrange for a meeting to take place after dark in the surrounding mountains or forests. During daytime, one's cover may be while the agent is gathering firewood on a hillside.

In short, the prevailing concrete circumstances must be taken into account and one must adapt to them. Officers should not mechanically copy the methods developed in the Soviet Union.

Principal Agents Directing Other Agents

Under what circumstances may we want to recruit and operate principal agents? This mainly occurs in the countryside, but it may also occur on trains or ships that go abroad, or wherever operational officers have difficulties arranging direct face-to-face contacts. Under such circumstances, officers may stay in contact with other agents through a principal agent intermediary who, after having assessed it himself, will forward their information to us. Principal agents may also be employed to maintain contact with agents inside the [enemy's] armed forces, where it may be difficult for our officers to stay in direct contact with our agent. A person to be used as a principal agent must be a politically reliable member of the Communist Party or Youth League, and his subordinate agents must all be directed and tasked one-to-one. A principal agent may be in contact with his subordinate agents in his cover capacity as a ship captain, for example, in which case their conversations are unlikely to arouse suspicion. Principal agents [*illegible*] develop and recruit agents, but may not organise them as a team. The direction of each agent must be one-to-one, and it is through the principal agent that the obtained intelligence will be passed on to the public security organs.

Questions and Answers

What are contact agents, 'route' agents, and identification agents?[71] Under what circumstances do we use such agents and what qualifications are required for each? (*Note*: These special terms are alternative ways of referring to the agents in question.[72])

> *Contact Agents*: In circumstances where an operational officer is unable to maintain direct personal contacts with an agent, a contact agent (also known as a communication agent) may serve as a go-between. For example, if an agent is dispatched to Taiwan, it may be impossible for an operational officer to maintain direct contact in person, hence the use of a communication agent is called for. (Wireless radio contact is something different.) In the case of an agent operating among bandits, the operational officer may find it impossible to maintain direct personal contact, so instead he will allow a contact agent under some suitable cover serve as a go-between. During the Great Patriotic War, in the struggle against the Ukrainian Banderists, the Soviet Union used contact agents extensively to stay in touch with those agents who had infiltrated the bandit enemy camp.
>
> *'Route' Agents*: These are agents who, with our instructions, carry out one particular kind of mission for specific periods in shifting localities. Their work may involve case-related operational activity or some other tasks. For example, when an operation faces a shortage of agent resources locally, a route agent may be dispatched temporarily to the

locality. Or when the quality of the locally available agent resources is inferior – if the local agents are of little use or if they are simply unsuitable – then a route agent with the right qualifications and abilities may be brought in from the outside. Having completed his mission, the route agent, in due course, will return to from where he came. Actual examples include investigations into instances of sabotage in factories located in the Mongolian and Tibetan regions. Here the existing agent contingent lacks the technical know-how and experience necessary to deal with arson, assassinations, etc., and hence agents who do have such expertise must be brought in from the outside. If maintaining personal contact with a high-level agent in instances like these becomes inconvenient due to the long distances involved, contact may be maintained by mail.

Identification Agents: Such agents are employed to deal with crimes against the state – involving counter-revolutionary elements as well as common criminals – and they are recruited primarily from among individuals who know the physical appearance of the enemy, such as fellow villagers, schoolmates, colleagues, or relatives. The ideal places to position identification agents are public spaces like train stations, passenger trains, ports, harbours, hotels, and so on, where the enemy is most likely to appear.

When an operational officer infiltrates the enemy camp from outside as part of a case-related mission, how should we lead and utilise him? Should he too be referred to as an agent?

An operational officer who has infiltrated the enemy camp from outside is not to be referred to as an agent. He is a salaried employee of the public security organs who has penetrated the enemy camp and who functions as an agent, and we should refer to him as a secret operational officer. Agents are not formal members of our staff; the cost of running them is covered by funds from the state's special expenditures budget and, unlike operational officers, they are not on the payroll of the public security organs.

How should we lead and utilise the secret operational officers?

Infiltration must be preceded by meticulous and detailed preparations to determine how to proceed so as to win the trust of the enemy. We must anticipate and consider how to respond to problems and how to establish and maintain contact with the officer. In particular, we must ensure that there will be no visits to any public components of the public security organ so as to avoid the officer's cover being blown or harm being inflicted by the enemy. Because the secret operational officer will be a Communist Party member, he will be reliable. Hence, his operation comes with numerous advantages. He may be expected to write his own intelligence reports. He should not be previously known to anyone in the locality where he will work, and ideally, he should be transferred in from elsewhere. His work is particularly demanding, and if we are careless, he will cease to be effective, and all the resources personified by the secret operational officer will have been wasted. For these reasons, this very important line of work must be conducted carefully and meticulously.

Part III

Best Practice

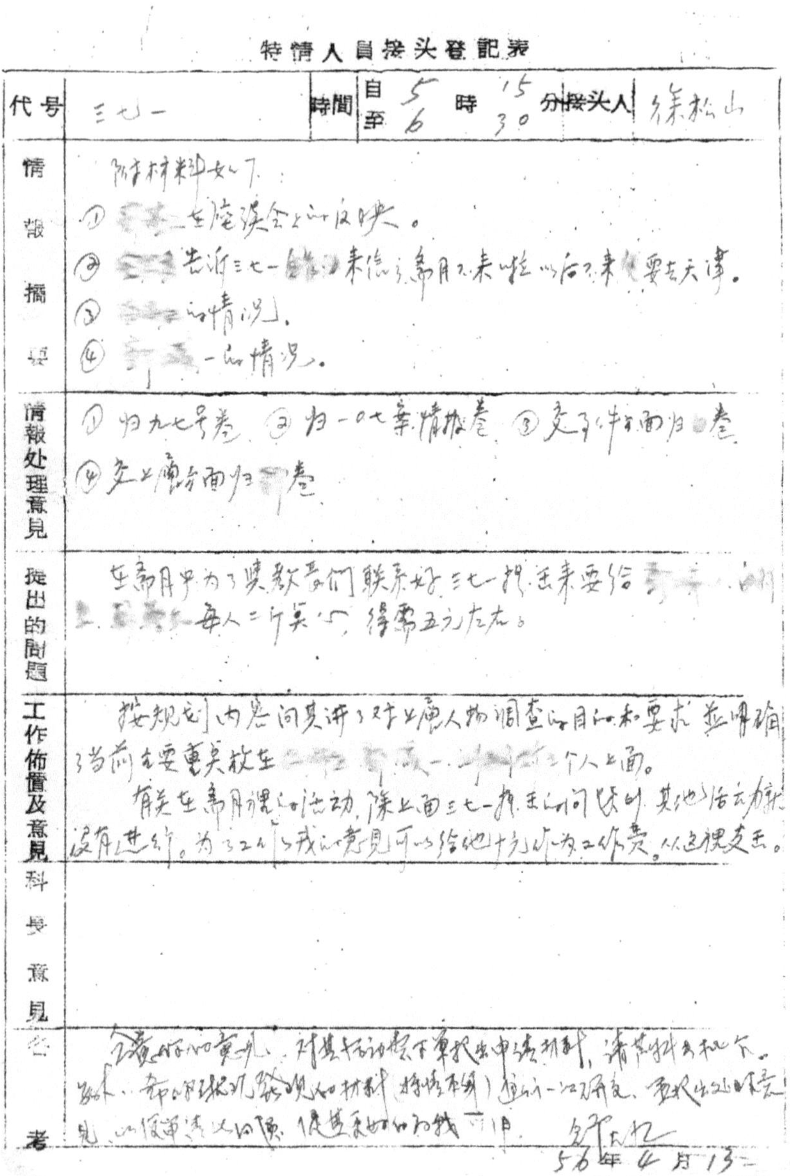

Figure 3 Intelligence registration and processing record (1956)

Introduction

During much of the Cold War, HUMINT capacity building did not have to survive public scrutiny. In order to be positively assessed by national governments, behind closed doors, its end product had to satisfy no more than a single requirement. What the Swedish security agency chief cited earlier called the 'spirit of the times' prevented agencies from making that requirement explicit: only in works of fiction could it be acknowledged that in intelligence and national security, an operation was a good one as long as it 'satisfied the only requirement of our profession: it worked'.[73] On no side of the iron and bamboo curtains in the real world did additional requirements – party political, statutory legal, ethical, religious, and so on – ever acquire more than secondary status. As motifically encoded in Part II above, capacity *building* entailed a diachronic process of identification, endorsement, and promotion of agent running tradecraft aimed squarely at increasing the advance odds that HUMINT 'worked'. In Part III below, the synchronic structure of corresponding relationships that ensued has been motifically encoded as *best practice*.

Some agencies needed remarkably long to put their HUMINT best practice on paper. It took the FBI, for example, until 1976 to produce a first edition of the 'privileged document' today known as the *Confidential Human Source Policy Manual*.[74] Individual case officers may in most countries have associated such manuals and guidelines with constraints of not entirely transparent rationality, red tape, and time-consuming paperwork, but today historians in a position to consult the editions that since the end of the Cold War have come to light in unredacted form (most notably successive *Richtlinien* from East Germany's *MfS*) find in them an indispensable key to the informed reading of primary sources. Recommendations and regulations that spell out the procedures meant to govern the handling, exploitation, preservation, and so on of agent *files* constitute a particularly rich repository of contextualising information on best practice. Knowing what best practice mandated was to be deposited in such files, for example, lets the historian avoid the error of merely pondering the significance of what is present in a particular file instead of also considering equally what is absent. Even fairly brief and condensed guidelines (Chapter 6) help us to not only draw tentative conclusions from what we find, but also to speculate with some authority about the possible evidential significance of what we don't.

Within their own ranks, security agencies promoted the adoption of best practice through the internalisation of texts that drew on the skill, judgement, creativity, and accumulated knowledge of their most experienced officers. Some texts were narrowly focused templates, like those guiding officers who had to make a suitability determination of a prospective agent based on presumed target dispositions. Others were samples of intra-bureaucratic communication (agent working agreements, periodic validation reports, etc.) that needed only minor modification to fit any likely scenario or context. Complementing such texts were write-ups of pilot programmes that merited wider emulation.[75] As in the case of the rules and regulations governing management of agent files, historians must develop a 'feel' for how courses of action were meant to develop in line with such model cases (Chapter 7).

Intimately linked to all of the above were security agencies' attempts at benchmarking and to adapt yesterday's best practice to changing circumstances. The need to develop ever more effective and sophisticated tradecraft necessitated what in the otherwise closed world of agencies was something of a paradox, namely the creation internally of an open information sharing environment in which professional vulnerabilities, solutions, insights, and new discoveries could safely be discussed by practitioners.[76] Where it came into being and survived, it has since been held up with pride by host agencies as an example of best practice. In the United States, in addition to updating officers monthly on the thought of agency Director J. Edgar Hoover, the *FBI Law Enforcement Bulletin* had already during World War II become a simple but effective variant of just such an information sharing environment. Developed within the CIA and subject to far greater restrictions in as far as access was concerned, is the classified agency quarterly *Studies in Intelligence* which during the Cold War was advertised as a platform for 'the permanent recording of our new ideas and experiences'.[77] In China, the early 1950s saw the birth of a number of classified public security journals offering officers what editorial boards called a space for 'exchange of experiences and findings', 'sharing of professional knowledge', and circulation of 'manuscripts published mainly for professional study and reference, rather than to immediately guide current practice'.[78] The discussions of performance and practical issues that survive from these fora are of particular value to historians where they expand on the implementation, or discuss pending or ongoing revisions, of existing practices (Chapter 8).

Introduction

Given the extent to which agent running on the ground often failed to meet the exacting elevated standard of 'best practice', historians also need to mine for information a complementary genre of primary sources in which agencies drew attention to what was regarded as *poor* tradecraft, human failings, transgressions, and deviations from best practice. A permanent background noise of policy reminders, this genre is easily sampled for 'contrary evidence' that historians may insert into a broader narrative to provide a semblance of balance and nuanced story telling. What occasioned these policy reminders was always something atypical, out of the ordinary, and not representative of the mainstream (Chapter 9) and in the end it is as such that they must be understood. Historians must resist the temptation to foreground them in a narrative to hint at the presence of a 'secret' true state of affairs behind a veneer of less outrageous, predictable behaviour that is dominant in the record as a whole.

6 Agent Files: *Management and Utilisation Regulations*

After the founding of the PRC, the process of identifying and codifying HUMINT best practice progressed to a point where, by the mid-1950s, the Ministry of Public Security was able to put the final touches on general guidelines with names like *Agent Work Manual* and more specific regulations such as the *Trial Measures Governing the Management of Agent Files*.[79] The *Trial Measures* covered essential aspects of the orderly administration of agent records, including their utilisation and protection as well as the procedures of documentation associated with agent recruitments, turnovers, terminations, and so on. They served as a blueprint for local regulations, often more detailed in their coverage, like those below, put on paper by the division of the Shenyang Public Security Bureau responsible for grassroots agent work in industrial enterprises and critical infrastructure. Where these regulations delve in passing on the recruitment of agents among 'engineers or higher', similar regulations drafted by divisions dealing with operational work in higher education or scientific research, for example, would here by analogy have referred to professors and senior academics.

Translated Text

Agents constitute an extremely important instrument utilised in operational work and security protection of infrastructure development. To fully bring their utility into play, a system of orderly management must be introduced, agent activity must be properly handled, and work must be prevented from descending into a state of chaos. Based on the Central Ministry of Public Security's *Trial Measures Governing the Management of Agent Files*, we have therefore drawn up the following temporary regulations.

Fourth Division, Shenyang Public Security Bureau, Circular No. 407 (1956), *Guanyu teqing dang'an guanli ji gongzuo zhidu de guiding (caoan)* (Draft Regulations Governing the Management and Utilisation of Agent Files). Mimeographed typescript, weeded out from the archive of a state-run enterprise in Shenyang on an unknown date.

Agent Recruitment, Clearing Out, and Turnover Procedures

1. The recruitment of an agent by operational line sections may only be initiated once a plan to do so has been scrutinised and approved by the section chief and endorsement has been sought and obtained from the division chief. In the case of [recruitment attempts targeting] engineers or higher, prior endorsement must be sought and obtained from the bureau director. The recruitment of an agent by protection sections may only be initiated once a plan to do so has been read and scrutinised by the section chief who must comment and sign off on it and then present it to the Fourth Division for endorsement. Agent recruitment may only proceed after the endorsements referred to above have been issued in writing to the recruiting unit.
2. The decision to clear out or suspend further utilisation of a non-performing agent should be initiated by the agent's case officer who, in a written report, must state the reasons and propose how to proceed. The report is to be presented to (and the proposed action may only proceed with the endorsement of) a leader equal in authority to the one who originally gave permission to recruit the agent.
3. If an agent is suspected of having turned on us and having sided with the enemy, or of actively engaging in destructive activities, or is found to owe a debt in blood, or is identified as a *tewu* suspect, and verification either calls for a formal investigation or for the agent in question to be arrested, the agent's case officer must record the findings of the verification, tentatively propose what action is to be taken, and obtain endorsement to proceed from a leader who is authorised to endorse agent recruitments. Once such action has been taken, the Fourth Division is to be promptly informed so that the agent can be written off.
4. When our work calls for the turnover of an agent from one case officer to another, endorsement must be obtained from the section chief. In the case of a turnover to a completely different unit, the section chief's endorsement must be reported to the Fourth Division where the agent will be written off. The turnover procedure may be dispensed when an agent's case officer is merely on temporary assignment elsewhere. In the case of agents transferred in from outside, their local presence should, in due course, be reported to the Fourth Division where they will be uniformly assigned serial numbers.
5. If an agent is relocated for reasons having to do with his [public] employment, his case officer should draft a report stating to what unit the agent is being relocated, and the case officer should present the report together with the agent's file to the Fourth Division, which

will then duly forward the relevant records. If an agent's entire workplace unit is relocated away from Shenyang and the running of him is assigned to a completely different protection unit, an *Agent Relocation Form* must be submitted to the Fourth Division where the agent is to be written off.

The Handling of Agent Files

1. An agent's file comprises the Agent Personal File and the Agent Work File. The basic element is one person, one file. The opening of a [new] agent file requires prior approval in writing from a leading officer at the appropriate level.
2. In practical terms, the agent's case officer is responsible for the opening of the Agent Personal File and the Agent Work File.
3. The registration of agent files, to take place at the division level, involves registration in the division's *Agent Files Registration Ledger*. The division chief is to assign responsibility for this registration to a specific officer. The operational line sections and protection sections may use their original index cards to register their files, and the section chief is to assign responsibility for managing this registration to a specific officer.
4. When a new file is to be opened, it is done by the officer identified by the division chief, based on a leading officer's endorsement, on a *File Creation Approval Form*, and it is to be accompanied by the provision of a file cover bearing a unique file number. The number on the cover of the file may not be altered at will.
5. Agent file contents:

    The Agent Personal File will contain, in the order specified below, records related directly to the individual agent.

    First part: Table of contents, agent registration form or equivalent, record of how the agent was recruited, the agent's written offer of service, plans for the utilisation and training of the agent, rules governing the rendezvous, communications, liaison, etc. with the agent, findings and results of the performance evaluations of the agent, decisions (stating the reasons) to reward or punish the agent, documentation on agent contact turnovers, and any record of formal endorsement of the clearing out or suspended utilisation of the agent.

    Second part: Records documenting the agent's past, his written autobiography, and special documentation concerning particularly important issues, records of investigations of the agent and related affidavits, rules to govern reimbursement of the agent, lists of recorded expenditures, [derogatory] information received concerning the agent's ideology, remarks, or activities, and registration of any financial items and/or other physical objects and documentation handed in by the agent. (The actual original financial items, identification papers, records, etc. may be stored separately.)

The Agent Work File will contain, in the order specified below, all of the information provided to the operational departments by the agent during the course of his operational activity. The file will include:

Table of contents, intelligence and reporting presented to the operational departments by the agent, written evaluations of the agent's intelligence and reporting by operational officers, records of oral debriefings of the agent, instructions issued to the agent by operational officers, disinformation prepared by operational departments for the agent's use, correspondence between the agent and officers, etc.

6. If one of the operational targets in a successfully concluded case investigation is to be recruited as an agent, the file documenting the case investigation may be filed in the archive, while the parts of that file containing the conclusive findings on the operational target in question and the opinion that he be recruited, together with the instructions of a leading officer, may be placed in the agent file as the item motivating the creation of that file. A note should then be added indicating where the original [case investigation] file of which this had been a part may be located.

Agent Work and Agent File Utilisation Routines

1. Changes involving the agent (e.g., transfers, agent contact turnovers, alterations in functions or status, etc.) are to be recorded on an *Agent Alterations Form* within three days and are to be presented to the Fourth Division so that the latter remains in control of the changing circumstances in the agent's work.
2. The case officer should rendezvous with the agent frequently, in principle once a week (absent special circumstances), and strictly avoid long lapses between contacts that may result in the officer losing track of the agent.
3. At each rendezvous with the agent, the case officer should always be on time, take careful debriefing notes, immediately edit the notes, and

6 Agent Files: *Management and Utilisation Regulations*   71

within two days of the rendezvous present the notes to the section chief for inspection and swift correction of any deviations.

4. On the second and seventeenth of each month, the operational line sections and protection sections are to report in writing on agent work during the previous half-month to the Fourth Division in order to allow it to exercise overall control. Line sections are to submit separate reports [on agent work], while protection sections (sub-sections) may incorporate the report on agent work in their comprehensive accounts. Reports are to mention the number of times agents have met with their handlers, what intelligence they have provided, what leads have been uncovered, and any problems that may have emerged in the running of the agent.
5. Every record added to an agent file must include information about the date of its creation and its source. The writing must be clearly legible and when it is in a foreign language, it must have attached to it either a full or a summary translation that has to be accurate.
6. When the number of pages in a file exceeds two hundred, separate folders may be created. File covers for these new folders are to be signed for by the section chief, and the slip containing his signature is to be Page Number One in the folder in question.
7. The officer in charge of the file should keep it in order, routinely organise its items, and, when appropriate, bind them together with string. He should remove any metal, and when binding the items together he should ensure that the text, dates, senior officers' instructions in the margins, etc. do not end up inside the binding.
8. When his [public] employment necessitates relocation of an agent, only his Agent Personal File is to be transferred with him. His Agent Work File is to be closed and deposited in the archive of the Fourth Division.

Routines to Safeguard Secrecy

1. If the work warrants borrowing or consulting a closed agent file that is deposited in the archive, prior permission must be obtained from the Fourth Division.
2. The *Active Agents Registration Ledger* is a top-secret document. Its personal safekeeping is entrusted to the officer in charge of agent registration. The other officers, who have nothing to do with it, are absolutely forbidden from consulting it.
3. Each agent will be assigned a code number by the division, and, with the exception of agent files, neither documents or telegrams nor the ledger of incoming and outgoing documents are to refer to agents by

name or to persons as 'agents'. Over the telephone or in ordinary conversations about work, agents are not to be referred to by name. Rather, their code number or alias is to be used. The goal is for only the case officer, section chief, and officer managing agent registration to know the true name of the agent. [An agent's identity] may not be shared with other officers who need not know it. This principle must be strictly adhered to in the context of research, investigation, and [counterintelligence] surveillance of an agent.

4. Agent records or telegrams are not to be typed up or mimeographed by typists. Rather, they are to be written in longhand by the agent's case officer. When an active agent's records or an Agent Personal File is to be forwarded, it is to be placed in an envelope, personally either by the case officer or by the officer in charge of agent registration, and then sent sealed, or delivered in person, to the recipient.

5. When part of the content of a report from an agent touches upon more than one case investigation, excerpts are routinely produced and shared. If the part to be excerpted is too voluminous and copying it is problematic, and furthermore, if it reveals neither the agent's name nor his circumstances, the entire original report (marked with its code number) may be [temporarily] removed from the Agent Work File, and a note indicating that this has been done should be left in the file for reference.

6. From the time an agent file is opened until it is closed and deposited in the archive, its safekeeping is entrusted to a specific officer who, when he goes off work, must not leave it lying about. Instead, he must place it in a designated file cabinet. The file may be removed from the office only with the permission of the section chief.

7. As stipulated, case officers are to record their oral debriefings of agents in notepads (operational line section officers are to use their work notebooks, whereas protection section officers may decide to use what they see fit). Blank agent forms should not be left lying about and should not be produced in an excessive number, as this may compromise secrecy.

Making Full Use of Agents

Senior officers at all levels should be involved in agent work, ensure its clandestinity, pay attention to the safekeeping and security of agent files, and conscientiously ensure that all comrades in their respective units register, safeguard, and utilise the files in accordance with these regulations. The Fourth Division will carry out regular inspections and make suggestions for improvements.

6 Agent Files: *Management and Utilisation Regulations*

In the process of their implementation, if these regulations are found to be imperfect in any respect or if they need to be amended, this should promptly be made known to the Fourth Division so as to allow for their revision.

The scope for trial implementation of these regulations is the Fourth Division and the protection organisations subordinate to it.

Fourth Division
Shenyang Municipal Public Security Bureau
20 September 1956

7 Recruitment: One Template and Two Profiles

The first of the three texts below lists the key points that Chinese officers were asked to keep in mind when contemplating recruitment of an agent from enemy ranks. Drawn up by the Harbin Public Security Bureau in 1951, copies of this particular template (*suoxie tigang*) were circulated nationwide as an example of best practice by the Ministry of Public Security through the end of 1953. The second and third texts, both from original operational files, illustrate what best practice looked like in the mid-1950s once it had been duly absorbed and adopted locally. In the first case (a 'Proposal to Recruit' from Liaoning province), the prospective agent is the brother-in-law of a Guomindang intelligence operative who, on the eve of the founding of the PRC, had fled to Hong Kong and in proximity of whose family, still in touch with him sporadically by mail, the Public Security Bureau of municipality Y wanted to recruit an agent for monitoring purposes. In the second case (a different 'Proposal to Recruit', this time from Heilongjiang province), in their psychological profile of the prospective agent, officers from a task force reporting to the Political Protection Division of the Harbin Public Security Bureau identify a member of the local intelligentsia as amenable to recruitment by appeal to patriotism rather than exploitation of any derogatory information.

Translated Text

Information to Be Collected About a Prospective Agent

A. Chronological résumé stating the person's name, assumed names, aliases, sex, age, family background, class status, educational level, ancestral home, original residential address, current residential address, and financial circumstances (including the size and financial circumstances of the family). Also state when (month and year)

Excerpt from 'Bannian lai Haerbin shi jingbao teqing gongzuo de jige juti gongzuo' (Some Concrete Operational Matters Encountered in Agent Economic Protection Work in Harbin during this Past Half-Year), September 1951, reprinted in *Jingji baowei gongzuo huiji*, Vol. 3 (January 1953), pp. 18–30.

7 Recruitment: One Template and Two Profiles

through whom and where the person joined his present employer and his current position. Describe his past education and his professional career.
B. The nature of what is at stake, the specific component of the enemy organisation involved, and his reactionary position within it.
C. Circumstances of past crimes and activities. What qualifications does he possess that allow him to get close to the enemy?
D. What doubtful or contradictory points about him are on the record?
E. Current circumstances
   1. Circumstances related to work, studies, and ideology.
   2. Who are the people with whom he is in regular or close contact? Who are the people with whom he has conflicts?
   3. Are there any of our own people, or in society more broadly, who are able to get close to him, and if so, are any of them Communist Party or Youth League members or participants in the revolution?
   4. What about his spending habits: any contradictions?
   5. Lifestyle and hobbies.
   6. Known conditions or *kompromat* that permit control.
F. Aim, conditions, and tactics of recruitment. When will he be able to serve as an agent and in what capacity?
G. What assets do we already operate in his proximity who will be able to gather counterevidence?
H. Substantive personal relationships.

Proposal to Recruit Zhao XX

In our investigations and research targeting those who fled abroad, we have identified the bandit Central Statistics Bureau *tewu* element Yang Nairui, who by 1950 had fled to a Hong Kong College of Theology (to do what remains unclear). Given that he had been a bandit operative in the past, he may still be an enemy operative. In 1951, he was in contact with his family by post. In order to investigate matters involving bandit Yang in greater depth as well as to control any developments involving his family and, in the course of doing so, to either discover additional matters or to create conditions facilitating future work, we must recruit a capable agent who is in proximity to bandit Yang's family. During our investigations,

---

Municipal Public Security Bureau document *Gong Zheng* No. 36 (1955), 'Wei qingshi jianli Zhao XX wei teqing gongzuo you' (Request for Instructions in the Matter of Recruiting Zhao XX as an Agent). Mimeographed 5-page typescript, weeded out from the archive of the CCP Committee of municipality Y on an unknown date.

we discovered that Zhao XX, married to one of Yang's sisters, is quite suitable, and we have tentatively identified and investigated him as a potential agent:

A. *Zhao XX's Background, History, and Family Circumstances* Zhao XX, male, age 32; family class status: impoverished urban resident; personal background: teacher; educational level: middle school graduate; ancestral home: XXXXX county, Shandong province.[80] Currently residing in Group 11, Residents' Committee 2, XXX district, where he manages a tobacco and liquor stall.

Zhao XX attended a village school from an early age, then entered Qingdao Junior Middle School at age fifteen and studied there until he turned seventeen and passed the entrance exam for the private Qingdao Business Middle School, from which he graduated at the age of nineteen. At the age of twenty, he obtained a teaching position in the private Yanhua School of Accounting in Beijing where he was assigned to teach book-keeping while, at the same time, he attended the school's advanced class on auditing. At the age of twenty-two, he moved to Tianjin where he held a position as lecturer in a private evening school of accounting. After a little more than one year, he returned to Yanhua School of Accounting in Beijing to teach auditing, which he did until the age of twenty-four. In 1945, after V-J Day, the Chiang Kai-shek bandits occupied the Beijing Yanhua campus and the school was dissolved. In December of that same year, he attended an accounting training class organised by the Northeast Field Headquarters of the bandits for two months until he was assigned a position in the Accounting Section of the Accounting Division of the Hejiang Provincial Government. In the summer of 1946, he was reassigned to head the Bandits' Authentication Sub-Section of the Accounting Office of Hejiang Provincial Peace Preservation Headquarters, and by 1947 he had been promoted to lead (with the rank of major) the Accounting Office's Accounting Section. In September 1947, he was transferred to Changchun to serve as quartermaster in the battalion of the Division Sector Office, still with the rank of major, as quartermaster. In May 1948, he served in succession as quartermaster major in the Third Regiment of Volunteers and in the combined stores and training battalion of the New Seventh Army and the Sixtieth Army of the bandits stationed in Changchun. In July 1948, he was assigned to be director of accounting (with the rank of major) in the cadre training class of the Songjiang Provincial Peace Preservation Headquarters, a position he held until October 1948 when the bandits stationed in Changchun rebelled, and he was made to attend a course organised by our [People's Liberation Army] teaching regiment for four months. In 1949, he settled here, with his family, as a civilian living first from the sale of fresh produce and then, up to the present, by managing a tobacco and liquor stall.

Family circumstances: Zhao XX's father is a businessman, his wife Yang XX is a former alternate member of the Guomindang Changchun Party District Executive Committee and currently is a housewife; the couple has four children, thus the household comprises seven people. Financially, they depend entirely on earnings from the tobacco and liquor stall, currently around *nn* thousand yuan/month, which places them in reduced circumstances.

B.   *Zhao XX's Substantive Personal Relationships*   Zhao XX's brother Zhao XXXX, originally a businessman. In 1948, he was a technician with the rank of second lieutenant in a communications platoon belonging to the 3rd Regiment of Volunteers of the bandits stationed in Changchun. After Liberation, he operated a hemp rope business and, in 1953, he attained his current status as a worker.

Zhao XX's sister Zhao XXX is currently a worker in the printing plant of Xinhua Book Stores in Changchun.

Zhao XX's cousin Yang XXXX is a [former] bandit Sanminzhuyi Youth Corps platoon leader.[81] During the Suppression of Counter-revolutionaries Campaign in 1951, he was involved in a plot to kill one of our Party cadres, and he was arrested and sentenced to nine years in prison.[82] He is currently undergoing reform through labour.

Zhao XX's cousin, Yang Nairui, was a member of the Central Statistics Bureau organisation in Changchun when, in 1948, he escaped to the South. He currently resides in Hong Kong and, until his escape, he maintained close relations with Zhao XX.

C.   *Post-Liberation Ideology and Conduct*   After coming here from Changchun in 1949, Zhao XX and his cousin Yang XXXX (arrested and sentenced to nine years in the Suppression of Counter-revolutionaries Campaign) co-funded and together set up a fresh produce stall. At the time, Zhao would often get together to drink with two other former bandit officers. Their relations were close, but at the beginning of the Suppression of Counter-revolutionaries Campaign he panicked. He tried to find out more about government policy in order to determine the likelihood of his being arrested and disposed of. In the end, he ceased to be in touch with any of those who had dodgy pasts. Also, he did not participate in the meetings of the local residents' committee (at the time, its members barred him from participation) that had announced that he was to be subject to probation for a period of two years. He behaved honestly, did not make any irresponsible remarks or behave poorly, and – abiding by the stipulations of the Probational Control Statutes – he regularly swept and helped clean up the neighbourhood streets. He actively aided the residents' committee and the Association of Industry and Commerce by writing slogans and drawing cartoons. His past reactionary position was known to have been quite senior (a bandit major), but no one had any knowledge of his having committed actual specific crimes and, as a result, after only two months, when the time came for a general assessment, probational control was lifted. After that, he did some work for a local school and, because he was a patient teacher and very meticulous, the overall feedback from the students was positive.

Zhao XX now regularly writes slogans and draws cartoons for the local residents' committee and the Association of Industry and Commerce, and he actively helps an amateur theatre group of the neighbourhood design sets, and so on. His attitude to tax collection and the purchase of government bonds is quite positive, and he now and then informs the local police station about what is going on in the community. He once remarked:

> The government has been lenient in its treatment of me. People whose reactionary positions were inferior to mine were all subject to probation for longer periods, and some were even arrested and sentenced. I have a profound sense that the government was lenient with me, and henceforth all I want to do is stand by the government, try to perform meritorious service to atone for my crimes, and become a new person. That, today, is my only way forward.

D. *Grounds for Recruitment* Zhao XX is the husband of bandit Yang Nairui's sister, Yang XX. While Yang Nairui studied in Changchun, Zhao was there as well (serving as a major with the bandit armed forces) and the two were in frequent and close contact. When Yang escaped to Tianjin in 1948, he sent Zhao a letter in which he shared the details of his escape. After they moved here, Zhao and his wife settled in an apartment right next door to the Yang family. Zhao was especially close to Yang XXXX (at the time, still undergoing labour reform) and together they went into business. Later, when he set up his own tobacco and liquor stall, Zhao relocated, but he still lives not far from the Yang family. In 1950, Yang Nairui wrote from overseas and inquired about family matters. Yang XXXX showed his letters to Zhao (interrogation records from the Suppression of Counter-revolutionaries Campaign have Yang XXXX admitting that the escaped Yang Nairui wrote five, maybe six, letters to his family in 1950 and 1951, but the investigation has so far failed to

7 Recruitment: One Template and Two Profiles

determine the precise number of letters) and also regularly discussed family affairs with him, in no way treating him like an outsider. To this day, Yang's mother regularly drops in on the Zhao family to chat and to help with chores. Zhao XX, in turn, does what he can to help Yang's mother who faces economic hardships. All in all, relations between Zhao XX and bandit Yang Nairui in the past, and between Zhao XX and Yang's mother in the present, are quite close.

Zhao XX has ample social experience and is good at socialising with people. From the age of nineteen, when he graduated from the private Qingdao Business Middle School and entered society to do business, all the way up to the time of Liberation he again and again found himself in unfamiliar territory (except when he arrived here in 1949 and already knew the Yang family), yet thanks to his 'socialising' skills, he always managed to quickly settle in and make many new contacts. Since setting up his tobacco and liquor stall, he has also managed to develop a larger than usual base of steady customers. From the moment his probation ended, he has been doing better and making more money than other comparable businesses in our city, and his stall is quite well run. Therefore, judging from the community information that he has been sharing with our local police station, he definitely has operational potential.

Zhao XX's reactionary position was quite senior and as a former bandit officer with the rank of major, he expressed panic and fear during the Suppression of Counter-revolutionaries Campaign. As soon as the government announced that he would be subject to probation for two years not only did he behave honestly and accept and respect the Probation Control Statutes but he also actively stood by the government and sought to atone for his past crimes by performing meritorious deeds – which is why his probation was suspended after only two months. The leniency shown by our government, its brilliant achievements in all areas these past few years, and the changing international situation have had a powerful influence on him. His current behaviour suggests that he is very enthusiastically standing on the side of the government (of course, we cannot lower our guard when dealing with him and we must remain vigilant). In addition, while his relations with the bandit Yang Nairui and the Yang family are very close, he is not a direct relative. Furthermore, Zhao appreciates the positive and negative factors that may determine his future. For example, on those occasions when we have sought him out to discuss certain matters, he has, without needing to be prodded, provided factual information concerning the bandit Yang, Yang's correspondence with his family after his escape, and so on. (Our own investigations have corroborated the information provided by Zhao.)

Zhao has also indicated to the government that he is willing to atone for his past crimes by performing meritorious deeds.

Given all of the above and given our operative needs and Zhao's potential, and assuming we train him rigorously and find a way of running him in an appropriate fashion, it appears likely that we will be able to achieve our aim (while remaining on guard and making sure he does not act fraudulently). Consequently, we are of the opinion that it should be basically possible to establish a formal relationship with him, reveal to him what his operational assignment will be, and prepare to recruit and utilise him as an agent. Please issue instructions indicating whether or not this will be appropriate.

XXXX Municipal Public Security Bureau
17 March 1955

Proposal to Recruit Yu X

A. Yu X (a/k/a XXXX), male, age thirty-three, from Dalian; Personal background: student; Family class status: rich peasant; Currently employed as an associate professor in the Department of Internal Medicine, XXXX University, and living with his wife and one small child in the university staff dormitory. Yu's wife, Xu XX, age twenty-six, a medical university graduate, is also from Dalian, and she is currently employed as a doctor by XXXX University. Yu has an unproblematic history and is a member of the [Communist] Youth League.

Yu studied in Dalian from a young age and graduated from Dalian No. 1 Middle School in 1938, whereupon he entered Manchuria Medical University in Shenyang, graduating in 1945. After the Glorious Restoration at the end of World War II, he served as a doctor of internal medicine in a Dalian hospital for three years, and then, in 1948, he went to XXXX University where he has since served first as lecturer, then as associate professor. In 1945, Yu joined the Dalian Medical Association and the Manchuria Medical Association. His special qualifications include a command of Japanese, English, and German, the ability to translate (written) Russian, and an intimate knowledge of Japanese affairs. He has known university employee Zheng XXXXX since childhood, when the two were classmates.

Final draft of 'Jianli Yu X de yijian' (Proposal to Recruit Yu X) as presented to the Political Protection Division of the Harbin Public Security Bureau. Deposited in a file on operation code-named Case 28. Closed file weeded out from the bureau archive on an unknown date.

7 Recruitment: One Template and Two Profiles

They maintain an excellent relationship, and he is well acquainted with Zheng's family.

B. The main aim of the recruitment is to have Yu serve as a bridge that will allow us to intensify work and launch a more in-depth operation targeting his colleague Zheng XXXXX's *brother*, who is based in Hong Kong and who is suspected of being a Nationalist intelligence operative about to return to China. We have conducted a probe and have found that one of the agents whom we already operate believes that to attempt recruitment would do no harm, only good, and that Yu would be of use to us. Our recruitment grounds and conditions are as follows:

1. Yu X and Zheng come from the same town and went to school together. Yu is intimately familiar with Zheng and with Zheng's family. Yu is also Zheng's primary contact here in Harbin, and therefore Zheng will believe what Yu tells him. Zheng is likely to entrust Yu with this and that and, more generally, rely on him.
2. Since Zheng and Yu both like Japan, know the country well, and share the same kind of infatuation with things Japanese, their relations are likely to deepen.
3. The family of Yu's wife hails from XXX, Harbin, and therefore, not surprisingly, she is very well-connected locally. Here too, conditions are conducive to the launch of a more in-depth operation.
4. Since he would be able to provide the brother of Zheng XXXXX in Hong Kong with things like 'affidavits' and 'corroboration of circumstances', Yu is well-placed to connect with him and to create conditions conducive to the successful mounting of an offensive.
5. Yu X has an unproblematic history and both the trials he has experienced and the forging to which he has been subjected over the years indicate that he aspires to be progressive, and he evidently has definite political consciousness, something that is particularly manifest under present prevailing conditions. As long as we explain our rationale to him, he will agree to work for us.
6. The relationship between Yu and Zheng XXXXX appears to be one of fellow townsmen rather than one of intimate and close bosom friends. In any case, given that our proposal does not entail a 'betrayal' of Zheng, we estimate that Yu will not compromise confidentiality.

C. Method of recruitment: principally through administrative channels, by way of extending an invitation (*yaoqing*) and offering an appointment (*pinren*).

Step 1: Have a senior member of the university administration talk to Yu in person, provide encouragement and education, and allow us to approach him in the name of the Public Security Bureau to explain our purpose. Then, after having invited Yu to serve as a Secret Asset in the Defence of the Motherland, educate him about important aspects of the international situation and about the need to safeguard clandestinity.

Step No. 2: Clarify the mission to Yu and make it clear to him that when the brother of Zheng XXXXX returns from Hong Kong, he should observe and note any suspicious points, and get to know the brother while maintaining friendly relations with Zheng XXXXX.

Please endorse if appropriate.

Case Group
27 January 1954

8   Agent Termination

This article from the journal *Inner Mongolia Public Security* is typical of the kind of texts touching on HUMINT that circulated in the information-sharing environment present within the Chinese public security sector in the mid-1950s. In this case, the two authors are concerned with rational agent termination and agent contingent downsizing, two hotly debated topics at a time when the Ministry of Public Security was calling for improved performance and a strategic realignment of domestic agent operations. The authors share their findings from trial runs of contingent 'downsizing and rectification' in Inner Mongolia's finance, trade, and communication sectors. Nationwide, the total number of agents in those sectors had peaked at 31,300 when, at the end of 1956, the Ministry of Public Security began to call for a reduction in the overall number of agents.[83] In articles debating the same topic in classified journals in the provinces of Liaoning and Heilongjiang, other case officers with firsthand experience expanded on what they maintained were ways of proceeding that, in terms of efficiency, merited benchmarking against comparable standards and practices elsewhere.

Translated Text

In order to determine how to carry out agent contingent downsizing and rectification even more prudently, we conducted trial runs in entities directly subordinate to the [Inner Mongolia] regional government's Department of Finance and Trade and Department of Communications. Below, for reference, we share some of our findings.

A.   Procedural Steps

Study the relevant documents and clear up any misconceptions among the involved officers. When agent contingent downsizing and rectification

---

Zhang Xinyi and Cheng Tingkui, 'Zai teqing gongzuo shang guanche shousuo fangzhen de jidian tihui' (Some Findings from Implementation of Downsizing and Rectification), *Neimeng gongan* (Inner Mongolia Public Security), No. 56 (1957), pp. 37–41.

was first put on the agenda, we found that, aside from correct understandings of it, two erroneous viewpoints were common among officers. The first regarded the process as simply the disposal of a burdensome load, and it maintained that agents are no longer of any use to us given that the threat level as a whole has changed fundamentally, the awareness of the masses has been raised, and case-related operational activity has been reduced. Adherents of this view favour simply discharging and clearing out most agents. A second, different view maintains that to recruit an agent is not a simple matter, and if most of the agents we currently operate were to be purged from the ranks, then many operational officers would find themselves idle. Adherents of this view favour clearing out as few agents as possible. At present, the former view is more common, the latter less so, but both are equally incorrect.

In order to make them abandon such erroneous views and make it possible for agent contingent rectification to proceed smoothly, we had the officers study the two parts of the documents from the Eighth National Public Security Conference [in December 1956] that analyse the present situation in our struggle and touch on agent contingent downsizing and rectification.[84] As a result, the following issues have been resolved:

1. Officers understand that while the threat level as a whole has declined and has changed fundamentally, there still exist some very cunning enemies (examples were cited).
2. Officers appreciated that downsizing the agent contingent as a whole will allow us to strengthen and improve the running of our most important operational agents.
3. Officers understand that, as a whole, the agent contingent is bloated with many weak agents. It must be downsized, but one cannot in one simple go discharge and clear out all agents (as some muddle-headed officers have suggested).
4. Officers understand that it is mainly the agents guarding critical assets and the secret investigation agents in units where conditions are already settled (i.e., where the political circumstances of critical staff have been clarified and our Party's presence is strong) who will be affected. Where conditions are not yet ripe, or where they are still needed, the agents will be retained temporarily.

In short, retrenchment and downsizing are to proceed in concert based on the actual prevailing circumstances and they are to be handled carefully, not blindly and rashly.

Investigate, sound out, and clarify each agent's circumstances. Some agents had to endure a struggle during the 1955 *Sufan* [personnel security risk assessment], and some case officers in turn received work transfers during the [subsequent] organisational restructuring of government departments.[85] As a result, agent direction was temporarily affected and so the actual circumstances of some agents are no longer entirely clear. Rectification must therefore be preceded, in each instance, by investigation. This investigation of agents is to be conducted one by one by the agent's original case officer (or, if that officer is no longer around, the task should be assigned to a specific officer) and assisted by the Party organisation, administration, and officers from the Protection Section in the agent's workplace. In addition, the agent's loyalty to us and his operational strengths and weaknesses are to be assessed by evaluating the overall quality of the intelligence he has provided. Substantive matters to be looked into are: (1) the agent's past performance and attitude; (2) his immediate circumstances (e.g., Does he have any problems? Did he have to endure a struggle during the *Sufan*? Was a formal conclusion reached concerning his past? Has he been compromised? What is his current state of mind? Has he been given a job transfer or a promotion? Has he joined the Communist Party or Youth League, etc.); (3) the degree to which the threat level in the agent's workplace may have changed; and (4) the agent's operational target(s) and the present and future operational environment.

Investigation and sounding out are central elements in the process of agent contingent downsizing and rectification. They are crucial, and they must be controlled directly by the component chiefs whose involvement will determine whether or not the general policy of downsizing the agent contingent can be correctly implemented.

Compile individual data by way of validation reviews and put forward reasoned opinions as to whether to retain or to let go. Opinions should be based on investigation and research and a command of the actual circumstances, with the officer in charge assuming responsibility. Start with a group discussion among the officers participating in the validation review (with the division chiefs present when called for), and once a consensus view has been reached, present it to the leadership for examination and settlement. Proceed in the same way when dealing with successive cases and settle them one by one.

B.   *Scope and Targets*

The state of the agent contingent is as follows: the total number of agents is not small, but the quality of agents is low and agent distribution is highly uneven. Changes in how our struggle unfolds, as well as changes among the agents themselves call for downsizing under the following seven circumstances:

1. Where agents were recruited to guard critical assets in units of limited size with staffs that by now are basically homogenous and where the Communist Party and Youth League organisations have a relatively powerful presence.
2. Where, at one point, there had been blind and chaotic recruitment of agents who today no longer serve any useful purpose.
3. Where Communist Party and Youth League members were recruited as agents, but they never functioned as such, and they have since been promoted or transferred elsewhere.
4. Where the original mission of an agent was merely to investigate a single person or a single issue, and the agent now no longer has any other mission.
5. Where an agent can no longer be utilised because clandestinity has been compromised or the regulations have been violated and the rules broken.
6. Where an agent is a counter-revolutionary element or other bad element who, in the course of the *Sufan*, was found to have consistently concealed issues, and today no longer retains any useful qualifications.
7. Where an agent was on a specific historical mission that has long since been concluded and, as a direct result, the agent retains no operational utility.

While reducing the size of the agent contingent as a whole, one should intentionally retain, in addition to the case agents, three categories of agents based on present and anticipated future needs. One consists of agents recruited among senior technicians who still have a role to play, be it as secret investigation agents or as agents guarding critical assets. Another consists of secret investigation agents whose covers permit them to investigate or control a particular sphere or an entire sector. Finally, agents who either guard critical assets in basic infrastructure-development sites or who serve as agents guarding critical assets in units where Communist Party and Youth League presence remains weak. Among the agents in this third and final category, the plan is to selectively assign permanent roles to the secret investigation agents among the senior technicians who are in a position to control a particular sphere (e.g., insurrectionists who [on the eve of the founding of the PRC] came over as a group to our side, senior intellectuals, elements in religious circles or reactionary cliques). In other cases, they are to be retained temporarily in anticipation of downsizing once conditions are settled, as in the case of agents guarding critical assets where the Communist Party and Youth League presence remains weak.

8 Agent Termination

C. Handling Principles and Methods

In general, agents are to be processed in accordance with the principles laid down in the documents of the [Second National] Conference on Operational Work [in July–August 1952].

1. When it comes to those agents whom we intend to retain and continue to utilise, we have re-examined and defined their respective missions and have permanently assigned a specific officer to each one of them to direct and train the agent and to consolidate and improve his performance so as to ensure that he serves a function. For example, after having been given a new mission and more effective direction, Agent XXX has already managed to win the trust of his operational target, and he has provided us with a significant amount of valuable intelligence that has allowed our case-related operational activity to make progress. Agent XXX has performed a major role in the Anti-Rightist Campaign.
2. When it comes to agents recruited from among Communist Party and Youth League members or basic segments of the masses that guard critical assets, we have opted for face-to-face conversation and education, and we have explained to them why the changing threat level prompts us to terminate the relationship and our utilisation of them as agents. But we have also left room for reactivation, telling them that if they encounter bad people or bad things, they should not hesitate to get in touch with us and report them. When we ended our agent relationship with some, we suggested to the former agents that they should try to join the Public Order Protection Committee in their workplace. Some have since become activists and they continue to play a role in that overt capacity.
3. As far as grey agents are concerned, we explained to them that we were terminating the agent relationship (again leaving room for reactivation) due to changes in the prevailing situation in our struggle against the enemy, and we lectured them on the strict need to safeguard clandestinity.[86] In the case of those who in the past played a definite role, we also used the opportunity to formally sum up what they had done for us, stressed their past achievements, and gave them due praise. At the same time, seeking truth from facts, we also pointed out flaws, suggesting how they might be overcome, and proposed a direction in which the agent might henceforth hopefully progress. In the case of agents who are unhappy with their present employment, we promised to get in touch with the relevant unit to see if a job transfer might be possible, while in the case of agents who have a hard time making ends meet, we promised to provide them with a suitable subsidy. Agents with whom we have dealt in this fashion tend to be content.

4. In the case of the small number of agents who either broke the law and violated discipline, leaked secrets, or kept counter-revolutionary issues in their pasts hidden from us, aside from subjecting them to ideological and political education and impressing upon them the need to safeguard clandestinity, we made a point of censuring them for their errors (if they had achievements to their credit, these were still acknowledged as such). In dealing with individuals of this sort, we have opted for the tactic of gradually distancing ourselves from them and (by no longer getting in touch) letting the relationship in effect end by itself. Meanwhile, we have asked their workplaces to keep an eye on them and prevent them from swindling and bluffing.

D. Points to Note

The handling of post-termination arrangements is of major concern, but it remains something of a weak spot. Some comrades prepare insufficiently for their conversations with agents about to be terminated, handle matters that arise in a simplistic and crude manner, and resolve ideological issues with insufficient depth and thoroughness. In some cases, implementation of the post-termination arrangements is too slow and is permitted to drag on for too long. None of this is unrelated to whether or not the person in overall charge assumes responsibility and makes agent contingent downsizing and rectification a priority.

There are two points that merit special attention when it comes to agent terminations. First, fully preparing for the conversation with the agent (in some cases it must be preceded by research) and setting it up differently depending on the individual rather than always following the same template. Even when the very same words are said, one must consider when to say them, how to say them, and who is to say them in order to gain the best results. Second, keeping the agent's economic and professional circumstances in mind and making a fair estimation of all of his past achievements. Agents pay a lot of attention to our attitude, and they will be moved simply by being given a fair estimation of their past achievements and an expression of concern for how their economic and professional circumstances might best be handled. For example, a certain grey agent in the Monopoly Trade Corporation (a former colonel division chief and participant in an insurrection against the Nationalist Party) said to us gratefully after having been elected to the local Public Order Protection Committee (he was ideologically progressive and enjoyed a good standing among the masses) that:

> My progress these past years is inextricably linked to the education and help I have received from the protection organs. That the [Communist Party] organisation

now shows such trust in me allows me to appear a bit more 'red' in the eyes of the masses. At the same time, I will certainly maintain my vigilance and continue to fight the hidden enemy.

If in our conversation we fail to engage with what genuinely concerns them and we fail to handle matters in an appropriate fashion, our agents are likely to feel resentment and hopelessness. For example, this occurred in the case of an agent whose professional [salary] ranking ended up being mishandled and as a result complained, saying:

> For your sake, I assumed a outwardly grey mien, with the masses all regarding me as a backward element. As a result, each time a promotion came around, I ended up being bypassed, and as for joining the Communist Party, that was out of the question. Only the organisation knew the truth [about my covert role]. Unless you now intervene on my behalf, I will have reached rock bottom!

In this particular case, we were able to correct the matter and, in addition to giving the agent an ideological education, we managed to find a new job for him and see to it that his rank was adjusted. The individual in question is now quite content.

Aside from the above, the process of agent contingent downsizing and rectification must, from start to finish, be guided by a spirit of investigation and research. It must begin with proper investigation and sounding out, and it must end with proper management of the post-termination arrangements. This is the key link. At the same time, when carrying it out, one must guard against certain officers' simple, impetuous, crude, and sloppy work style as well as against simply letting research behind closed doors take the place of arduous and meticulous investigative and ideological work. Leaderships must supervise and conduct timely inspections to discover and rectify deviations and flaws, educate their officers, advance their work, and improve its quality.

E. *Disposition of Agent Files*

Agent files should be regarded as our public security property and, as such, they should be properly managed and preserved. They must neither be rashly destroyed or allowed to go missing nor be transferred to other departments at will, as they touch upon numerous confidential matters (in particular, concerning operational means and what has been reported on issues involving specific individuals) and retain historical reference value. Therefore, regardless of the *kind* of records involved, agent files must be properly put in order, deposited in the archive, and assigned a number that will allow for their retrieval.

9   Tradecraft Dos and Don'ts

The four short policy reminders below are examples of what may be called the internal representation of 'worst practice' in the information-sharing environment of the Chinese public security sector. Here it competed with best practice as a topic of conversation centred on tradecraft-related flaws, deviations, limitations, errors, and so on. The first policy reminder was prompted by what the Shenyang Public Security Bureau rightly regarded as an example of dangerously poor tradecraft: a section chief in one of its municipal district branches allowing a case officer to receive agent reports through the ordinary post (rather than, as regulations mandated, at face-to-face meetings) and, as a result, one agent's confidential report on a person of interest going missing. In the second, the Ministry of Public Security in Beijing told units responsible for the protection of critical infrastructure to refrain from recruiting senior CCP cadres as agents, given that, in any case, they were compelled to provide their government with the sought-after information. In the third, the Heilongjiang Public Security Bureau cautioned officers not to simply clock up countless evenings of socialising in the name of agent assessment and development. In the final policy reminder, the editorial board of *Heilongjiang Public Security* tells case officers to always, at the very least, and no matter how busy they may be, make sure they know whether their agents are actually still among the living...

Translated Text

Do Not Send Agent Reports through Ordinary Post

To the heads of operational line sections, economic protection sections of municipal district branches, and protection sections (sub-sections) of factories and enterprises:

We recently discovered that Comrade Piao Wenxiang in the Economic Protection Section of West of the Tracks Municipal District Branch, in

---

Shenyang Public Security Bureau Second Division general circular *Gong Jing* No. 769 (1953). Mimeographed typescript weeded out from the archive of a state-run enterprise in Shenyang on an unknown date.

the course of his work of operating agents, for fear of jeopardising secrecy by having face-to-face meetings with them and with the permission of the protection section chief, Comrade Deng Shirui, ordered agents to send their reports to him through the post in the form of ordinary letters. On 10 August, agent Zhang X's report on the activities of a suspicious element went missing, and despite repeated inquiries with the post office, it still has not been located.

This serious incident illustrates the degree to which our economic protection officers still have a muddled understanding of the clandestine nature of agent work. Minister Luo [Ruiqing] pointed out early on that 'agent work is top secret work that cannot be conducted without complete secrecy'. Yet some of our officers, including leading officers, still have not conscientiously taken on this high-level instruction. They regard clandestinity as a 'minor' matter, and they make decisions surrounding it on their own without bothering to request instructions from, or report to, the higher levels. As a result, clandestinity ends up being jeopardised, and this adversely impacts our work. In addition to now ruling that sending agent reports through the ordinary post is impermissible, we also hope that all recipients of this circular will learn a lesson. Recipient units must educate their staff and point out to officers that as they direct their agents, they must always and everywhere pay attention to safeguarding clandestinity and see to it that there will be no more such incidents.

It has hereby been announced.

Second Division of the Public Security Bureau of
Shenyang Municipal People's Government
5 October 1953

Do Not Recruit Senior Party Cadres to Serve as Agents

Our Ministry's fact-finding missions report that, in the course of opening up agent positions in factories, mines, and enterprises, economic protection units have in many cases recruited senior [Communist] Party cadres and leading managerial cadres (secretaries of Party committees, Party branches, and Youth League branches, trade union chairmen, factory managers, and deputy managers who are Party members, etc.) as agents. This is not merely unnecessary but also inappropriate given that such comrades are rarely in a position to serve as agents and, furthermore, their recruitment might well have a negative impact on the influence of the

---

Ministry of Public Security notice, 'Gedi budei jiang wo dang zheng fuze ganbu jian wei teqing' (Do Not Recruit Local Senior Party and Government Cadres as Agents), *Jingji baowei gongzuo huiji*, Vol. 12 (May 1955), p. 46.

Party among the masses, or might end in the masses developing mistaken impressions of the Party. The fact that they are senior Communist Party members does itself already mean that these cadres share counterespionage responsibility and need not be recruited as agents. We therefore urge economic protection units to investigate and promptly cancel all recruitments of leading Party and government comrades as agents and explain why to the individuals in question. In the future, such cadres are not to serve as agents.

Central Ministry of Public Security
22 February 1955

Refrain from Lavish Wining and Dining

In our struggle against the enemy, agent entertainment is but one of numerous operational means employed by us. When our work calls for it and depending on the agent involved, we very much need to engage in successful entertainment in a directed and well-prepared way. For this purpose, we are able to draw on the public security special expenditures budget.

However, it is inappropriate to make a habit of engaging in purely material entertainment while neglecting political education. There is, for instance, no need to let the case officer invite his agent to wine and dine in a restaurant or at a state-run canteen every time they meet without giving any thought to what might be called for by the mission or by the target, or to always provide a lavish offering of liquor, candy, and sweets at the clandestine premise. If an officer behaves in this way, not only will it not improve the desired performance of our agents but it may also give some of our high-level agents a mistaken impression. In the past, some of our politically progressive agents had already raised critical objections to this kind of entertainment, saying that the practice did not have any political meaning and did not fit in the overall mood of today's new society.

Some comrades maintain that they entertain agents as part of their work and that it is an entirely legitimate way of rewarding agents who have made achievements. Agents who perform well do indeed and of course fully deserve to be given gifts and rewards so as to spur them on to do their work for us even more efficiently. But the form of the reward must not be limited to simply wining, dining, and entertaining. One should think this

---

Heilongjiang Public Security Bureau General Office Secretariat, 'Yong chichi hehe de fangfa zhaodai teqing duibudui?' (Is Wining and Dining with Agents Appropriate?), *Heilongjiang gongan* (Heilongjiang Public Security), No. 26 (1956), p. 17.

over and then make a determination based on what is warranted by the nature of the mission and the circumstances of the individual agent. For example, an agent whose professional position is that of a senior technician may be presented with a commemorative gift or a book that has high political significance, while a politically progressive or ordinary agent employed by an organ or enterprise may be given a material reward (including an amount of cash). None of this is set in stone, and it must all be decided based on our operational needs and the agent's concrete circumstances.

To sum up, we must rectify the way we go about entertaining our agents. We need to discriminate and consider whether the work calls solely for wining and dining in a restaurant (or a clandestine premise) without paying any attention to ideological or political direction. The practice amounts to a significant waste of state property and does not have much of a positive role when it comes to bringing into full play the activism of our agents.

Secretariat of the General Office of
Heilongjiang Provincial Public Security
Bureau
1956

A Case Officer Schedules a Rendezvous with a Dead Agent

Recently something quite bizarre occurred involving the handling of an agent by one of our operational officers.

In January of this year [1957], the officer in question heard that an agent whom he handled had fallen ill, had been bedridden for quite some time, and was in a precarious state. The officer then forgot about this, as countless other tasks kept him busy. In mid-February, however, it was time for another scheduled contact meeting with the agent. The officer proceeded to their regular rendezvous premise where he paced back and forth, glancing at his watch and now and then looking out the window for the agent who was, however, nowhere in sight. Disappointed, the officer finally decided to leave the premise. As he was walking away, he began worrying whether he had arrived too late, but he concluded that no, there had been nothing wrong with his timing. Then he suddenly remembered that maybe his agent still had not recovered from his illness. He would no doubt find out at their next scheduled meeting, he thought, and so he decided to return home.

Zao Bai, 'Yi wei zhenchayuan he si teqing "jietou"' (An Operational Officer's 'Rendezvous' with a Dead Agent), *Heilongjiang gongan*, No. 25 (1956), p. 17.

In early March, it was again time for a scheduled meeting and the officer, following the regular routine, set out for the rendezvous premise. He again waited for quite a long time, but as on the previous occasion, his waiting was in vain. Impatiently, he paced back and forth: 'Why has he still not showed up?' he asked himself. By this time, he was quite furious and so he decided his agent 'really deserves a serious dressing down!' 'Could it be that he's still ill?' he asked himself. 'No, that can't be it! Such a long time has passed, he should have recovered by now.' The angry officer silently cursed the agent and said to himself: 'If he is unable to meet, couldn't he have at least sent me a note?' But the officer also realised that his own anger would not solve the problem. Therefore, in the end he had no other option but to shake his head, sigh, and again walk away disappointed.

After some more time had passed, the officer one day suddenly remembered that it was time for a meeting with his agent, and in a rush, he approached the rendezvous premise where, again, there was no sign of the agent. By now the officer could no longer keep his anger bottled up. After making some inquiries, it was at this time that he finally found out that the agent had died well over a month earlier. Stunned and dumbstruck, the officer stood there not knowing what to do next.

How is it possible for something like this to have occurred? Our agent work is meant to be conducted meticulously, but in this case the operational officer had clearly gotten into the habit of merely following his own familiar routine, and he was unwilling to conduct the investigation and research that would have allowed him to stay on top of the everyday life of his agent. We often stress that officers must understand the background, state of mind, and employment situation of the agents whom they manage, but this does not mean that officers do not also need to keep themselves informed of, and care about, the everyday life of their agents. After all, unless we have a complete understanding of our agents' circumstances, we will end up on the defensive in our work. Once we have ceased to conduct our agent operations in a targeted fashion and our utilisation of them has deteriorated, even our very best agents will be of little use to us.

Part IV

From the Agent Work File

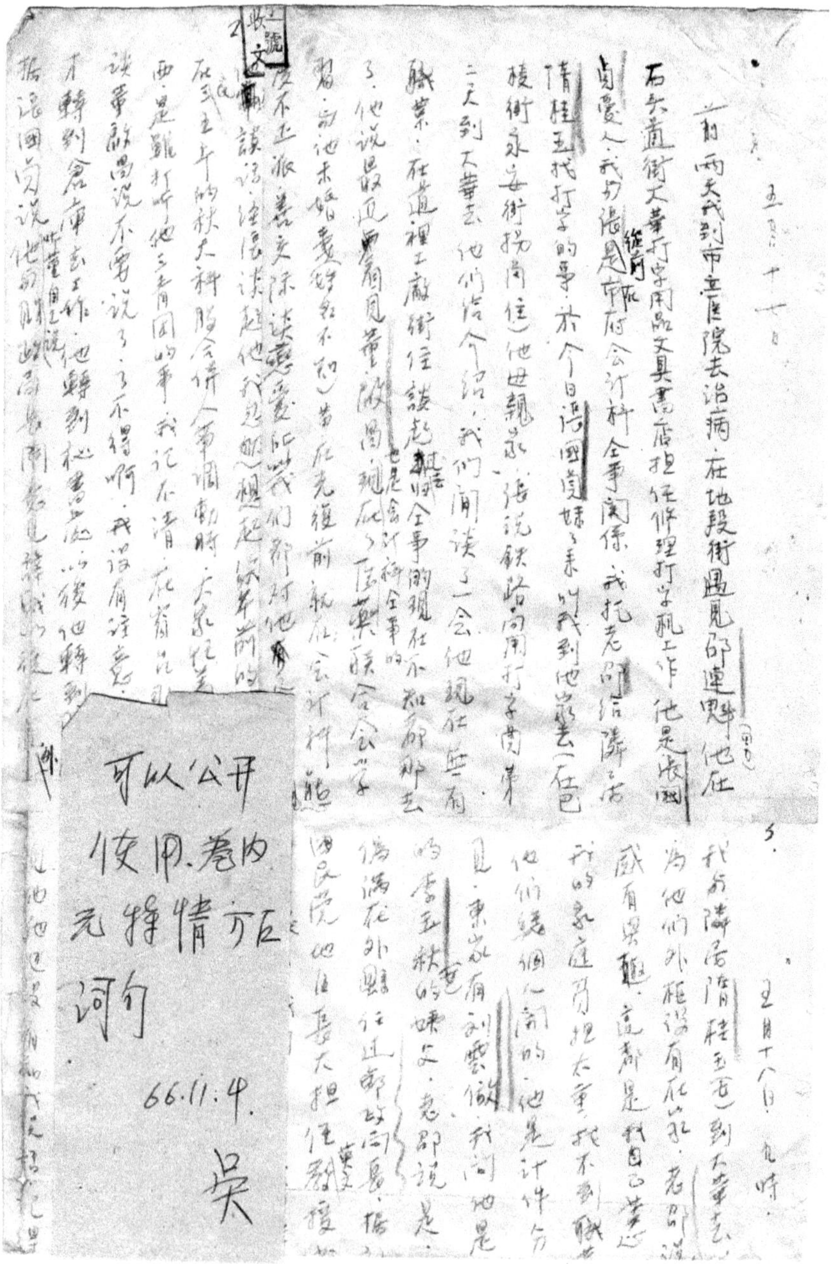

Figure 4 Information shared with case officer (1950)

Introduction

Records of the kind translated in Part III above do not emanate immediately from the running of sources/agents/informers, but on their own they nonetheless successfully illuminate crucial aspects of the 'machinery' of HUMINT. A history foregrounding such records can convey the broad picture, including of policy changes and the evolution of security agencies as organisations. What has to be kept in mind, however, is that formal doctrine, rules and regulations, and experience written up expressly to document Cold War stakeholders' views of how HUMINT *should be* (or, which in this case is no different, should not be) conducted, are not evidence of how it was. Historians eager to get closer to the agent running praxis itself therefore must also interrogate sources of a very different kind, starting with the unevaluated and uninterpreted information produced by the agents and their handlers on the ground. If our interest is in the Cold War FBI, we will find it deposited in bureau files and institutional subfiles on assets as 'information furnished by the informant'.[87] In the Soviet Union, 'reports written by an agent, and an operational officer's notes on meetings with the agent' ended up in what the KGB referred to as operational working files.[88] And as already indicated in the *Management and Utilisation Regulations* translated above, in Cold War China it was placed in what the Ministry of Public Security called the Agent Work File, the repository of 'all of the information provided to the operational departments by the agent during the course of his operational activity'.

What has long frustrated historians grappling with officially declassified archival records is that such 'raw' evidence from the agent running praxis rarely survives in the files to which agencies n years after the event may grant access to the public. Often this is not because it, in a particular file, is judged to be particularly delicate or sensitive; once it had been exploited and become part of a finished intelligence product, an agent report, for example, had limited long-term value and therefore typically failed to survive assaults by a first wave of agency archive weeders entrusted with a mission no more sinister than to create more shelf-space. When a second wave of weeders later entered the same archive as part of a declassification initiative, much of the original file content had already disappeared. 'There has been substantial destruction in this classification', the authors of a guide to the records and classification system of the FBI note in their comment on the records that 'taken as a whole, well document how the Bureau recruited informants and evaluated the information given by them'.[89]

As a kind of intellectual shorthand, it is convenient to speak of reporting as the primary content of Agent Work Files. But what does this 'reporting' actually look like? After studying a substantial number of files from East Germany's *MfS*, one German researcher in the end designated the entire diversified corpus of agent reporting as simply one of agent 'texts'.[90] There is no such thing as a *typical* agent report, and what in each national instance is deposited in agency archives are texts that can be very heterogeneous and at times look like pages from a diary or resemble an open-ended chronicle (Chapter 10).

Agent meetings always involved far more than the delivery and reception of information, and Agent Work File content allows the historian to develop quite a multifaceted picture of the praxis of agent 'handling'. Detailed contact reports present a picture of the case officer as the all-important man or woman in the middle who must reconcile the needs, aspirations, and motivations of the agent with the demands of the HUMINT machinery more generally. Case officers must constantly monitor agent morale to determine whether any problems may be forming. At every meeting between handler and agent, the most important item after the debriefing is what a British writer on the subject calls 'welfaring'.[91] Agents 'need to be welfared, they get afraid, they get family problems', and what this entailed is well documented in the Agent Work File (Chapter 11).[92]

Once the tasking of the agent becomes more complex than simply 'give us more information on X' and begins to include what the KGB called 'active measures' (and J. Edgar Hoover spoke of as intentionally subjecting operational targets to 'a certain amount of mental anguish, suspicion, distrust, and disruption') the historian's work with primary sources becomes ever more challenging.[93] Decoding what survives (Chapter 12) can be frustrating when minutes of meetings, notes on operational planning, and so on were only ever meant to be understood by a narrow readership already supremely 'in the know'.

The case officer contact reports in the institutional files of agents based on university campuses are among the most straightforward in terms of readability. When the Cold War was over, a fellow at St Antony's College, Oxford, observed that: 'Of course there must be people, in Oxford, at other universities, and in other walks of life, who have this second, part-time job, this bit of secret life. All secret services, everywhere, need their contacts and informers.'[94] A Canadian academic's study of the praxis on Canadian university campuses in the 1960s found that agencies' 'preference for informers was not students, who came and went and were less reliable and trustworthy but permanent staff, especially academics, who had a long-term presence on campus and an interest in controlling unrest'.[95] On this point, the preference of the Royal Canadian Mounted Police tallied well with that of other countries' security agencies (Chapter 13).

10 Raw Intelligence: All Quiet in the Northeast Linen Mill

Translated in full below are the weekly reports of an agent recruited by the Economic Protection Division of the Harbin Public Security Bureau to monitor the movements of one Yang Kun, a twenty-two-year-old technician in the Northeast Linen Mill.[96] Yang's pattern of life had raised questions by matching what one senior division officer insisted was the signature profile of an individual involved in pre-incident counter-revolutionary activity. In the end, the reports of the agent – who shared dormitory and office space with Yang – contributed to an informed decision, in the summer of 1951, to suspend further surveillance of Yang and to conclude that he had *not* been engaged in conduct with a counter-revolutionary nexus. The reports rarely do more than note that at such and such a time on such and such a date, Yang Kun was observed doing X or overheard saying Y. The agent largely refrains from speculating about what his own observations might mean and, in this respect, his dull matter-of-fact reporting actually illustrates good tradecraft; the officer who recruited him appears not to have told him anything specific about what he expected him to hear and see and, as a result, the agent does not ambitiously attempt to substantiate an already decided-upon political 'finding' involving his target.

Translated Text

On 4 October, at half past eight in the morning, Yang Kun went to the post office to mail a pictorial magazine; he did not return until after half past eleven. He then sat at his desk for over twenty minutes doing nothing, appearing as if he was contemplating or thinking about something. When the time came (at twelve o'clock), he went off to have lunch.

On 5 October, he sat at his desk working on a text. Also, on his desk at the time there was some stationery. On a scrap of paper that he had tossed

---

Collection of handwritten agent reports from a file of the Harbin Public Security Bureau on the case of the *Letters from the Northeast*. The text on the collection's cover reads: *Teqing gongzuo huibao 50 niandu ji 12 ye* (Agent Work Reports for the Year 1950, Twelve Pages in Total). Closed file weeded out from the bureau archive on an unknown date.

in the lavatory waste basket, I was later able to make out the words 'Comrades, we face a glorious task!'

On 6 October, Yang Kun received a letter from inside the Great Wall, handed to him by the linen mill dispatcher.

On 8 October, before lunch at eleven o'clock, Yang went out, and he did not return until four o'clock that afternoon. I do not know where he went.

On 9 October, at half past six in the morning, Yang went out and did not return until half past twelve. Then, on 12 October, he went out at eight in the morning and again did not return until noon. When I asked him where he had been, he responded that he had gone to the hospital to treat a bad toothache. He let me have a look at his tooth, and I could see that it was swollen.

At a meeting that day, the director said that Yang had messed up the figures for some lumber. Yang, however, insisted that he had actually calculated the figures quite well.

I found a discarded draft of something he had written, and on it were words like '*tewu*', 'Sanminzhuyi Youth Corps', and so on. On a different scrap of paper that he had thrown away I could make out the words 'Struggle of Two Worlds' that had been written with a fountain pen.

XXXXXX 14 October 1950

On 15 October, as it was a Sunday, Yang Kun did not go to work. He went out, and when he returned, he said: 'I am having cotton-padded leather shoes made', but I did not ask him where.

On 16 October, Yang Kun happened to be at his desk writing a letter when Director Wang showed up. Yang then stopped writing and put the letter in his desk drawer. From what I had seen, the letter said things like 'I am very busy at work, which is why I did not write earlier ... Recently four [Soviet] experts have arrived at the linen mill ... The mill has set up a night school ...' and so on. The day before yesterday, I spotted the letter again, still there, in his desk drawer.

On 18 October, at eight o'clock in the morning, Yang Kun went out. When he returned to the mill at eleven o'clock, he said: 'I went to have my tooth looked at, at the hospital of the medical university.' He then went to the inner office to talk about something with Xue Ruiyuan.

On 18 October, Yang Kun and Xue Ruiyuan spent the evening reading the two reports, published in *Northeast Daily*, entitled 'People of Korea Shed Tears of Blood and Vow Revenge; Seoul Turns into a Hell on Earth' and 'Leader of the Italian Communist Party, Togliatti, Addresses the Situation in Italy'. Yang Kun read the newspaper very carefully, paying great attention to what it said, and he appeared to be gravely concerned. When he was done, I grabbed the newspaper to look at the reports. At that point, he looked over at Xue Ruiyuan and raised his left arm as if to give him some sort of signal that I could not make out.

On 18 October, at half past six in the evening, there was a mass meeting of all the staff in the linen mill at which Mill Director Ren delivered a report on current events. In it, he spoke of how the 'American imperialists raise *tewu* in the same way other people raise dogs. They send them to the Chinese mainland where they direct their ferocity at the People.' He also noted that 'There are *tewu* elements here in our linen mill as well, and every member of the staff must remain vigilant', at which point Yang Kun looked in all directions and spoke with resentment to another Southerner about these observations. Yang continued to listen in silence, with his head resting on his hands. What I find suspicious is that both he and the other Southerner appeared to be panic-stricken.

On 19 October, during the lunch break, at half past eleven Yang Kun and Xue Ruiyuan walked off together in the direction of the administration building. By one o'clock, they were back in the office. (As I was observing their movements, I remembered that I had seen them leave during the lunch break the day before as well.)

On 20 October, Yang Kun and Xue Ruiyuan again walked off in the direction of the administration building during the lunch break, but they were back in our office by one o'clock.

On 20 October, shortly after seven o'clock in the morning, Yang Kun went out. By two o'clock in the afternoon, he had returned to the linen mill. He said he had been to the dentist.

Person reporting: XXXXXX (XXXX), 21 October 1950

On 29 October, in the evening, Yang Kun went together with Xue Ruiyuan and others to see a movie. They watched *The Heroes of Lüliang*.

On 31 October, shortly after eight o'clock in the morning, Yang Kun went out. When he returned to the office at eleven o'clock, he brought with him two pairs of cotton-padded leather shoes. One pair was his, the other belonged to Gao Xing. (He said that the shoes had been custom-made in a shoe shop near the Nangang district trolley station.)

On 1 November, at seven o'clock in the evening, a mass meeting of all staff in the linen mill was held. During the meeting, a man in Seating Area No. 3 who was wearing glasses handed to Yang Kun copies of a mimeographed list of people's addresses that looked something like this: [*drawing*].

On 2 November, at eight o'clock in the morning, Yang Kun left for Zhaolin Theatre to attend a memorial service. He was back at the mill by ten o'clock.

On 2 November, I spotted Yang Kun's temporary graduation certificate. It looked something like this: [*drawing*].

2 November 1950

On 1 November, at half past seven in the evening, a mass meeting of the staff at the linen mill was held. It was there that I saw Tao Yiwei give one copy of the list of people's addresses to a staff member, a Southerner who was sitting in Seating Area No. 3, and a second copy to Yang Kun. The list looked something like this: [*drawing*]

[Stamped with personal chop of] XXXXXX 5 November 1950

On 3 November, during the noon lunch break, Yang Kun went to the office to attend a meeting of the Youth League branch.

On 4 November, at half past eight in the morning, Yang Kun left the mill to attend a meeting of the municipal Youth League Committee. He returned to the mill around one o'clock.

On 4 November, after lunch at two o'clock, Yang Kun went out (to attend a meeting at the mill, he reported). Sometime after four o'clock, he was back in the office.

On 4 November, at around three o'clock in the afternoon, Yang Kun wanted to borrow some money from Ding Weixin, but Ding replied that he did not have any. I later asked him: 'Were you able to borrow some money? I can lend you some if you (Yang Kun) need it.' I then ended up lending him 300,000 yuan.[97]

Note: I have recently discovered that Yang Kun sometimes leaves the mill on his own (he says he is going to see a dentist), but this does not occur at anything resembling regular hours. This deserves to be investigated because sometimes Yang Kun says: 'I'll visit the dentist tomorrow' and then, on the next day, he does not go. Why is that? (I cannot figure it out.)

5 November 1950

On 5 November, Yang Kun left the mill in the afternoon. When he returned, he was carrying a lot of books.

On 6 November, he left at half past seven in the morning, but he was back at the mill by half past nine (after having visited the dentist).

On 7 November, he left at half past eight and he was back at the mill by half past eleven.

On 7 November, at about six o'clock in the evening, the students in the Russian-language class organised a party to celebrate the October Revolution in the Soviet Union. A total of some thirty people took part, including Yang Kun, Fang Zheng, Li Yuanjing, Tao Yiwei, and Cheng Zhengmin, while the remainder [of the students] were attending a meeting somewhere. None of the five – Yang, Fang, Li, Tao, and Cheng – addressed the party.

On 9 November, he left at seven o'clock and was back at the mill by eleven o'clock, carrying a book in Russian.

On 11 November, there was a meeting for all those who had come to the mill in Harbin from inside the Great Wall. Also present at the meeting were the mill's two directors, Ren and Zhang. Yang Kun delivered a long progressive statement, saying things such as: 'We will resolutely hold our positions, do our jobs well, and when the organisation needs us, we will be

10 Raw Intelligence: All Quiet in the Northeast Linen Mill

ready to sacrifice everything ...' and so on. He tries to come across as a progressive and is eager to win the trust of his superiors.

On 11 November, he went out before lunch (but I cannot remember at what time).

On 11 November, in the afternoon, Yang Kun said in front of me, Xue Ruiyuan, and Zhao Yaonan, that: 'Today on the tram I heard two Southerners who were saying: "If I had known then that it would be like this up North, I would never have come to the Northeast in the first place".' Yang's point was that the North is no good.

On 11 November, around four in the afternoon, Yang produced a list of people's addresses and wrote a letter. When he and I went together to Daoli city district to watch a movie, we passed Yuxing Foreign Tailors where Yang Kun entered a shop to buy some postal stamps. As it turned out, they were all out of stamps, so he was unable to mail his letter. In Daoli, we then watched a movie.

On 12 November, Yang Kun left at eight o'clock for the municipal Youth League Committee to attend a meeting. This may have been when he posted his letter. He was back at the mill shortly after half past two in the afternoon.

On 13 November, he went out at eight o'clock in the morning (he said he had to visit the dentist) and was back at the mill by noon.

[Stamped with personal chop of] XXXXXX 13 November 1950

On 14 November, Yang Kun returned to the mill at around four o'clock in the afternoon. (I don't know what time he had left or where he had been.)

On 14 November, in the afternoon, Na Xiaogong said he had taken Yang Kun's cotton-padded overcoat to have it mended. At the time, Na brought with him a pair of cotton-padded trousers belonging to Wu Geng for Yang Kun to borrow and wear. Not long thereafter Na Xiaogong left, and Yang Kun phoned to explain to Wu Geng about the cotton-padded trousers and overcoat.

On 15 November, at half past seven, Na Xiaogong came to return the cotton-padded overcoat to Yang Kun.

On 15 November, Yang Kun went out at eight o'clock in the morning, saying he had to visit the dentist, and he was back again at the mill by half past eleven.

On 15 November, shortly after eight o'clock in the evening, Yang Kun was at his desk writing a letter. He finished the letter very quickly, and then he put it in his pocket.

On 16 November, Yang went out at eight o'clock in the morning and he was back at the mill at eleven fifteen. (Without having mailed the previous night's letter.)

On 17 November, shortly after eight o'clock in the morning, Yang Kun went out. At around two o'clock in the afternoon, he was back in his office. (He still had not mailed the letter written on 15 November.)

On 17 November, at half past three in the afternoon, Na Xiaogong showed up again. He spoke with Yang Kun for a while, measured his trouser leg, and then left.

On 18 November, at eight o'clock in the morning, Yang Kun went out, taking the letter with him. When he left, he said he was going to see the dentist.

On 18 November, at six o'clock in the evening, Yang Kun went to the Cinema of the Northeast to see a movie.

[Stamped with personal chop of] XXXXXX 19 November 1950

On 20 November, at three o'clock in the afternoon, I saw Yang writing a letter. As soon as he finished writing, he placed the letter in an envelope.

On 21 November, at half past eight in the morning, Yang Kun put on his cotton-padded overcoat and went out, taking with him the letter he had written on 20 November and intending to mail it. He was back in his office by ten o'clock.

On 22 November, at about nine o'clock in the morning, I spotted the newsletters (four copies, eighteen pages), *Letters from the Northeast*, sent to Yang Kun. Yang put on his cotton-padded overcoat and went over to the administration building carrying the newsletters. But when he then showed up at the Harbin office, he no longer had them. This proves that he had already distributed the newsletters.

On 25 November, shortly after six in the evening, I went together with Yang Kun and two children (Zhao Yaonan's little brother and sister) to the Cinema of the Northeast to watch a movie, and when we got there, we saw that Yang Ke and the others were there as well, all watching the movie.

On 26 November, at eight o'clock in the morning, Yang Kun went out together with Xue Ruiyuan, taking the radio. They planned to attend the Youth League municipal committee lecture and then go to the Public Security Bureau to register the radio. They came back to the mill after half past three that same day and explained that 'We were not able to attend the Youth League lecture because we could not find where it was being held.' The radio has now been registered; I saw the permit with my own eyes.

XXXXXX 28 November 1950

On 29 November, during a study session from four to five o'clock in the afternoon the topic of the discussion was the disarmament proposal put before the United Nations General Assembly by the Soviet Union. Xue Ruiyuan said: 'Why doesn't the Soviet Union take the lead by disarming? Isn't it all talk and no action? This is something we can discuss.' At that point, He Yonggui and Yang Kun said in unison: 'Right! Let's each say what we think!' He Yonggui said the aggressor is sending *tewu* to our territory to carry out assassinations, sabotage, and so on, then so why can't we also send *tewu* to the enemy's territory to engage in sabotage? Yang Kun said: 'How do they decide the composition of the General Assembly and Peace Observation Commission? Surely there will be people from this side going over there, but perhaps they have not yet had a chance to engage in sabotage?'

On 1 December, at eight o'clock in the morning, Yang Kun walked off in the direction of the administration building. He was back on site at ten o'clock, telling everybody: 'I heard Cheng Zhengmin say that there has been a major victory in Korea, and the American army has suffered a massive defeat. More than 50 American aircraft flew over and bombed the liberated areas. The People's Army used its self-propelled anti-aircraft guns from the Soviet Union to shoot down 48 aircraft.' Yang Kun explained: 'A friend of Wu Shiheng's just returned from Korea, and it is from him that Cheng Zhengmin heard this.'

On 1 December, shortly after seven o'clock in the evening, I discovered that Wu Geng was talking to another guy about where the provisions are stored. This is what the guy looked like: in his early thirties, massive stocky build, round pudgy face, and above medium height.

On 2 December, at six o'clock in the evening, Yang Kun headed for the public bath house on Fourteenth Street in Daoli district, but we split up before we got there. When I returned to the mill together with Zhao Yaonan and Li Fengqing at half past eight, Yang Kun had already returned, and he explained that he did not go to the bath house on Fourteenth Street but instead went to a bath house in Majia district where he had something to eat in a little restaurant before returning to the mill.

Evening, 3 December 1950

On 13 December, at three o'clock in the afternoon, I discovered Yang Kun writing a letter. He did not finish the letter, but he continued writing that same evening.

On 13 December, at the study meeting, Yang Kun said: 'They are not going to drop an atomic bomb on Korean territory; their bombs have already flattened Korea. They might still drop one on Chinese territory, however.' He asked: 'How many men are there in our Volunteer Army over in Korea?' and he said things like 'the Americans are bound to stage a comeback', and so on.

On 16 December, at five o'clock in the afternoon, I went together with Yang Kun, Xue Ruiyuan, and Zhao Yaonan and his sister-in-law to the Cinema of the Northeast to see a movie. Afterwards, we went to a restaurant for a meal and then we returned to the mill by trolley car.

On 17 December, in the morning, Yang Kun asked me to take the letter he had written on 13 December and post it outside the mill. The letter was addressed to one Yang Ying at 2 Back Street, Wujiang county, and the sender was given as Yang Kun at [Northeast] Linen Mill, Harbin.

XXXXXX 17 December 1950

11 Welfaring Agent 107: 'She Now Has Misgivings ...'

The case officer contact reports below have been selected from the Work File of Agent 107, operated by the Political Protection Division of the Harbin Public Security Bureau, to hint at some of the frustrations in agent-handler relationships. When she was recruited in the summer of 1950, Agent 107 was twenty-eight years old, married (but living with her mother, not her husband), and a former member of the CCP who at some point in the past had deserted the Communist cause and in the eyes of the Party become a so-called 'renegade element'. Her handler (male) now expected her to monitor former Nationalist officials and their families in Harbin's Daowai district, a section of the city known for its prostitutes and drug smugglers.[98] Specifically, her task was to look for anomalies indicative of preparations to peddle disinformation and spread distrust among the grassroots community. Her reporting was as overwhelming in quantity as it was underwhelming in quality. With her handler, she shared notes on personal encounters, snippets of conversations, and remarks recalled accompanied by her own personal observations. Early in 1951, one of her case officer's superiors noted that: 'She should not write down her information in the form of a diary. Nothing is served by doing that, it is a waste of time, and much of it lacks content.' Interesting to the historian is the external matter that ends up competing for attention with her reporting. She hopes that the Public Security Bureau will reward her by resolving her financial difficulties, but the bureau leadership merely expects her case officer to use a promise to 'resolve her issues' as leverage to extract more information from her.

Translated Text

Case Officer's Contact Report

I met with 107 on 20 September. She now has misgivings and is depressed. She does not think she can provide us with anything, and she

Operational records in an Agent Work File maintained by the Political Protection Division of the Harbin Public Security Bureau. Closed file weeded out from the bureau archive after the Cultural Revolution.

11 Welfaring Agent 107: 'She Now Has Misgivings ...'

fears that the government may have overestimated her value. She recently noticed that, unlike herself, some former members of reactionary organisations have already managed to find employment. Every time she meets with us and is unable to provide us with anything, she finds the criticism difficult to take.

I should explain that 107 has a petit bourgeois background and does not take direct criticism well. Under the circumstances, I have opted for education and encouragement, and I have tried to explain to her that her own past crimes were the result of Guomindang society and that she should bring herself to see clearly what they amounted to, and today she should stand on the side of the People. She must face up to what is happening and realise that it is her responsibility to share with the government things that she may pick up that are not beneficial to the People. I also told her that her progress will be tested in the process. As for finding a job through the government, I said she was free to look for a job herself and that the government would not stand in her way.

At our next meeting, I must carefully consider her state of mind, educate her, and make sure she reactivates her old contacts.

Wang Delu

Given her circumstances, we should resolve the job problem to facilitate her continued utilisation.

[Reports Officer] Jiang Yong, 21 September 1950

Let her look for employment on her own. We can help her prove that she has already registered with the authorities, but we should not become involved in her job problem. She should be given encouragement and advice as to how to do her work for us, and she should be told that as long as she is successful in her work for us, the job problem will, in the end, resolve itself. Given that she is someone who has not yet made a commitment to the People or had her citizen's rights reinstated, for now there must be no more talk of the government helping her find a job.

[Reports Officer] Liang Jinrong, 21 September 1950

Case Officer's Contact Report

At 10 a.m. on Tuesday, 31 October [1950], I met with 107 on Eighth Street in Daoli city district:

She told me that [the suspected Sanminzhuyi Youth Corps member] Xu Qingzhi still operates his pushcart, but recently the cart broke down. Xu's wife told her that there are people looking to hire individuals to transport goods, at 200,000 yuan a day.[99] Apparently, Xu wants to wait, but he may need to take them up on it for a few days. His attitude now is that 'Times are hard and no matter what happens, the fighting is only becoming worse. From our mountaintop, we watch the tigers fight; when two tigers fight, one of them is certain to be wounded. I do not bother to ask questions or to listen to what people say. I will just buy and sell and deal with whoever shows up.' In other words, Xu does no more business than he must in order to survive. There will be no way, he says, to fend off aircraft and artillery.

107 said that a few days ago, her husband told her that when he went to Changchun, it was in the company of Liu something (he did not tell her his first name) who now works in the Harbin Bookshop. The two of them used to be very close, but after her husband got a job with the Metals Mining Bureau, they no longer see that much of each other. 107 will try to find out more from her husband about Liu's circumstances.

107 is now very gloomy about her work prospects. Recently, she has been looking at private schools as an option, but to no avail. She has presented her proof of residence to the Labour Bureau, but she did not receive any job offers. By far, she is most anxious about finding employment.

I have told 107 to focus on Xu Qingzhi's substantive personal relationships and, through her fellow schoolmates, try to get closer to Xia Zhenguo and Liu something.

Wang Delu

Instruct 107 to connect one by one, in her mind, all of Xu Qingzhi's contacts known to her and see whether anything problematic comes to mind. She need not actually go and look them up herself. Tell her that, as long as she is successful in her work, finding a job or securing an income will not be a problem. Lead her by the hand to work for us.

Liang Jinrong, 1 November 1950

Case Officer's Contact Report

At 10 a.m. on Wednesday, 8 November [1950], I met with 107 in Beilin Park. On this occasion, she had some information to share about the following individuals in the Harbin Bookshop:

Zhao Fumin. He currently runs the Harbin Bookshop, but at the time of the illicit Manchukuo regime, he ran a book sales branch in Xinyang. Zhao attended the Kingly Way Academy and after the Glorious Restoration at the end of World War II, he joined the Northeast Youth Society organised by Yu Zhian (Yu Zhian was a professor in the Kingly Way Academy).[100] Later, Zhao launched another bookshop.

11 Welfaring Agent 107: 'She Now Has Misgivings ...'

107 still does not know his first name, but Liu something also works in the Harbin Bookshop. He returned to the Northeast from inside the Great Wall in 1948 and lived for quite a long time in Changchun. He knows the husband of 107.

Xu Qingzhi still operates his pushcart, and he has not changed. A fellow villager from his ancestral home in Keshan dropped by and told Xu what it is like in Keshan, where, he said, the Soviet army has arrived and is preparing to fight the Americans. From what 107 understands, the villager in question, whose last name is Liu, suffered pain and punishment in Keshan.

In my opinion, 107 should try to find out more about Zhao Fumin and Liu something here in Harbin, or otherwise find out what Xu Qingzhi may be up to, and also come up with a way to get closer to Xia Zhenguo.

Wang Delu

After discussing 107 at our last officers' meeting, we decided, if possible, to recruit and utilise her husband. This would benefit our work; we are now waiting for higher level approval to proceed.

Liang Jinrong, 9 November 1950

Attempt to recruit [her husband] XXXXXX approved.

[Section Chief] Zhang, 10 November 1950

Case Officer's Contact Report

At 10 a.m. on Thursday, 23 November [1950], I met with 107 on Eighth Street. 107 had been to the Rural Services Agency on Jingyang Street and had applied for a job as a typist. During her work interview, when she was asked about her past, 107 did not say anything about the blemishes on her record.

Now is the time to look into the matter of her employment and decide if it will be OK for her to get a typing job, if we should tell her to admit the blemishes on her record, and if we should provide her with a letter of introduction. These matters really need to be dealt with quite urgently.

Wang Delu

We are not going to become involved in her search for a job. Regardless of where she ends up, she will need to come clean about her historical issues, since she is an element who has lost her rights as a citizen, and, as such, no state entity anywhere will be in a position to take her on. She does not need our help to find employment in the private sector. She needs to have it pointed out to her that unless she scores some successes in her work for us, the government will not be prepared to put its trust in her. If she is successful and performs well, we may be able to appeal to a higher court on her behalf and request a reprieve or a reduced sentence.

Liang Jinrong, 24 November 1950

Case Officer's Contact Report

At 10 a.m. on Friday, 1 December [1950], I met with 107 on Eighth Street. She still has not been told whether or not she will actually get the position as a typist. I told her that no matter where she is looking for a job, in any state-run entity she must come clean about her past and not conceal anything. I also told her that she is the one who can really do something about her rights as a citizen, and by performing well in her work for us, she may be able to see her rights reinstated early. 107 responded by saying that she will now no longer make finding employment her priority, but rather she will concentrate on being successful in her work for us, and then she will look for a job. I would say, based on our conversation, that she is performing very well.

Wang Delu

The last time around, the section team agreed to have a group leader investigate the reason why all this continues to be bogged down and never goes anywhere. Other duties have so far prevented the group leader from doing this, but at the next meeting of the section team we need to investigate how we will be able to make some progress here.

[Reports Officer] Wang Yuhu

Agreed.

Liang Jinrong & Qi Lumin, 2 December 1950

Case Officer's Contact Report

At 10 a.m. on Saturday, 16 December, I met with 107 on Eighth Street. While she knows Luan Xinde and Xia Zhenguo, for now she is unable to get closer to them. During our conversation, I tried to find out more about her own contacts as well as to get a more detailed understanding of the people whom her husband knows. Based on her written submissions, we should identify the key targets on whom she should concentrate.

At present, she still has this idea that some people whose 'crimes are far more serious ... enjoy more freedom than I do'. She asks why someone like herself, whose 'crimes are slight, still must go on like this?' I have explained to her the difference between her crimes and those of other people, and I sternly pointed out to her that while at one point she may have been a member of the Communist Party, she then joined the

Guomindang and carried out reactionary activities. As a result, she became a hidden traitor and Party renegade element. Therefore, her crimes are different from ordinary crimes. In the end, she said that she would make every effort, adding that she recently felt that she was discovering things that people had kept to themselves when they had to register with the authorities.

I asked her to write down the names of her new contacts and identify and focus on her priority targets.

Wang Delu

Based on what was learned from this meeting, it seems likely that her husband already knows of her contacts with us. So, for example, she says 'I never told him directly, but he senses what I do, and he has told me to make an effort with it.' That 107 is short of any means to carry out her work is quite possible. We believe attempts to talk her husband into serving us should be intensified, and this would help her. 107 insists her crimes are slight; she must be convinced of their severity. She should be told that 'given your crimes, the court may want to interrogate you again. All it takes is one sentence from us, but it all depends on your performance.' Perhaps putting it like that would work.

Wang Yuhu

Efforts to recruit her husband XXXXX should be intensified.

Liang Jinrong, 17 December 1950

Case Officer's Contact Report

At 10 a.m. on Thursday, 28 December, I met with 107 on Eighth Street. The last time I met with her, I had her write down the names of the reactionary elements she knows and to settle on a few priority targets. From what I understand this time around, her scope is still too wide, but she has managed to gather some information as well as to get in touch with quite a few of her targets. Under the present circumstances, 107 has a problem because almost every day she ends up having to travel quite some distance from where she lives. This makes her mother very unhappy, and she quarrels constantly with 107, accusing her of running around doing everything except looking for a job. 107 says that while she is capable of handling her mother, she has to ask herself: 'If I go on like this, but still do not get any results, then what should I do?'

I explained to her that if she is sincere, honest, and makes an effort, the government will take notice. The government will decide on the basis of her actual performance whether or not she is a sly one. I reminded her that she herself still must look for a job, but that the government can provide her with proof of residence. She said that if she does find employment, finding the time needed to carry out this kind of [information gathering] work may become problematic. My own analysis of her situation is that on the whole, she wants us to help her find employment. If she is to continue to serve us as well, it must be a job that will allow her enough time to do both. Under the circumstances, she herself is simply incapable of finding such kind of employment.

The information that 107 has been able to gather is in her written submission.

In my opinion, in order to get her mother to stop quarrelling with her and to make it possible for 107 not to have to rely on her mother for money, we really should provide her with suitable employment and give her some comfort. In this way, in the future she will be able to do her [agent] work for us more effectively.

Wang Delu

Judging from the information she has given us, 107 has gone just about everywhere, but to no avail. For now, we are not going to help her find employment. The court is about to suspend her sentence because of her work for us, but it has not yet implemented its decision. In another matter, one should select some priority targets for her. About visiting the oil plant to look for people she might know, tell her not to go there again. Let us double-check the residential address of Xia Zhenguo and then tell her to look him up at home.

Liang Jinrong, 29 December 1950

I am not clear about the concrete circumstances under which one might find employment for 107, but I will ask the leadership to give the matter some thought. As for the information she provides, it is no more than a jumble of factoids, all of which need to be analysed separately.

[Reports Officer] Shao Guozheng, 29 December 1950

Case Officer's Contact Report

Met with 107 this morning. She submitted a self-assessment of her work thus far, and from her work one can tell that her attitude is honest and that she is making efforts to improve. She is able to overcome her problems, and we should consider that she is a good agent.

Furthermore, she has to manage a variety of tasks and cannot concentrate, which means that even though she has reported many things, so far she has been unable to really proceed in depth. Consequently, when I met with her, together we looked at her situation and her problems and then tentatively set some work priorities for now. At the same time, based on her present circumstances, I gave her encouragement and guidance. We determined that, as of now, she should focus primarily on the following individuals:

Xu Qingzhi, currently residing on Baoding Street, who attended school in Japan. He [later] attended a Guomindang training course for military and government cadres in Changchun. He is now making a living operating a pushcart. He is very dissatisfied with the government and often speaks of not wanting to do anything at this point but wait for the return of the Guomindang. His wife, Lü Guifang, registered with the authorities as a member of the Sanminzhuyi Youth Corps, but since coming to Harbin she has still not reported to the local authorities. Her brother, meanwhile, lives on Taiwan.

Fu Baochen. From what 107's classmate Wang Xiuqing has said, Fu had been a member of the Guomindang, but whether he mentioned this when he registered with the authorities is unclear. He now works in the government Electric Power Bureau.

Xia Zhenguo (Lianzhong), currently residing on North Eighth Street, was at one stage a member of an espionage outfit that would pass on intelligence to the Guomindang in Changchun (according to information from 107's classmate Liu Yuzhi). He has recently been released from a government reformatory, and he is a very unsavoury character who wheels and deals in copper. His wife is a nasty piece as well, and rumour has it that while in Changchun, they were involved in counterfeiting currency.

Zhang Peilin. After the end of the war, he maintained excellent relations with some crucially placed Guomindang officers and travelled to Changchun on business. Whether he himself is a member of the Guomindang is unclear, but his brother certainly is a member of the Guomindang.

Liu Zehan, who served as director of the illicit Manchukuo regime's Jilin Provincial People's Livelihood Bureau, is currently at home, unemployed, and regularly in touch with some of his former colleagues. Rumour has it that he has kept a lot of documents (I don't know if they are from the illicit Manchukuo regime or from the Guomindang).

Others, such as Dong Qichang and Li Shaobo: 107 should develop an understanding of them, while also focusing on the above individuals.

This time around, 107 was even clearer in her attitude and she wants to do all in her power to perform her work well. In this way, she will atone for her past crimes.

Below is 107's own assessment of her general situation since agreeing to work for us. Basically, this is not bad, and it does have some substance. All in all, in the future she should be given some training and encouragement in her work.

Shao Guozheng, 25 January 1951

Agent's Self-Assessment

A.   Work Situation   Quite some time has now passed and even though I have managed to get close to people whose thinking used to be backward and who used to be members of reactionary organisations, all I have been able to obtain is general information about their daily lives, employment, and so on. I still do not know much about their real attitudes or their political thinking. Some of them engage in side-line economic activities or labour and are merely seeking a quiet, safe life, and they are unwilling to participate in revolutionary work. They are obviously distancing themselves from the government, but because their actual educational and political theoretical levels are high, this reflects their backward attitudes. As for myself, my political level is inferior, and I am far from being able to analyse problems. I cannot come up with any concrete examples. I hesitate to be bold and I fear my analyses will be incorrect.

People with whom I was in touch, and those about whom I have inquired indirectly and who have since been in touch with me, have not revealed anything. I always try to visit them at home and then to produce a timely report, but I feel that my reporting is very insubstantial. People give me the cold shoulder and do not share anything substantial with me, which I find disconcerting. This is altogether wrong of me, and it shows that I am simply too impetuous. I keep it to myself, however. Once I return home, I think about what kind of tactics I could use to tease out the truth from them, but I cannot come up with anything. In this respect, I suffer from a lack of experience and insufficient training. It becomes an ideological burden and my work yields no results. Thankfully, nobody appears to have become suspicious about me.

When it comes to new acquaintances, my excuses for staying in touch are not good enough. For example, I have used buying and selling as a reason for looking up old Xia (Zhenguo), who has the bravery of a frightened thief, trading as he does without a licence. My first step was simply to become acquainted with him, but in the future, I will somehow need to find a better excuse for staying in touch with him. He may be uneducated, but he is particularly careful when it comes to details. If the superiors can give me instructions as to how I should proceed in a case like this, I will definitely complete my task.

B.   On What I Have Achieved in My Work   I feel particular shame because my contributions to the People have been so small, and for this I have to make a deep self-criticism. At every meeting, the superiors always earnestly and tirelessly help me, while I seem all along to be running around in the dark without producing any concrete results.

What I achieve is far too little. Due to (1) seriously insufficient study and yielding to too much household work, and (2) my lack of political theory and muddleheaded nature, I am not making any progress. At this stage, I should be able to have an 80 per cent success rate or more, but the way I see it, I am only hovering around 20 or 30 per cent. The obstacles mentioned above are flaws I must quickly overcome, and I need to modestly improve my work.

C.   *Pluses and Minuses, and Deviations in My Work*   I do not study sufficiently, my political mind is not sound, and I am incapable of correct analyses and judgements. Given these weaknesses, my work has not yielded any results.

My biggest weakness is that I am unable to judge the thinking and attitudes of the people whom I encounter. I am incapable of assessing their social contacts with sufficient accuracy and precision.

When I met Zhang Xian and Bian Baowen, I did not engage them in conversation. Even now, I still have not been able to explain to myself exactly why. Was I being too individualistic, telling myself they are really not people of any importance, and, in any case, they too are going to have to register with the authorities? My thinking was wrong: I underestimated the enemy and did not understand him well enough. All these weaknesses of mine are impacting my work, I know, but I am confident enough to come clean about them.

My relations with my contacts are too shallow. Emotionally and practically, I am too rigid and not flexible enough. Again, because of these weaknesses, I have no concrete achievements to show. Plus, I am not bold enough. I am prone to deviations.

I do not feel that I have anything positive to point to. I do want to make contributions to the government, and, in my mind, I am single-mindedly focused on picking up truthful information everywhere. No matter how difficult this may prove to be, I will in the end succeed.

D.   *How to Do My Work in the Future*   I must study and become proficient, be careful and overcome my impetuousness. Most importantly, I hope the government will give me in-depth instructions, since I myself lack actual experience and have limited resources. If the need is for me to continue as before, I need to be able to approach people in a more flexible way in order to understand what they are really up to (given that they not only keep me in the dark but appear irritated with me). This is crucial. The remedy must suit the case, and one must choose one's approach depending on the actual circumstances. Hence, on this point too, I hope to receive instructions (this is a minor point of criticism that I wish to raise). For instance, when I looked up Lu Huaizhang, I barely managed to engage him in small talk before finding him prepared and on his guard ideologically. Are all these individuals who already have registered with the authorities still hyper-vigilant? Or do they simply find that people chatting with them are a nuisance? Again, take old Xia, with his past history and activities. Although he is an uneducated man, after having spent time in a government correctional facility, he is very vigilant. He is really cautious and to approach him will call for something special. In short, all the people who know they have problematic pasts are taking precautions, hence, in these cases, getting at the truth can be very difficult. One must come up with all kinds of ideas in order to obtain a deeper understanding.

As the American imperialists confront massive setbacks in their occupation of Korea and must reconsider their plans for expanding the war, the victories of the Chinese and Korean People's Armed Forces are victories for lovers of peace all over the world. The setbacks of the American imperialists have provoked them into a last desperate attempt that has exposed their weaknesses – the insufficient power of their soldiers and the morale of their army that has declined by 90 per cent. All they can do now is threaten with bombardment from the air, but this will not turn the tide. With accurate preparations, we will be able to block their advances, and through close mutual cooperation, we will carry out the most powerful rear-area work. In order to secure the doom of the running dogs of the American imperialists, they must be crushed by way of practical actions. Our study needs to be strengthened in order to ensure our execution of tasks, since unless we study, we shall not have sufficient resources.

As for how I need to act from now on, ideologically, I have already unburdened myself and, under the circumstances, as long as I have what is called for, I am sure the government will provide me with the means. Therefore, in my current environment, if the government thinks working as a teacher will be appropriate, I am delighted. I would have a better chance of engaging in [political] study, even though I dare not make sufficiently bold demands on myself. Again and again, I find myself thinking that I just do not have what it takes. So far, I have not made any contributions and, as a result, for me to ask the government to resolve my problems is asking too much. On this point, I hope the higher levels will take my circumstances into consideration when deciding.

XXXXXX 25 January 1951

12 Tasking Agent 371: Active Measures

Security agencies would on occasion give their agents tasks more complex than merely to serve as quasi-passive providers of information on people or events. A Chinese textbook from the final decade of the Cold War period describes such missions as including 'standing outside the vortex of contradictions while discreetly exploiting those contradictions to manipulate (*baibu*) the enemy'.[101] In 1956, the Political Protection Division of the Harbin Public Security Bureau assigned such a mission to Agent 371, an educated man in his twenties who had kinship ties with many of the people about whom he had already been reporting for some time. A Muslim, he was not only meant to develop community intelligence but also to discreetly undermine contacts between one particular Harbin imam and a member of the Muslim community in Tianjin. Translated below are records of the briefing and debriefing of the agent, as preserved in his Agent Work File. In addition to structuring his carefully written reports in the form of one item, one subject (hereby facilitating the filing of reports and avoiding the headaches for archivists caused by the diary-type format employed by Agent 107 in the previous chapter, which called for endless cutting-and-pasting of pages), he also, for the benefit of the secular public security officers who would be reading his reports, occasionally glossed Muslim religious terminology used by his operational targets, and now and then submitted his own appraisals of what they were saying.

Translated Text

Case Officer's Minutes from the Briefing of an Agent

At 1 p.m. on Friday, 6 January 1956, at the premises on Third Street, [Political Protection] Division Chief Lu Bo and [Political Intelligence] Section Chief Lu Junjie met with Agent 371.

Operational records in file maintained by the Political Protection Division of the Harbin Public Security Bureau. Closed file weeded out from the bureau archive on an unknown date.

At this meeting, Division Chief Lu issued instructions in preparation for the agent's upcoming visit to Tianjin. Specifically, he took into account that the agent had already spoken to [the operational target's] Cousin X [here in Harbin] about intending to travel to Beijing to pick up the wife and children of one of his in-laws. The following are Division Chief Lu's instructions to the agent:

I. Today, once you are back home, find an opportunity, when the children cannot listen in, to talk only to your wife and your mother, and tell them the following: 'During the upcoming vacation, people at work who are from out of town will be going home, while those who live with their families here in Harbin must attend study sessions as part of the *Sufan* [personnel security risk assessment]. To me, this may prove awkward and therefore, before it is announced, I will ask the president of our school for a few days' leave to travel to Beijing to pick up our relatives. In that way, I will be out of town during *Sufan* study, and by the time I return, the study sessions will be over. If anybody from outside asks, just tell them I have gone to pick up our relatives.' Explain to your family that you have borrowed the money for the trip elsewhere, that you do not have to repay it for a long time, and that no one in the family should be concerned in any way. Just tell them 'It's no big deal!'

II. Tomorrow (Saturday, 7 January), you visit Cousin X at home and tell him that your Beijing in-laws 'have conferred and insist that I come [to pick up the wife and children and bring them to Harbin with me]. One of the in-laws is terribly busy in the trade union, while the other cannot get his factory to approve his leave. They point to me, saying that you get a teacher's vacation. They have pooled their resources and are able to put up 30 yuan. This means I still must borrow 20 yuan.' Tell Cousin X you are not yet sure if the school will approve your leave and insist that he keep your plan to stop over in Tianjin a secret! Then go to the school and ask for leave, giving as your reason that you must pick up your relatives in Beijing.

III. On the day after that (Sunday, 8 January), you visit Cousin X at his home and tell him it was not all that easy to get the school to agree to give you leave, but in the end you managed to secure permission. Tell him: 'I will be leaving either tomorrow night, or if not then, definitely the morning thereafter. If there is anything else, just let me know!'

IV. On 10 January, you [the agent] are to come to the premises on Third Street at seven in the morning. Be sure *not* to tell Mullah Han, and, when you leave home, make sure you look as if you are about to set out on a journey.

Record produced by Xu Songshan, 9 January 1956

Case Officer's Minutes from the Briefing of the Agent

On Tuesday, 10 January [1956], at the premises on Third Street, Division Chief Lu Bo and Section Chief Lu Junjie met with Agent 371. This is an account of what took place at the meeting:

Agent 371 arrived at the premises at a quarter past seven in the morning to report on implementation of the tasks he had been assigned by Division Chief Lu at their previous meeting. At approximately eleven o'clock, Division Chief Lu issued instructions to Agent 371, discussing the next steps in his assigned mission and whether he was to first go to Tianjin or first go to Beijing. In the end, it was decided that he would first go to Tianjin. In case [the agent's operational target in Tianjin] X Jr was then to suggest the two of them travel to Beijing together, the agent was to come up with a way of dissuading him and, most importantly, ensure that they would *not* travel on the same train. The division chief also further clarified the agent's mission in Tianjin. It was primarily to build closer relations with X Jr in order to create favourable conditions for future operations. Section Chief Lu briefed Agent 371 in concrete detail about his tasks, the means by which he was to execute them, and the issues to which he was to pay particular attention.

The agent's first task: mainly to find out just what kind of a person X Jr is by way of paying him a cordial visit, carrying a letter, and taking him up on his request to spend a few days in Tianjin.

Operational steps:

I. In order to understand X Jr's present circumstances and his opinions, the agent is to concentrate primarily on observing the following: (1) how X Jr views the arrest of his father; (2) his opinions about the future of his medical clinic, the Muslim community, and so on; and (3) his attitude about current events, including about the collectivisation of agriculture, the socialist transformation of private industry and commerce, the international situation, and so on.

II. Make a note of the matters that X Jr asks about and shows an interest in. Which issues concern him the most?

III. What kind of life does he lead? What is his attitude towards his father, X Sr, and that of his family clan towards his friends and relatives? What is his social life at present?

The agent's second task: to create conditions during the visit to Tianjin, on which to base future work.

Operational steps:

The agent's opinions must tally with those of X Jr. In some matters, he should first state his own opinion, for example, that the lesson to be learnt from the arrest of X Sr is that it came about as the result of a failure to differentiate good people from bad people. The agent should also let X Jr's family feel that he may be of use to them by becoming involved with them in somewhat greater depth, for example, by offering to lend him some money, looking out for him, advising him about how to act, or sharing some ideas.

The agent's third task: to find out who are the people in Harbin that X Jr likes, how much he actually knows about what is happening here, and which people does he not like, and so on. The same goes for people and circumstances in other cities.

Finally, Division Chief Lu told the agent to prepare answers in case X Jr raises any of the following subjects:

1. The development of industry in Harbin.
2. How Muslim businesses are faring.
3. The circumstances in our city's elementary schools.
4. What is happening here with respect to the collectivisation of agriculture and the transformation of private capitalism.

The agent was asked to spend three or four days in Tianjin, to arrive in Beijing on 16 January, and to spend two days there before returning to Harbin.

Record produced by Xu Songshan

Agent's Own [Post-Mission] Analysis and Suggestions

Analysis of X Jr, based on my Tianjin visit:

1. I gained even deeper insight into the reactionary elements in his thinking.
2. He has a particularly deep yearning for a changed climate, and he listens to enemy radio broadcasts for consolation and hope.
3. He associates with some foreigners and Chinese whom, assuming there is a future change in the climate, he believes will be of use to him to prepare the ground and conditions for him to work his way up.
4. We may now conclude that X Jr is a *tewu* who may be spoken of as managing a counter-revolutionary organisation. This conclusion amounts to very significant progress.
5. X Jr is sly, and he is of the opinion that now is not the time to act. His idea is to become a long-term covert sleeper.

6. Right now, X Jr employs double-dealing tactics. On the surface, he pretends to be committed and honest, and he plays the part of a law-abiding and moderate person.
7. X Jr is terrified when it comes to his own crimes, however. He gets some comfort from the fact that his father was sentenced to a mere six months for illicitly hoarding grain [and he was not charged with counter-revolution].
8. As a consequence of the *Sufan* and what happened to his family because of the people with whom they associated, both father and son will in the future be acting even more carefully and with even greater cunning.

Suggested Direction of Future Efforts:
Apart from whatever instructions the leadership may issue, I maintain that:

1. The enemy is sly and careful, and therefore we must act with even greater cunning and care if we are to win his deep trust and be able to penetrate [his organisation].
2. Existing basic and favourable conditions should be exploited for us to stay on top of all of the enemy's activities and plotting.
3. In order to corroborate the existence of his counter-revolutionary organisation, we must start from the enemy's substantial personal relationships and then proceed in greater depth to clarify his liaisons and patterns.
4. In order to determine whether or not activity is ongoing, we must focus on what he routinely pays attention to and what he takes an interest in, and then proceed from there.
5. We should make X Jr and his father our priority target, adopt the tactic of a full-frontal attack to achieve clarity about essential matters, while employing an outflanking tactic to secure from their substantive personal relationships the facts surrounding their past and present activities.

XXXXX 23 January [1956]

Task Force's Assessment

Upon his return from Tianjin on 20 January, Agent 371 in addition to orally reporting to the leadership on the main circumstances also, as requested by the division chief, submitted a detailed record of his work and made some suggestions [in the document above, dated 23 January] about what to do next. His main suggestions were as follows: to continue efforts to win the enemy's deep trust and penetrate [his organisation]; exploit existing basic conditions to stay on top of all of the enemy's activities and plots; in order to corroborate the existence of his counter-revolutionary organisation, start from the enemy's substantial personal relationships and then clarify his liaisons and patterns; and in order to determine whether he is active or not, focus on what it is that he routinely pays attention to and takes an interest in, and proceed from there.

We basically concur with these opinions, although the concrete [operational] steps needed [to meet our goal] are still missing. Based on the letters that X Jr has sent to Cousin X about wanting to visit Harbin when his father is released from prison, and in line with the spirit of Division Chief Lu's instructions (and before deciding on our next operational steps), at this point we tentatively propose directing Agent 371 to focus on the tasks below, and we ask the leadership to indicate whether or not they are appropriate:

I. When we researched all of the contacts with whom X Sr has been in touch, as well as the Muslims connected to him, we found that Agent 371 knows all of them personally and is more or less in touch with all of them. This includes a single Han contact whom Agent 371 knows only through Cousin X. In accordance with Division Chief Lu's instructions, Agent 371 may be directed to remain further intimately in touch with these contacts and to observe and understand which ones have, since X Sr was arrested, distanced themselves from him and his family and which ones remain in touch. This will help us understand the circumstances of the contacts maintained by X Sr.

II. On 28 January, X Jr appealed to Cousin X in a letter, saying he should have listened to him and not loaned any money to Wang Liming and Liu Zhensheng. In a second letter, on 29 January, he expressed major dissatisfaction with the kind of friends that Cousin X keeps. In his letter, he wrote: 'You do nothing but hang out with people like that, so no wonder you get in trouble! Just you wait, your days of really big trouble have not yet arrived. Look at what happened to X Sr. He disgraced himself and lost all face!' When Agent 371 was in Tianjin, X Jr expressed similar sentiments and said one must be careful about the kind of friends one keeps. Since his return, the agent has not yet spoken to X about X Jr's letter, nor has Cousin X as yet mentioned it to the agent. For this reason, we plan to direct the agent to side with X Jr, express concern for his family's attitude, find an opportunity to tell Cousin X what X Jr asked him to do, and clarify with him the dangers of making friends like that, while also, at the same time, expressing approval of how carefully X Jr is handling things. If it turns out that X has spoken about the context of X Jr's letter, then he is to tell Cousin X that he must not be angry, that X Jr means well for the family, and he should let that be a lesson. We want the family to have a positive impression of the agent.

III. Before he went to Tianjin, Agent 371 had already agreed with Cousin X not to let anyone know that he would stop over there [on his way to Beijing], but Cousin X's wife ended up mentioning this when she was in Xiangfang Women's Mosque and, as a result, Ma Tongzhi, Yang Maoting, Yang Xiyuan, and others all found out. In order to show how careful he was in handling things, and in the context of the above matters, the agent should, in conversation with Cousin X, hint at how sloppily things had been dealt with. Although it was only a minor matter, one should, nonetheless, have been more careful. Depending on the result of all this, we should consider having the agent write a letter to X Jr to tell him about what is happening in Harbin. The drafting of the letter in question merits a separate discussion.

Group Four, 1 February [1956]

Section chief's comment: Agreed. Division chief, please comment and instruct. When briefing the agent, tell him as follows: Judging from the circumstances, X Jr was angry with Cousin X because of the kind of friends he keeps and X Jr simply had to lecture him. At that point, his younger brother may suspect that we are responsible and start to distance himself [from the agent]. In such an event, we should have a strategy to be ready to deal with it.

Lu Junjie

Division chief's comment: In the days to come, the following matters are to be dealt with: (1) mainly directing the agent to move in on and get to know X Sr's key contacts, and (2) developing a strategy to deal with a possible visit by X Jr to Harbin.

Lu [Bo]

Tasking of Agent (Excerpts from the Case Officer's Memoranda)

[On 7 February 1956] I told the agent to primarily stay on top of the activities and the contacts of the X family, plus to gather some intelligence on what Mullah Han may be up to. I also instructed him to monitor X Sr's interactions with his *old* contacts and the circumstances regarding any *new* ongoing encounters between Yang Shengqing and Cousin X. Next time, it is planned that a strategy, based on due research, will be devised for the agent's tasks during the Spring Festival and later a possible visit [to Harbin] by X Jr.

[On 10 February 1956], as instructed by the division, I had Agent 371 write a letter [to X Jr], based on a text drafted by us, that he will post this afternoon. We also worked out how, during the Spring Festival, the agent should develop and expand his contacts with X Sr's family. If he has a chance, he is to share with Cousin X some useful hints about how to behave in public, not only to make X Jr realise that the agent cares about Cousin X's somewhat immature behaviour but also to let him know that the agent can be of assistance.

[On 16 February 1956] our conversation centred on Chen Xuefu, who is a teacher at Xiangfang city district school and a Youth League member, albeit a very backward one. If Chen begins to spend a lot of time with Cousin X, this may in the long run prove to be dangerous. In order to shield Chen and not let this go so far that he becomes influenced by the X family, in my view we should direct Agent 371 to sabotage the relationship for the good of the family, for instance, by suggesting to Cousin X that he should be more vigilant and stressing that Chen is after all a Youth League member and that although he may be backward, one never knows what he may say at Youth League meetings! (Whether feasible, please instruct.) My tasking of the agent, this time around, was mainly to have him find out more about some trends and attitudes of the members of X family. Also, if there are urgent matters, I told the agent to promptly report them to me.

[On 20 February 1956] according to plan, the tasks were laid out to deal with two possibilities. One is that X Jr comes to visit Harbin, the other is that he does not. Our overall aim is to break up and undermine his current contacts with X Sr and with Chen Xuefu in particular. The difference lies in how to go about this. I clarified to the agent that if X Jr comes to Harbin, then the agent should take his side, help him from there, and support his view, explicitly stating what he should think about when making friends. If, on the other hand, X Jr does not come to Harbin, then the agent should draw inspiration from the visit to Tianjin, combining this with what X Jr would want to see done on his behalf, asking X Sr to explain to him the dangers of making the wrong kind of friends.

[On 25 February 1956] I suggested to the agent, on the basis of intelligence, that he talk at length with X Sr on Sunday (the twenty-sixth) with the aim of breaking up and undermining his contacts. In his discussions with X Sr, I told the agent to begin by stressing the insights and attitude of X Jr. I also tasked him with probing the attitude and circumstances of Mullah Han.

[On 28 February 1956] Agent 371 suggested that Mullah Han's leaking of what should have been a secret has worked in our favour and has helped isolate X Sr and undermine his contacts. Less favourable is that it also has put X Sr on guard and therefore it will complicate our work in the future. I tasked Agent 371 with finding opportunities to raise and really talk the matter through, and to have X Sr truly understand the dangers of making [the wrong kind of] friends, plus to become clearer about just what kind of nominal kinship exists between Chen Xuefu and the X family. As a second point, I told the agent to find out just how far Mullah Han had leaked the secret. I also made it clear to him that in order to be able to undermine and isolate X Sr, he will have to create the right conditions in a number of respects. Therefore, as of now what Mullah Han has done will indeed benefit our work.

[On 7 March 1956] my original plan had been to have the agent advance on X Sr as well as on Cousin X, but it has proven difficult to launch such advances as they appear likely to arouse suspicions among members of the X family. Under these circumstances, I instead tasked the agent with primarily controlling and understanding where X Sr seems to be going. The original plan is still on the agenda and should the opportunity arise, it is not to be abandoned. The X family has not told the agent the entire truth about receiving the letter from X Jr. I tasked the agent, according to plan, with finding out where X Sr is going and what he is plotting at each juncture as well as to observe his contacts with X Jr and other people. The agent's *modus operandi* will be to closely observe and study the day-to-day activities and remarks of each member of the X family so as to be able to retain the initiative and meet our demands.

Agent's Memorandum

After his release from prison, X Sr asked me in the course of a conversation at his home on 26 February, when no one else was present: 'When you went to the mosque, did Mullah Han mention visiting the Public Security Bureau branch in Daoli city district?' (I replied saying that he mentioned it and that Mullah Han is prepared to talk to him about it in detail when he finds the time.) X Sr then said: 'I heard Mullah Han say that Bai Wenquan had committed errors and was disciplined because he shared with us what was said in the letter. This was all meant to be secret, yet news of it spread. At this point, that is really bad!'

I told X Sr: We are one and the same family – the peaches may go bad, but the apricots are fine – on top of which you are my elder. None of our backgrounds are good. We have all endured disciplinary measures, in Changchun and here in Harbin. We are in the same boat and as close as we can be! We share mutual responsibilities. When something happens to you, I myself, Cousin X, and the others all become equally worried. When I visited Tianjin on the way to Beijing I spoke in detail to X Jr about what is going on. X Jr may be young, but in some respects, he is indeed informed and intelligent. We see things in the same way. You have already regained your freedom, but from what X Jr has said and from what I myself have seen, in the past you were too honest and tolerant. You were not cautious enough when you picked your friends. Some come to see the doctor, others come to perform an act of *niyah*, others come to ask for money, but the number of those who really have what is best for the Muslims at heart are very few.[102] Most come to perform an act of *niyah*, and when you give them money, they are happy; those to whom you give less money are disappointed and far from happy. When you upset one of the Han people (*Hanmin*), they will bear a grudge. But now there is opposition among the Muslims as well. For this reason, I feel that in the future we must be more circumspect when it comes to the people with whom we are in touch and we must keep some of them at a distance. If you plan on making new friends, then you must start by considering whether or not they are trustworthy. What happened this time around taught us a lesson, teaching us that we need to analyse people – who to keep at a distance, who to keep close, whom to call a friend, whom not to befriend, and who is reliable and who is not.

X Sr then said: 'Right, I have also thought about this, and it is how things have to be done as of now. During these past few days, quite a few people have called on me, but from now on, I will tell the ones hoping to perform an act of *niyah* to go to the mosque, where it is up to Mullah Han to decide. We will then give our money to Mullah Han. In conversations from now on, we need to be even more circumspect. It does not matter in the case of people whom we know really well, like you (he pointed at me) or Mullah Ma. Here you can talk about anything. It is with the other people, around whom we really must not say anything.'

XXXXX 26 February [1956]

Agent's Memorandum

I asked Cousin X: 'Did you know about the things the Mullah and my uncle talked about?'

He said: 'My father had mentioned them to me!'

I said: 'One day last week I had already discussed them in detail with my uncle. As of now, you too must pay particular attention, especially when it comes to the people with whom you are in touch. We already suffered because we had failed to draw a clear line when it came to the people we met. In the future, in my opinion, we must be more circumspect when it comes to the people with whom we are in touch.'

He said: 'My father and I have already appraised the situation, and from now on, when people show up again hoping to perform an act of *niyah*, we will tell all of them to go to the mosque. We will also have to be more careful about what we say.'

I said: 'When it comes to conversations, the main thing is to always be clear about with whom you are talking. I'll give you an example. Only the day before yesterday did I find out just *why* there is a nominal kinship between us and Chen Xuefu, something I had not known before. This is why, when we spoke the last time, I did not dare say anything.'

He said: '[Chen's] thinking is really backward! When they asked him to come to Xinli village to be the dean of instruction, he turned them down and became all moody. His relations with us are fine, even recognising one of us as his nominal father, but from now on, we need to pay more attention.'

I said: 'You're right. After all, he is a [Communist] Youth League member, which is scary, since at meetings of the Youth League, they do not keep secrets from each other. We cannot compare him to Wei Youdong who may be a Youth League member as well, but Youdong is one of us.'

He said: 'At one of the League meetings, Youdong directly questioned him about this matter of ours, but no matter how hard he tried, he could not get him [Chen Xuefu] to answer.'

I said: 'Can one guarantee Chen Xuefu will not spill the beans at a meeting of the League?'

He said: 'Right, when dealing with these members of the Youth League or the Communist Party, one must be much more careful about what one says.'

(At the family clinic, conversation on 4 March, 8:10 a.m.–9:20 a.m.)

XXXXXX 7 March [1956]

13 Debriefing Agent 594: Monitoring Campus Unrest

In May 1966, Agent 594 had just begun his third year as a HUMINT asset of the Cultural Protection Division of the municipal Public Security Bureau on one of Harbin's college campuses. An ambitious teacher in his mid-twenties from a non-proletarian family background and engaged but not yet married, Agent 594 started out hoping his overall career would benefit from serving as an agent, but the head of the Cultural Protection Division had not been particularly impressed and informed the officer who had recruited him that 'from the looks of it, this guy is willing to do the job, but he has only limited skills'. Agent 594 met his case officer regularly once a month and, on the whole, had very little to report, but suddenly all that changed in early June 1966 when the CCP leadership in Beijing announced that regular teaching had been suspended and students on campuses all over China would be called upon to henceforth concentrate full time on conducting a Great Cultural Revolution. The two then met regularly every two weeks. Translated below are the meticulously edited contact reports that Agent 594's case officer shared with his component chiefs between May and October 1966.[103] When it turned out that the covert operation of the agent might have been compromised (and debate ensued in the Division about how to handle the matter), his handler did what he could to ensure that he was protected.

Translated Text

Case Officer's Contact Report

On 20 May 1966, from 10 a.m. until noon, I met with Agent 594 at the Second Division's Point No. 21. The contents of the agent's (nineteenth) oral report and my oral replies to his questions are as follows:

Operational records in Agent Work File maintained by the Cultural Protection Division of the Harbin Public Security Bureau. Closed file, weeded out from the bureau archive after the Cultural Revolution.

13 Debriefing Agent 594: Monitoring Campus Unrest

Today, the agent reported the following to me:

Most of the masses in the No. 1 Medical School are critical of the staff study tour of Dandong Medical School. They say that the aim of the study tour, arranged by the school authorities, was unclear. They say that to emulate other people's professional skills and to copy their syllabi does not give prominence to politics. The staff had not used the tour to learn how Dandong managed to revolutionise teaching and to let it penetrate to the frontlines (the rural areas). In the end, they blamed the leadership; it should not have assigned Sun Bingcong (a clinical instructor) to lead the study tour.

On May 17, Sun Bingcong addressed a meeting of all teachers and staff at the No. 1 Medical School. He shared what he had picked up from the experiences of Dandong Medical School. He said: 'True, making cultural revolution is important, but educational reform is rather more immediate.'

During discussions that same afternoon, Sun told the group of teachers who had been on the study tour with him: 'It is people like us who are at the helm.' Teacher Fan Yusheng promptly retorted, saying: 'Our helmsman should be the Communist Party', whereupon Sun blushed and became all quiet.

At the end of my meeting with him, I asked the agent to note what the relevant individuals are saying about the Great Cultural Revolution.

Li Jingui, 23 May 1966

Case Officer's Contact Report

On 2 June 1966, from noon until 2 p.m., I met with Agent 594 at the Second Division's Point No. 21. The contents of the agent's (twentieth) oral report and my oral replies to his questions are as follows:

The agent reported that some teachers and staff (at the No. 1 Medical School) have recently voiced strong objections to the school leadership's failure to deal with the extramarital affairs of the physical education instructor XXXXX. The most vocal objections have been made by teacher Wang Zhenjin. He had previously written to the Xiangfang Municipal District Branch of the Public Security Bureau about XXX's extramarital affairs (involving female students and staff) and had asked for him to be criminally sanctioned. Wang has called on the school leadership repeatedly to intervene and deal with the matter. In the afternoon of 31 May, Principal Liu invited Wang Zhenjin to his office to discuss the matter. When Wang arrived, Education Administration Section Chief Liu, General Affairs Section Chief Ma, and one other person were present. Principal Liu asked Wang to state his opinions on the matter. Wang responded by saying that this was not an isolated matter to be judged simply as it stands. Its swift resolution, he said, must take the past behaviour of XXX into account. No one present agreed with Wang. In the end, Principal Liu told him that while his outrage was commendable, this matter must be resolved in line with the [CCP Centre's] *Twenty-Three Points* that caution against linking historical issues (such as XXX's expulsion from the Youth League for expressing reactionary opinions) to current errors. This prompted Wang to question why, given that Sun's behaviour illustrates how class struggle manifests itself in educational circles. After the meeting, Wang said to his colleague Tang Guochen: 'As soon as I said that to the principal and the others, they shut up.' [The agent added that] Wang is now stirring up his colleagues by posing questions such as 'Why didn't the school leadership act right away? Why don't they let the masses have a say in the matter of XXXXX? What is the problem?'

The agent agrees with the view expressed by Wang Zhenjin and maintains that the school should not suppress the matter.

The agent had no information to share about the unfolding of the Cultural Revolution movement on campus. He said that currently it is not a major topic of discussion. The intensity with which the [extramarital affairs of] XXXXX are being debated is however noteworthy, he said.

What the agent is saying makes me wonder if the issue is not really due to Wang Zhenjin's agitation? Why is he so concerned with the school's inaction towards XXXXX? Is it perhaps because Wang wants to draw attention away from the Great Cultural Revolution, bearing in mind that in the past he himself wrote critically about Chairman Mao's *On Practice*? Is he afraid that the Great Cultural Revolution will land him in trouble? This would explain his deliberate attempt to urge the school leadership to deal with XXXXX's conduct.

At the end of my meeting with the agent, I asked him to focus on garnering responses about the Great Cultural Revolution, especially Wang Zhenjin's views and what he says in private about the movement.

Li Jingui, 2 June 1966

Case Officer's Contact Report

On 8 June 1966, from noon until 2 p.m., I met with Agent 594 at the Second Division's Point No. 21. The contents of the agent's (twenty-first) oral report and my oral replies to his questions are as follows:

The agent said that now the Cultural Revolution movement at the No. 1 Medical School is very sluggish. On [Saturday] the fourth, all staff and students went on an outing organised by the school and then they had the next day off. Classes resumed on the sixth. That afternoon there was a meeting to debate what had been learnt during the outing. This provoked the students into putting up big-character posters at the entrances to the Party Branch, the school administration building, and the principal's office, questioning their attitudes towards the Great Cultural Revolution. The vice-secretary of the Youth League, Yuan Wenfang, in turn, accused the students (who had put up the big-character posters) of being 'paranoid', whereupon the students put up even more big-character posters, asking the vice-secretary *who* it was that he believed was 'paranoid'?

13 Debriefing Agent 594: Monitoring Campus Unrest   133

On the seventh, Zou Tianfu (head of a group of instructors) organised a meeting with sanitation staff, telling them: 'At the moment, the big-character posters are attacking the wrong targets. Some take aim at our school [leadership], which is not good. We must actively lead the students in the right direction, ask them to reject the tactic of exhaustion, and strike a balance between work and rest.'

The agent reported another incident involving the blackboard bulletin *Staff Life*: Wang Zhenjin (who is seriously afflicted with revisionist thinking and is an opponent of Chairman Mao's *On Practice*) had drawn a red banner masthead on which, in the middle, he had drawn a pink-coloured circle without Chairman Mao's portrait in it and written: 'Hold high the great red banner of Mao Zedong Thought!' Next to it, he had drawn [the revisionist] Deng Tuo and a pen penetrating Deng's heel, not his heart.

At the end of our meeting, I told the agent to pay more attention to what Wang Zhenjin may be up to during this Cultural Revolution movement.

Li Jingui, 11 June 1966

Case Officer's Contact Report

On 12 June 1966, from 10 until 11 a.m., we met with Agent 594 at the Second Division's Point No. 21. The contents of the agent's (twenty-second) oral report and our oral replies to his questions are as follows:

At our meeting today, the agent's main concern was whether or not we would allow him to employ the medium of a big-character poster to expose the operational target Wang Zhenjin (seriously afflicted with revisionist thinking and an opponent of Chairman Mao's *On Practice* and other writings).

In the end, we told the agent that as far as the matter of Wang Zhenjin is concerned, for now it would *not* be appropriate for him to expose Wang. We also told the agent that he himself was really not in a position to write an overall refutation of Wang's views given that they are based on a considerable volume of research. In order to successfully refute Wang's views, we told the agent, he would need a lot of time. He would have to go through a lot of material, in particular, things that Wang has shared with him as a friend and things that that other people are not aware of. Once you begin to expose those issues of his, we said to the agent, relations between the two of you will sour, which in turn will have an impact on what you will be able to do for us in the future. Also, we explained to the agent, the school Party Branch is aware of Wang's issues. It has documentation, and it will be able to mobilise people to expose Wang and to refute his views one by one. Once that happens, we said, you can still join in and expose Wang. For now, it is more important for you to focus on the primary task of exposing and denouncing the 'black line', the reactionary [bourgeois academic] 'authorities', and the proxies of the bourgeoisie inside the Party (Principal Liu has already relayed [provincial First Party] Secretary Pan Fusheng's instructions), so that you and everyone on campus will remain in step with the movement unfolding in other cities and provinces.

Last, we told the agent to properly and meticulously study the editorials published in the *People's Daily* since 1 June, to study and grasp their spirit and raise his own ideological awareness. We also asked him to reflect on whether or not, in his teaching these past years, he may have deviated from the education policies of the Party Centre and said incorrect things in class. He should be ideologically prepared and if he had deviated, he should draft a conscientious self-criticism and calmly adopt a correct attitude towards any big-character posters criticising him that the masses might put up.

Chen Xianqing[104] and Li Jingui, 12 June 1966

Case Officer's Contact Report

On 22 June 1966, from 9:40 a.m. until 11 a.m., I met with Agent 594 at the Second Division's Point No. 21. The contents of the agent's oral report and my oral replies to his questions are as follows:

Today the agent reported mainly on the progress of the Cultural Revolution movement at the No. 1 Medical School during the past two days:

On 20 June, the masses started to bring internal school matters to light. Their first target was the former secretary of the Party Branch, Pang Shuo (who has already been transferred to the No. 3 Medical School to serve as its principal in charge of general affairs). They accused him of not implementing the spirit of both the general and the specific education policies of the Party, of not sharing Chairman Mao's directives of 3 July [1965, on student workloads] and 26 June [1965, on public health] with the masses, and of abusing his power in pursuit of personal gain. The masses also unmasked some of Pang's supporters, including Dai Shuzhen (former General Branch secretary of the Youth League), Zhao Shumei (Protection Section officer), Li Shuzhen (former General Branch vice-secretary of the Youth League), Qu Guilan (current General Branch secretary of the Youth League), and Sun Hengyuan (physical education instructor).

On 21 June, Youth League Committee Clerk Liu Chenshi (a member of the school's *ad hoc* Cultural Revolution Leading Group, according to the agent) put up a big-character poster exposing Wang Zhenjin (seriously afflicted with revisionist thinking and an opponent of Chairman Mao's *On Practice*), branded him an anti-Party anti-socialist element, and called for his writings to be denounced. Many teachers and staff then wrote big-character posters denouncing Wang Zhenjin's views. As a result, the number of big-character posters exposing Pang Shuo declined.

Other big-character posters exposed the shortcomings and errors of ordinary teachers and staff. They asked why, for example, Zhao Shumei in the Protection Section did not manage to provide newly enrolled students with residency registration permits on time, and why it always took her so long to issue border region travel passes to students returning home for vacation?

The school personnel cadre, Zhao Yulian, maintains that the big-character posters these past two days have been problematic in that their targeting has been incorrect and that people should not attack the wrong targets. Teacher Liu Xizhi also says that this is a troubling trend and that one should not focus on ordinary shortcomings and errors but rather concentrate on resolving major issues of principle.

This morning, Wang Zhenjin also put up a big-character poster in which he compared himself to a big poisonous weed and admitted that his past views had amounted to erroneous, revisionist stuff.

At the end of our meeting, I told the agent to stay on top of Wang Zhenjin's attitude and to write a big-character poster denouncing him by amplifying arguments others have already put forward.

Li Jingui, 22 June 1966

Case Officer's Contact Report

On 26 June 1966, from 9:30 a.m. until 11:30 a.m., I met with Agent 594 at the Second Division's Point No. 21. The contents of the agent's oral report and my oral replies to his questions are as follows:

The agent today had the following to report about the Cultural Revolution:

Wang Zhenjin (seriously afflicted with revisionist thinking and an opponent of Chairman Mao's *On Practice*) is mainly writing big-character posters criticising himself. He has also made public the letter he sent to the CCP Centre and Chairman Mao [on 2 December 1961]. In the letter, according to the agent, he essentially argued as follows: 'Chairman, in my opinion the Twenty-Second National Congress of the CPSU is not revisionist. Instead, it is Marxist. Khrushchev, furthermore, is not a revisionist element.' Wang later admitted that he had been wrong and that his letter was a big poisonous weed.

XXXXX (physiology teacher and new bourgeois element who in the past maintained links with White Russian expatriates) has recently become the target of many (well over one hundred) big-character posters put up by students and teachers. The first one was put up by students and was entitled: 'XXXXX Is a Big Rascal!' It accused him of teaching the male reproductive organ obscenely to a class made up entirely of female students, telling them how the male reproductive organ erects, what a sexual impulse is, and how illness may reduce the sex drive of the male, and so on. The students have branded him a big rascal and have forbidden him from teaching classes (he has since not dared to teach again).

At the moment, the school has asked for big-character posters directed at Wang Zhenjin and at XXXXX to be put up in the canteen. Other big-character posters are being put up in the auditorium.

The agent, when reporting on the above, commented that as a physiology teacher, it was not improper for XXXXX to lecture on the reproductive organs and the erection of the male reproductive organ, since, after all, once they have graduated, the students will be expected to propagate contraception. I snapped back, telling the agent that the students had been right to put up their big-character posters and that XXXXX should not have brought up such vulgar things in class in the first place. What is the point, I asked the agent, in teaching female students these things? Do they need to know all those details to be able to propagate contraception to the masses? In the future, I said, lecturing to girls about stuff like that should not be permitted.

Finally, the agent mentioned that some students and teachers recently put up a dozen or so big-character posters aimed at the agent and his links to XXXXX, querying his attitude towards the Cultural Revolution and asking why he had not exposed any of XXX's issues? The head of a group of instructors, Li Zuoping, once said to the agent in conversation: 'You and XXXXX are very close. You once joined forces and did something quite major. If it were to be uncovered, the two of you would be stunned! I am saying this just to test your attitude; if you were to take the initiative and go public yourself, the negative impact on you would be limited.' The agent then told Li Zuoping: 'I'll expose what I want, and you can expose whatever you want. If you think you are on to something big, just go ahead and expose it!' Li nodded and said: 'Of course, of course!' whereupon the agent added: 'I promise you, I have done nothing major together with XXXXX!'

I ended our meeting telling the agent that he can expose whatever it is that he knows about XXXXX, and in whatever fashion he wants. But I emphasised once again that 'No matter whose issues you expose and no matter who exposes yours, you must keep our relationship in mind and you absolutely must not jeopardise clandestinity. This is an organisational matter of principle.' The agent promised not to jeopardise clandestinity.

Li Jingui, 26 June 1966

Case Officer's Contact Report

On 30 June 1966, from 9 a.m. until 11 a.m., I met with Agent 594 at the Second Division's Point No. 21. The contents of the agent's oral report and my oral replies to his questions are as follows:

About XXXXX (a new-born bourgeois element openly spreading poison in class):

When the agent went to see him on the twenty-fifth, XXX asked: 'Why did you come? Aren't you afraid?' The agent replied: 'Why should I be afraid? Who are you and what should I be afraid of?' XXX said that it would be best not to come around, and he told the agent not to visit him until the movement was over. XXX told the agent that a factory worker (name unknown) who was at home on sick leave had dropped by a couple of times. He was pessimistic about the prospects of overcoming his illness and he was deeply distressed. XXX consoled him and sought to encourage him to fight his illness. Several days ago, the worker showed up again and XXX then told him about having become the target of big-character posters on campus and why he was no longer able to look his colleagues in the eyes. The worker said: 'Look, you have given me courage, but now you yourself have been defeated. Let me ask you, are you an ox-monster or a snake-demon?' XXX replied 'No!' whereupon the worker asked what he was afraid of?

To the agent, XXX explained that the worker's remarks had grabbed his attention and made him think: 'My mind may be seriously full of bourgeois ideology, and I may pursue individualism and a bourgeois lifestyle. But I do not agree with those who claim I oppose the revolution, oppose the Party, and oppose the people.' The next day, the worker returned and gave him a copy of Chairman Mao's *Talks at the Yan'an Forum on Literature and Art*. Now XXX is studying the talks and writing down what he learns from them.

When they were having lunch in the canteen on the twenty-eighth, Wang Zhenjin (seriously afflicted with revisionist thinking and an opponent of Chairman Mao's *On Practice*) said to the agent: 'Now, look at those guys (pointing at the people who had put up big-character posters aimed at him), see how they have all gone quiet.' Two days later, while Wang was writing a big-character poster in his office, the agent went to see him. He offered the agent a custom-rolled Harbin brand cigarette. This led the agent to ask: 'How come you are buying cigarettes?' Wang responded by saying 'I am happy now.'

In the morning of the twenty-eighth, Tang Guochen (who wants to avenge the execution of his father and is resentful about the present) said to the agent that the issue of XXX is only his bourgeois ideology and there is nothing else to it. When he wrote the character Jiang *Cun* instead of the character Jiang *Qing*, it was merely a slip of the pen, but now they are attacking him for it. We too should attack him, but when we are done, we should attack *them*! For now, we have no choice but to attack old XXX, given what is happening. Tang then told the agent: You have the brains to do it! So, write down the dates and contents of the big-character posters targeting you in case we need to defend ourselves when they are no longer up there.

Feng Kezheng (a casual labourer in the boiler room) has told the agent to be careful now that he has become the target of a number of big-character posters. He has told him to watch out and not be swept up by the current or branded a member of this or that faction. According to the agent, this boiler room worker once studied traditional Chinese medicine and idolises life in the Soviet Union.

I tasked the agent and told him to (1) concentrate on observing Wang Zhenjin in the movement and his current circumstances, because, for now, there is no need to pay attention to anyone else specifically, and to (2) submit a comprehensive report about his own contacts with Feng Kezheng.

Li Jingui, 2 July 1966

Case Officer's Contact Report

On 3 July 1966, from 3 p.m. until 4:30 p.m., I met with Agent 594 at Point No. 21. The contents of the agent's oral report and my oral replies to his questions are as follows:

Protection Section officer Zhang Dongqin has apparently told the agent that Ma Yongshan, head of the school's General Affairs Section, is aware of the agent's work for the Public Security Bureau as is also possibly Party Branch clerk Yang Xiuzhi. The agent asked me for instructions about how to respond, and I said that I would look into it and take care of the matter. It appears the school principal Liu Liandi had mentioned it at a Party Branch meeting. We asked the principal to stress the need for everyone to safeguard clandestinity, which he promised to do.

On 2 July, at around 10 or 11 o'clock in the evening in conversation with the agent, Wang Zhenjin said as follows about how he was dealing with the movement: Some of my problems do involve revisionism, but some do not. I object to being called a pure anti-Party anti-socialist element. One day, when such charges have to be substantiated, the truth will come out. I come from a good family background, I joined the [revolutionary] endeavour as a teenager, and all along I have been fostered by the Party. Yes, when I wrote my first letter to the Party Centre [in December 1961], my understanding was flawed. At the time, the *Programme* of the CPSU's Twenty-Second Congress had not yet been made public. But once it was, when I realised that what I had written in my letter was wrong, I wrote a second letter [in the first quarter of 1962] to the Party Centre and admitted as much. When the Twenty-Second Congress adjourned, Chairman Mao sent a congratulatory message and called the *Programme* a 'grand programme'. This is in the newspapers, if proof should be needed.

Wang continued: No one really understands my problem. When the time comes, I will need to produce my own denunciation of it. Right now, my denunciation is already very harsh. I have elevated my problem to the level of principle. Yang Xiuzhi (the Party Branch clerk) told me: 'Young Wang, you need to cool off a little!' and he suggested that in my big-character poster entitled 'Opposing Activism', I had pinned big labels on myself rather unnecessarily. Later, when I thought about it, I realised that the labels had indeed been too big. Why had I not been able to maintain a cool head? Why had I let myself get trapped?

A few hours later that same night, at around 2 o'clock, the agent was again visited by Wang who said that he had been unable to sleep. The more he thought about it, he said, the more he regretted pinning those labels on himself. He wanted to publicly annul his own big-character poster 'Opposing Activism' and declare that when he had captioned the big-character poster (in which he quoted from his [December 1961] letter to the Party Centre) 'Look, This Is My Sinister Stuff!' he had fallen into a trap set for him by XXX. What he should have done, he said, was caption the poster 'Look, This Is My Naïve Stuff!' He also said he wanted to write a big-character poster exposing Liu Chenshi (leftist and Youth League Committee clerk) and demand that he immediately return the 100-page manuscript that he had stolen from Wang's bookcase several years earlier. According to the agent, Wang, who wants to put the manuscript on public display, had told him that when he took the manuscript, Liu was seen by (the copyist) Yu Delu. Wang had confronted Liu who admitted to handing over the manuscript to the Party Branch. (Meanwhile, Wang's big-character poster [exposing Liu Chenshi] is said to have already been put up.)

Tang Guochen has said to the agent: 'Our close relations with XXX are limited entirely to [vocational] study and nothing more. Whatever he has in terms of being anti-Party and anti-socialism, it is not something he can hide from us. He and I are both accused of running a sinister shop, and you (referring to the agent) are referred to as our pawn.' There are indeed big-character posters saying as much, so 'We should expose them and go public with what we know. XXX is an idiot. Just look at his behaviour in the movement.' Tang Guochen is concerned about the agent becoming involved in the activities of XXX. Wang Zhenjin has also suggested that XXX XXX's behaviour in the movement is barefaced, idiotic, and regrettable.

Furthermore, the agent reported that Zhao Yuling (personnel clerk, Party member, and deputy in charge of the class also taught by the agent) mobilised the students on Saturday [2 July] to petition the higher authorities to dispatch a work team [to lead the movement at the school]. Zhao's husband, Yang Wenzhi, used to be head of the dean's office, but he engaged in factionalism and was transferred elsewhere when he turned against the principal and the Party Branch. Zhao's present activities may have something to do with this, and the school leadership has been asked to take note.

Given what was happening, I tasked the agent as follows: Keep an eye on Wang Zhenjin and Tang Guochen, try to find out more about Tang's intentions, and if conditions permit, find out what it was that Zhao Yuling said when she mobilised the students (who are also taking the agent's class).

Chen Xianqing, 4 July 1966

Case Officer's Contact Report

On 8 July 1966, from 9 a.m. until 11 a.m., I met with Agent 594 at the Second Division's Point on Anshun Street. The contents of the agent's oral report and my oral replies to his questions are as follows:

Today, the agent reported on the individuals cited below:

About Wang Zhenjin (seriously afflicted with revisionist thinking and an opponent of Chairman Mao's *On Practice*):

In the morning of 5 July, people from the No. 1 Medical School visited Harbin Medical University to see the exhibit on the medical sector's war preparations. During the visit, Wang asked the agent: 'What do you think will come out of my public declaration [about the big-character poster "Opposing Activism"]?' The agent replied that he had not heard any reaction, whereupon Wang added: 'The aim of my declaration was to annul the things that I had written and also to warn Liu Chenshi not to use what he had stolen from me to attack me.'

That evening, Wang again asked the agent: 'What do you think of the present movement in our school?' The agent said: 'It's all so chaotic, I can't really make out where things are going.' Wang then asked: 'What do you think of my declaration?' The agent said: 'In my opinion, what you are trying to do is merely have the verdict reversed.' Wang disagreed: 'No, my declaration is correct. Also, I want to teach Liu Chenshi a lesson. Didn't he give me a hard time? I want to show him who is boss!' Wang went on and said that XXX had written a poem about the bitter fate of a frog, a poem that goes something like this:

> I do not want to boast,
> my build may be small, but my resolve is immense;
> For the sake of teaching, I perform
> autopsies, decapitations, and amputations. Fearlessly!
> Suddenly, a giant hand appears, obstructs half the sky,
> lifts the cover of my cage, and lets me see through his fingers;

Short of food and out of water, regrets come easy,
had I not realised that even on dry land, one must stretch one's legs?
The moment has arrived, the sacrifice must be done, ideals realised!
I bare my innermost, the law of nature, before my students.
Not knowing the geography,
I took a wrong turn and lost my way!
Oh, how I miss my mates! Now, who will show me the way?
Day in and day out, time has no end.
If I cannot break out of my cage,
Then let them fry me in shallow oil …

Wang said he is convinced that XXX had not intended to be vulgar [when lecturing on the reproductive organs], but he asked the agent to please not write a big-character poster denouncing him.

Wang told the agent: 'The stuff I have written (opposing Chairman Mao's *On Practice*) is as sophisticated as it gets. Marxism, Leninism, and Chairman Mao's works – they are all highly sophisticated. Aside from my first letter to the CCP Centre and Chairman Mao that was muddleheaded, all my other writings are correct.' Lowering his voice, Wang again asked the agent not to put up any big-character posters denouncing him for saying this. The agent reassured him he would not.

On 7 July, Wang took the agent to read one of his big-character posters, entitled 'In Reply to Student Queries', in which he explains that it was entirely for reasons of his own – and not because of what anyone else might think – that he was withdrawing his big-characters posters, 'Opposing Activism' and 'My Sinister Stuff!' Wang admitted that some of the things he had written did not tally with the facts, while other things (such as what he had said about looking at postponed marriages and family planning from a class point of view, and about refuting bourgeois notions of superiority and inferiority by invoking the proletarian understanding of happiness) may have been flawed, they must not be called sinister stuff. They were based in part on Chairman Mao's views of class struggle. To call arguments aligned with Chairman Mao's views 'sinister stuff' is wrong! To do so at a time when the issues involved have not yet been resolved is irresponsible, Wang said, and no self-critical examination will at this stage get to the bottom of things given that 'without investigation, no right to speak'.

Wang said that 'some people looking for targets want to draw attention to me and somehow make me out to be "the cream of the crop"'. He then lowered his voice, adding that 'I have my supporters, though, who support my withdrawal of my big-character posters.' The agent asked if he meant Yang Xiuzhi (Party Branch clerk assigned to the office of the Cultural Revolution Group), and Wang said: 'Yes, she understands me. All my writings, apart from that first letter [to the CCP Centre], are correct. Once they start challenging them one by one, you will see what I mean. My writings are like the Chairman's: they target specifics. Bourgeois notions of superiority and inferiority were questioned by Norman Bethune, and when the time comes, I will show them whom they are actually refuting! The Chairman's [arguments] rest on an ideology of struggle, while those of Li Dazhao rest on people's [economic] livelihood.'[105]

About Tang Guochen (who wants to avenge the execution of his father):

In the afternoon of 5 July, Tang said to the agent: 'I have studied the big-character posters aimed at me point by point, and not found anything serious. About my family's past: my oldest brother was a decorated model soldier of the illicit Manchukuo regime, my second brother was an active counter-revolutionary, and my father committed suicide in an attempt to escape punishment during land reform. Those are all facts, but they have little to do with me. The remaining charges don't really amount to much. They are trying in vain to shut me up with their big-character posters. I may not be saying anything now, but I will in due course.' He then told the agent: 'From now on, choose your words a bit more carefully. Also, note down everything they say in those big-character posters aimed at you.'

About Feng Kezheng (casual labourer in the boiler room):

In conversation with the agent, Feng revealed some things that are problematic, including his admiration for the Soviet Union. Also, on 2 July, Feng said the following to the agent: 'I worry about you. You have now become a target of big-character posters that even mention you by name. In the future, you must be more careful about what you say and do. Try not to become involved with those people (meaning XXX, Tang Guochen, and so on). It is not worth your while.'

About Liu Liandi (the principal of the No. 1 Medical School):

Teachers and students have lately put up more than two hundred big-character posters aimed at Liu, focusing on ten issues. He is being asked why he resists the Cultural Revolution the way he does. Many big-character posters compare him to a tiger blocking the road, and they raise issues like the following:

1. Liu has said repeatedly at several school assemblies that 'demons will not get away even in the absence of big-character posters. Just because you accuse someone of being a demon in a big-character poster, that alone does not make him one.' On 1 July, he said at an assembly that in another two weeks, the school must start to divert attention away from the movement towards reform of the educational system. He then said that when the movement is over, teachers will still be teachers and students will still be students. He also said we should appreciate some of Khrushchev's works.
2. Liu's view of the issue involving former Party Branch secretary Pang Shuo is problematic. In his opinion, the issue has to do with not implementing in time the spirit of the Party's general and specific policies.
3. When asked by the students why he had not insisted on Pang Shuo coming back, Liu asked the students in return: 'Why do you want him [to come back]? To take charge of our Great Cultural Revolution?'
4. Liu once announced in a campus broadcast: You may put up big-character posters criticising whatever you think is not in accordance with Mao Zedong Thought, including problems in our canteen, bedbugs in the dormitories, and so on.

5. He once said to Xiang Fujin (surgery teacher): 'Any more big-character posters and I'll fall ill!' (By now, it has already been three days since he was last in his office.)
6. [Some big-character posters] asked Liu why he has made such a mess of the movement.
7. He was asked why he said: 'I am new here and neither close to nor distant from anyone. It is not yet my time to put up big-character posters.'
8. He was asked why, since coming to our school, he has only focused on matters of people's livelihood and has failed to give prominence to politics.
9. He was said to be full of bourgeois ideology, decorating his office beautifully, and he was asked why he did not take Comrade Jiao Yulu as his role model.[106]

At the end of our meeting, I told the agent to continue with the tasks I had already given him. I stressed that he should limit contact with Zhang Dongqin (who manages protection work on campus) in order to avoid jeopardizing clandestinity. We did not decide when to schedule our next meeting. Attached is a written report from the agent in which he asks about a possible job transfer. I would say it merits consideration, but I ask that the leadership decide and issue instructions.

Li Jingui, 7 [sic] July 1966

Case Officer's Contact Report

On 15 July 1966, from 10 a.m. until 11:45 a.m., I met with [the agent] XXX at Point No. 21 on Anshun Street. The contents of his oral report and my oral replies to his questions are as follows:

First of all, the agent reported that the movement on the campus of the No. 1 Medical School is cooling off, and the number of big-character posters is down. Wang Zhenjin has declared that he will remain 'firmly silent'. Meanwhile, the masses have exposed something else involving Tang Guochen. During the outing organised by the school on 4 June, when the students went to the north shore of the river, according to XXX, they caught some frogs that they gave to Tang Guochen after they had returned to school. Tang is said to have put the frogs in a box with a lid made of a piece of plywood that had a picture of Chairman Mao's portrait on it. This led the masses to put up a big-character poster entitled 'We Do Not Tolerate Anyone Defiling the Portrait of Our Leader.' When the agent asked Tang about the masses bringing this matter to light, Tang denied doing it on purpose, and he said it was simply because at the time he had not found anything else to use as a lid. He went on to say that our newspapers have our great leader's portrait in them all the time, so why should one not dare to use newsprint to wrap things? Aren't there a lot of people who do just that?

Second, the agent discussed casual labourer Feng Kezheng. The agent has met him on three occasions since 9 July, and on one of those occasions they ended up drinking together. In conversation with the agent, Feng said the following things:

1. He said that whatever is in your file is something you will carry with you [your entire life], until the day the [political] climate changes.
2. While serving a prison sentence, Feng got to know an inmate who had been a [Nationalist] bandit army captain surgeon. The surgeon is currently unemployed, and Feng asked the agent if he could get him a letter of introduction so he would be able to find a job.
3. Feng hails from a big landlord family in Anda. The brother of his grandfather used to be the head of a local guild and his cousin, Feng Kejia, is a municipal bureau chief.
4. With each [political] movement, the Communist Party is making more and more enemies. In addition, there are many inconspicuous people not on the mainland who are just biding their time. In a future war, people will be prepared to collaborate from within with the forces from without.
5. When change comes (meaning, when the old regime stages its comeback), I will be nothing like what I am now. At the very least, I will not live in a house like this, all wretched and without a proper job.
6. Feng told the agent to remain silent and not to put up any big-character posters. He said: 'Look, you put up a big-character poster aimed at XXX but ended up being accused of trying to reverse the verdict on him! Lie low and write nothing, no matter how much they try to provoke you. Nothing good ever comes from writing anything, and no harm is done if you write nothing. Even if they call you a loyalist, just remain silent. Likewise, if they say you are no more than a pawn of XXX, just remain silent and wait until the end of the movement. What point is there in offending those people?'
7. Feng said he can barely stand the sight of anything these days.

Third, the agent raised with me the matter of his own [agent] status. That he does work for us has become known, he said, to the following people in the No. 1 Medical School: School Principal Liu Liandi, Education Administration Section Chief Liu Yuzhen (member of the Party Branch), General Affairs Section Chief Ma Yongshan (member of the Party Branch), Zhang Dongqin (Party Branch clerk and head of the Protection Section), and Yang Shuzhi (member of the Party Branch). Previously, no one knew about him except Protection Section officer Zhao Shumei (who is now participating in the Socialist Education Movement off campus) and [former] Party Branch secretary Pang Shuo (who is no longer at the school).[107] When the [Cultural Revolution] movement was getting under way, the agent asked for the [school] leadership to be informed at an appropriate time, and we agreed to tell only the school principal. We spoke to Principal Liu in person and asked him to keep it secret, but he ended up revealing it at a meeting of the Party Branch. When we found out, we talked to Principal Liu once again. Subsequently, at another school Party Branch meeting, Liu remarked that the agent's relationship with the Public Security Bureau had been terminated because his relationship with XXX was unclear (which was something we had suggested he should say). After that meeting, when the agent reported on some school-related matters to Yang Shuzhi (member of the Party Branch), she told him that his status was known to her, and she revealed to him everything that principal Liu had said about him at the two meetings.

144   IV From the Agent Work File

The agent is under immense pressure, suspecting we no longer trust him, but he is prepared to submit to a security check. When I confronted him and asked him what he thought of the matter, he took a step back and said that he did not believe what XXX had said was true, and if the organisation did not trust him, there would be no need to give him any new tasks. I said that whether or not the organisation trusts him depends on the work he does for us. I added that I had nothing more to explain anyway since he was unlikely to believe what I say. He immediately responded that he did not harbour any doubts about the organisation.

Upcoming tasks: With regard to the movement, I said to the agent that his main task remains to keep an eye on Wang Zhenjin and Tang Guochen. As for Feng Kezheng (whose ideology is reactionary and who has approached the agent), I told the agent not to draw too close to him and to let him take the initiative. When you meet him, I said, do not volunteer information about yourself and let him do the talking as much as possible. If he becomes too arrogant, hint that he should back off, so he does not think of himself as too important. Rip off his mask and find out exactly what he is up to.

Chen Xianqing, 15 July 1966

Case Officer's Contact Report

On 18 August 1966, from 1 p.m. until 3 p.m., I met with Agent 594 at the Second Division's Ansong [*sic*] Point. The contents of the agent's oral report and my oral replies to his questions are as follows:

About Wang Zhenjin (severely afflicted by revisionist thinking and an opponent of Chairman Mao's *On Practice*), the agent reported as follows:

On 16 August, the Red Guard Rebel Regiment (today renamed the Red Guard Combat Regiment) organised a 'To Rebel Is Justified' rally at the No. 1 Medical School. It was attended by well over a thousand people from the No. 2 Medical School, No. 3 Medical School, School of Electric Power, and College of Engineering. The rally was managed by students who put on Pang Shuo a tall hat bearing his name and hung a billboard around his neck that read: 'Ox-Monster and Snake-Demon Pang Shuo.' As the meeting proceeded, the Red Fire Combat Regiment of the Medical School handed the organisers a note calling for Wang Zhenjin and XXX to be forced to endure a struggle. At that point, Wang Zhenjin appeared at the entrance and was surrounded by female students who attempted to drag him onto the stage. He resisted at first, but then the male students from the School of Electric Power managed to drag him and XXX to the front of the stage. When Wang Zhenjin's anti-Party remarks were read out, he protested, raising his hands and shouting 'I serve the people', and he denied he had ever said anything of the sort. The students then put a tall paper hat on his head, but Wang proceeded to pull it off. They put it back on, but Wang pulled it off repeatedly, no less than six times. Finally, after he had tossed the torn paper hat quite far away, two male students stepped onto the stage, placed his hands in a clasp behind his back, and put the hat back on his head, but all along he was refusing to bow. One male student, joined by a few others, grabbed his hair and pushed him to the ground and gave him a solid beating. The rally lasted from 5 p.m. to 8 p.m., after which Wang was escorted to the dormitory for single men. In addition to a student guard by the door, surveillance was deployed outside his window until the next morning. To prevent Wang from escaping, his door was locked from the outside. After discussion among the members of the Combat Regiment in the afternoon of the 17th, the surveillance was called off and Wang's dormitory door was opened, allowing him to move about. Later that day, he went to the General Affairs Section, asking that they convert some of his local grain ration coupons for national coupons (something they refused to do) and give him 5 yuan in cash (to pay for meals off campus). At about 6 p.m., Wang arrived at the campus gates carrying a blanket. The students guarding the gates asked him what he was up to, and he told them he was going to return a blanket that he had borrowed from someone. He was allowed to pass and still has not come back. According to Feng Kezheng (casual labourer in the boiler room, from a landlord family whose members have a dodgy past), Wang had told him (suggesting that their relationship is close) that he was going home, and he asked that Feng not tell anyone. In my opinion, he was not going home but instead he was going to Beijing, either to lodge a complaint or to ask for help from the Soviet revisionists.

At the end of our meeting, I told the agent to adopt a correct attitude toward the revolutionary activism of the students. I said to him that the orientation of their struggle is correct and that although there may be problems with some of their methods, those are all problems that they will run up against as they move forward and that can be solved by way of study. At present, I told him, we must study Chairman Mao's works in earnest, especially what he has to say in the *Report on an Investigation of the Peasant Movement in Hunan* about 'It's terrible!' and 'It's fine!' and the question of 'Going too far'. This will help us develop the correct attitude towards the revolutionary passion vented by the students. It will also be helpful to study the Centre's 16-point 'Decision Concerning the Great Proletarian Cultural Revolution' and the Communiqué of the Eleventh Plenum of the Eighth CCP Central Committee.

Li Jingui, 18 August 1966

Case Officer's Contact Report

On 30 August 1966, from 1:30 p.m. until 2:30 p.m., I met with Agent 594 at the Second Division's Ansong [sic] Point. The contents of the agent's oral report and my oral replies to his questions are as follows:

The agent reported the following:

Wang Zhenjin is a member of the No. 1 Medical School staff whose ideology is extremely revisionist, who has been the target of numerous big-character posters, and who, when the students forced him to endure a struggle in the evening of 18 [*sic*] August, no less than six times pulled off the high hat the students had placed on his head and, as a result, received a good beating from a number of students. Wang fled the following day and has since written a letter in his brother's name to Feng Kezheng, the casual labourer in the school's boiler room, to which Feng has replied. The contents of Feng's reply are unclear.

Feng Kezheng told Zhang Dongqin that four bureau chiefs and eighteen counter-revolutionaries have been dragged out in the Xiangfang Municipal District Branch of the Public Security Bureau.

At present, only slightly more than 20 students remain on campus, while more than 350 have gone off to Beijing and elsewhere to exchange revolutionary experiences. Now there is nothing happening on campus, and aside from occasionally attending mass rallies arranged by other units, people go about their days as they please.

I did not give the agent any concrete tasks; I merely told him that for now he should concentrate on studying the Centre's 16-point 'Decision Concerning the Great Proletarian Cultural Revolution' and Chairman Mao's works.

Attached are some drafts of big-character posters written by Wang Zhenjin.

Li Jingui, 31 August 1966

Case Officer's Contact Report

On 6 September 1966, from 3:30 p.m. to 4:50 p.m., I met with agent XXX at the Second Division's Point No. 21. The contents of the agent's oral report and my oral replies to his questions are as follows:

Wang Zhenjin (whose ideology is revisionist) has been located and escorted back to the No. 1 Medical School (from his home in Baichengzi, where had gone in the second half of August after having been forced to endure a struggle at a rally) by two staff members on 1 September. Although Wang was resentful of the students who had molested him, he told the agent that they had failed to understand what was really going on, and he blamed the powerholders at the school for instigating the students and he said that the rally had been an attempt to divert the movement from its correct course. He told the agent: 'My revisionist views have been strongly influenced by Li Zuoping' (an activist in the movement) and he said that he would explain his understanding of the events when, at some point in the future, he is given permission to tell his side of the story. Feng Kezheng (the casual labourer) is encouraging him to do so. Wang insists that his problem is one of understanding and he says that he has already made a self-criticism for his past letters to the CCP Centre and the College of Traditional Chinese Medicine.

The students have put up a big-character poster copied from the municipal Bureau of Public Health that exposes Principal Liu Liandi of the No. 1 Medical School as a former puppet regime director of the Xingnong cooperative in Tonghe county. After Liberation, he was brutally beaten at a mass rally, which is when he developed the back pain from which he is still suffering. When the big-character poster was read, a lot of people drew connections between what it exposed and his performance in the present movement, and they charged Liu with intentionally obstructing the movement and seeking to divert the movement from its correct course. The Red Guard Rebel Regiment is now planning to 'bombard the headquarters'.

Teacher Wang Yingxia says Yang Zhizhou was beaten to death by the students. Some people, she said, had incited a few students to do this because Yang was about to expose issues involving the school's core leadership and the provincial Party Committee.

I assigned the following tasks to the agent:

1. Find out exactly *when* Wang Zhenjin is supposed to have written a self-criticism to the Centre and to the Party Committee of the College of Traditional Chinese Medicine. If he kept copies of what he wrote, find a way of finding the copies to look at them.
2. Find out what the reactionary or revisionist viewpoints are that Li Zuoping is supposed to have shared with Wang Zhenjin.
3. Find out where Wang Yingxia heard about the [*illegible*] of Yang Zhizhou.

I gave him no further specific tasks; I merely told him to find out what he can about what is happening in the movement.

Chen Xianqing, 6 September 1966

Case Officer's Contact Report

On 4 October 1966, from 3 p.m. until 4 p.m., I met with agent XXX from the No. 1 Medical School at Point No. 21. The contents of his oral report and my oral replies to his questions are as follows:

The agent mainly reported on recent developments at the No. 1 Medical School:

The [newly appointed] principal XXX and former Party Secretary Pang Shuo are locked in a struggle, and Pang has been beaten up. At first, he was simply responding to the questions put to him according to the facts, but then, when he tried to argue in his own defence, he was repeatedly beaten up. In the end, he simply admitted to everything.

From what the masses have uncovered, the concurrent head of the Protection Section, Zhang Dongqin, appears to be a loyalist. He has put up quite a few big-character posters in his own defence (the Protection Section reports directly to the Xiangfang Municipal District Branch of the Public Security Bureau) and he has threatened to quit. Meanwhile, he is joining the students who have gone to help with the harvest in the countryside.

At the moment, only a handful of people remain on campus, guarding the school. Everyone else has gone to help with the harvest in the countryside.

[Before the Cultural Revolution] the core leadership of the school was divided and the Party Branch was split into two factions. An inspection team from the municipal Bureau of Public Health came to investigate and ended up reprimanding the section chief of the Education Administration and the General Affairs section chief and their respective factional followers. Those who were reprimanded at that time are now in power, and they are attempting to reverse the verdicts. Word has it that the earlier Education Administration section chief, Yang Lianyou, has turned up, and he gave a talk that lasted an entire day.

The students have raided homes and confiscated property as follows:

Pang Shuo (who used to insist that he lived in strained circumstances). This time around, the students who raided his home discovered lots of woollen clothes, corduroy and fine cotton fabrics, as well as nylon hosiery and leather shoes.

Tang Guochen (known all along to be the son of a counter-revolutionary and resentful about the present). During the raid on his home, they discovered books on law, in Chinese (printed by the Nationalists) and in Japanese, from the time when his father had served as a chief justice. They also found address books and clothes from when his father had been a student.

XXX (a neo-bourgeois element known all along to habitually take leave, feigning ill health, while busy translating foreign language works). During the raid on his home, they discovered high-heeled shoes and satin quilts as well as well over one thousand photographs (of himself and his wife).

Wang Zhenjin is seeking to have the verdict passed on him overturned. He is known to have revisionist views, and he has written articles opposing Chairman's philosophical writings. Now he is trying to argue on the basis of the Centre's 16-point Decision Concerning the Great Proletarian Cultural Revolution (where it says that 'it is not allowed, whatever the pretext, to incite the masses to struggle against each other') that the old school leadership had forced him to endure a struggle and that the original verdict passed on him should be reversed. His documentation appears partly reasonable and suggests that there are some problems with the work done by the old leadership. Fundamental issues, however, were managed well.

Li Jingui, 6 October 1966

Case Officer's Contact Report

On 22 October 1966, from 1 p.m. to 2 p.m., I met with Agent 594 at the Second Division's Ansong Point. The contents of the agent's oral report and my oral replies to his questions are as follows:

About Wang Zhenjin (seriously afflicted with revisionist thinking and an opponent of Chairman Mao's *On Practice*): the agent reported that Wang had recently written something called 'A Plot Laid Bare', in which he refutes the points raised by the Red Guards who forced him to endure a struggle on campus. Having completed a first draft [on 2 October], he showed the agent what he had written and asked for his comments. The agent was able to prepare a copy for us.

The agent had no further issues to report, and I did not give him any new tasks. Attached is the text (10 pages) of Wang Zhenjin's 'A Plot Laid Bare', as copied by the agent.

Li Jingui, 24 October 1966

13 Debriefing Agent 594: Monitoring Campus Unrest

Agent's Letter to the Section Chief

Section Chief Chen [Xianqing]:

Greetings. Recent developments in our school have been more or less the same as developments in other schools. The conflict on campus between the two [rebel] regiments remains intense, with much verbal abuse and even physical violence. Now the students have departed in droves to exchange revolutionary experiences. From what they say, they are all headed past the Great Wall to Yan'an, Jinggangshan, Chairman Mao's hometown, and so on.

Zhang Dongqin and I, the two of us, spend all day writing billboards with Chairman Mao's quotations. Last Wednesday morning, Wang Zhenjin came to see me and he took me outside the garage where we work. He said to me: 'I hear you are in contact with the Public Security Bureau?' I asked him 'Who told you that?' He said: 'That I can't tell you.' I replied: 'I have nothing to do with the Public Security Bureau', and then I added: 'You and I don't have to keep any secrets from each other. You say I am in contact with the Public Security Bureau: Who told you that?' He smiled and said: 'That I cannot tell you at this point!' Saying no more, he then left. (I maintained my composure and appeared calm and natural throughout.) In the evening of the following day, Wang Zhenjin knocked on my door. We did not talk, and he said he had merely come over to see if I was around, and then he left.

These past few days, Wang has not spoken to me when our paths have crossed, nor has he visited me at my home. It strikes me that this may well be a serious matter. After our last conversation, I began to pay attention, but he always seems to avoid me. This is how I see it: First, perhaps I was not careful enough and somehow made him suspicious. But having gone over every detail of our meeting in my mind, I am quite certain that this is not the case. Second, [Principal] Liu Liandi has already told Yang Xiuzhi (political instructor, Party member), Liu Yuzhen (Educational Administration section chief, Party member, and member of the Party Branch committee), and Ma Yongshan (General Affairs section chief, Party member, and member of the Party Branch executive committee) about our connection. Whether these people have, in turn, mentioned it to others, I cannot say. But personally, I suspect Ma Yongshan, who is on good terms with dining hall attendant Zhang Kecheng, who, in turn, gets along well with Wang Zhenjin. Zhang Kecheng used to talk to me about everything, but this is no longer the case. Then there is Liu Yuzhen: one time when I was writing billboards with quotations in the garage, old Zhao, the driver, and Liu Yuzhen dropped by. Old Zhao said he does not care much about politics, and, in his opinion, our billboards are useless because they are all over the place and nobody takes any notice of them. Liu Yuzhen then took old Zhao outside and murmured something to him. When they returned, neither of them said much. Old Zhao later observed: 'This room is heated. From now on, you stay here and write. I for one support your writing of quotations.'

That is about it. I hope you will give the matter some thought. I wanted to give it a few more days but then I decided not to, lest something comes up unexpectedly and makes things difficult. I look forward to receiving your instructions, as I am deeply concerned.

At the moment, I spend my days writing billboards of Chairman [Mao] quotations. Please contact me by telephone. For now, the students are keeping all telephones on campus under surveillance. If you contact me, please say that I am urgently needed at home because something has happened. That should be enough, but also mention that I am writing billboards so that the students know where to find me.

Greetings,

XXX 7 November

Section chief's comment on the letter: Comrade [case officer] Jingui, please investigate the matter and propose how to handle.

Chen Xianqing, 7 November 1966

Case Officer's Letter to the Section Chief

Section chiefs Chen and He,

About the matter raised by [the agent] XXX, I would say his cover has already been blown, and that is a fact. Based on earlier circumstances, the most likely culprits would appear to be those members of the Party Branch. I therefore suggest we begin by talking to them. Even if it turns out they are not the source of the leak, we still may want to talk to them about the importance of safeguarding clandestinity and of remaining quiet. Once we have arrived at the truth, we can investigate the matter further and decide how best to respond.

In addition, could we not also ask the agent to issue a flat denial in some suitable form? While this may be problematic, I still believe it may work. In any case, we cannot simply leave the agent to fend for himself in the midst of all of this.

Li Jingui, 7 November 1966

Section Chief's Note to the Division Chief

Based on what I observed during my own encounters with him, the agent is unlikely to have blown his own cover. He was most likely unintentionally compromised by the Party Committee of the school, which suggests that we need to learn a lesson from this when conducting operational work in units of this kind. As of now, we shall no longer be able to make use of this individual; all we can do is temporarily drop him. During our next several meetings with him, we should educate him about the need to safeguard clandestinity, express concern for his [*illegible*], and make sure that he has no reason to feel resentful, should we [*illegible*] suspend all further utilisation of him.

Comrade [Division Chief] Wang Ke, please read and issue instructions.

Chen Xianqing, 3 December 1966

Division Chief's Instructions to the Section Chief

Find a way of getting in touch in person with the agent and educate him on the need to safeguard clandestinity. Under no circumstances must he give away state secrets. If he faces no other choice, tell him he can admit to having acquaintances in the Public Security Bureau.

Are the members of the Party Branch really very clear about our contacts with the agent? On the whole, if they only know a very little, then there is no need for us to talk to them since if we do talk to them, it will just further corroborate the facts. In such a case, it is better to say nothing at all. If back when the agent was recruited, the Party Branch had actually been involved, then I agree that we should proceed as suggested by Comrade Jingui.

If, at some future point, the whole thing is traced back to the public security organs, we could cover ourselves by making something up.

I maintain that we should gradually rid ourselves of agents of this kind. As of now, exercises like this are redundant.

[Cultural Protection Division Chief] Wang Ke, 3 December 1966

Section Chief's Note to the Case Officer

I have already spoken to the agent. If anyone makes any inquiries, he will say that after fearing that Wang Zhenjin might try to commit suicide, the public security organs instructed him to keep an eye on Wang and that is all there is to it.

Chen [Xianqing]

Part V

From the Agent Personal File

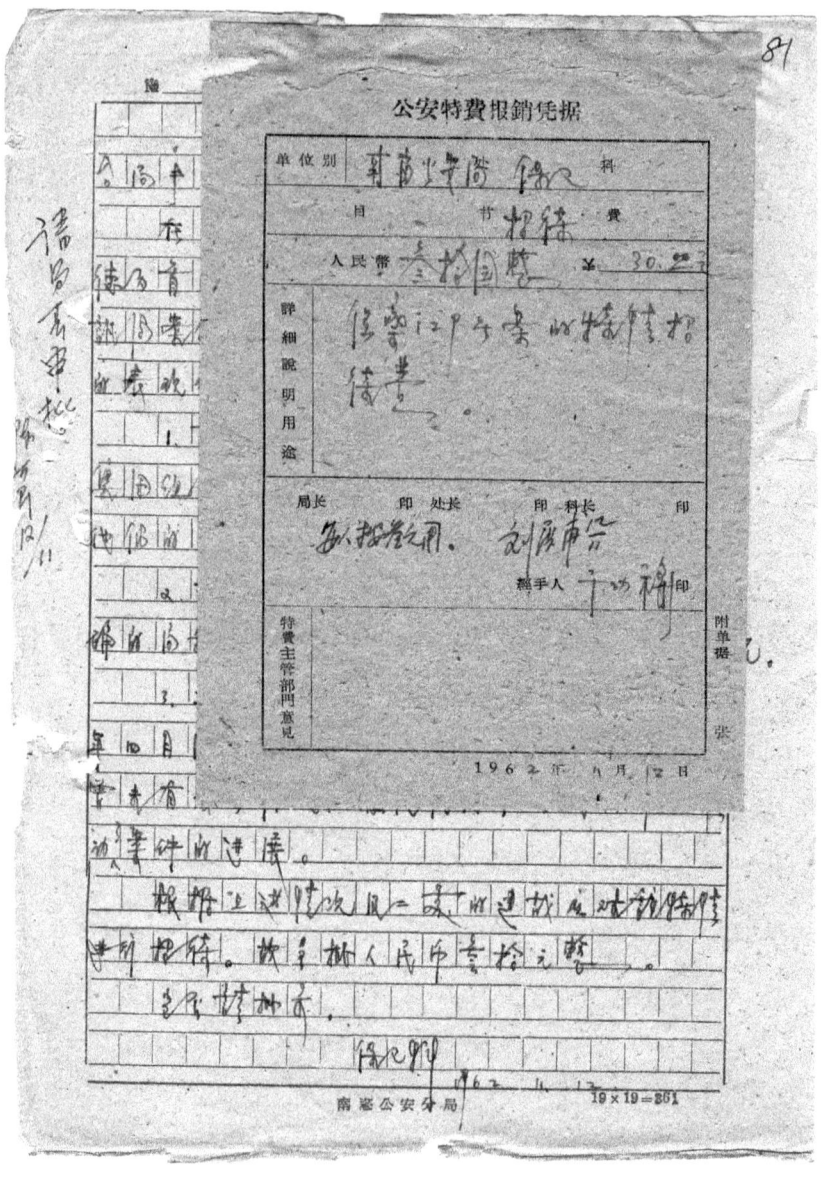

Figure 5 Drawing on special budget funds to reward an agent (1962)

Introduction

Agent Work Files document how agents executed their missions, but they reveal precious little about the agents themselves. When properly maintained, they indicate neither an agent's real name nor any biographical information about the person behind the code designation. No pre-recruitment profiling data of the kind called for in Chapter 7, for example, is included in the Agent Work File, nor is any information on the agent's post-recruitment circumstances, such as what kind of life he or she led when not performing agent duties. The retired Swedish security-agency chief who boasted of his nationwide Cold War 'web of agents' said it had included, in addition to 'pillars of society', men like the 'local convenience store manager [*ICA-handlaren*], bank clerk, or factory employee and active member of the village bandy team'.[108] How were they recruited and what were their rewards? What kind of personality traits did these anonymous 'concerned citizens' possibly share? As individuals, how did they deal with the moral dimension of their mission when it included what He Xia in Chapter 2 identified as informing on 'relatives, close friends, or colleagues at work'? For answers to such questions, historians must set aside the Agent Work File and in its stead mine a different primary source, the one that in the United States, the FBI maintains on its HUMINT assets as an 'administrative' file. In the Soviet Union and in China, its equivalent is the so-called Agent Personal File which, in the words of *The Soviet Intelligence Officer's Handbook*, brought together 'documents with personal data on an agent' and, as explained in Chapter 6 above, held the 'records related directly to the individual agent'.[109] It was here that agencies deposited the ridiculously multifarious paperwork that documented the full cycle of an agent's career, from the first spotting, assessing, and pitching of the would-be target, through the ups and downs of his or her service, and ending in a closed file with the agent's termination.

The Agent Personal File makes it very clear that no one was ever *only* a human 'agent' – the agent persona is never more than one part of the individual and it is not necessarily dominant. The widespread perception that the recruitment of a person as an agent will henceforth be key to all

156   V From the Agent Personal File

other dimensions of his or her biography is mistaken. But while keeping in mind that the Agent Personal File is maintained by an anonymous 'administration' and is never seen by the agent (who has no way of correcting or influencing what may be recorded in it), it does constitute the historian's primary source of information on the agent as such. In the case of the file of a long-serving agent, its content allows historians to draw, more than any other source, refined and differentiated images of the agent persona.

The present set of records is not an attempt to familiarise the reader with the contents of an Agent Personal File by combining records representing constituent parts from different files. All the items in Part V have been translated from the file of a single long-serving agent, a secular Muslim member of the non-Communist intelligentsia in Harbin, recruited in 1950 and active well into the mid-1960s. The translations are merely meant to serve as an advertisement for what *can* be found among the primary sources: the life and service of no two agents were never the same, and no two Agent Personal Files ever shared exactly the same kind of content.

The first record (Chapter 14) throws light on what a KGB officer would have called the *situatsiya verbovochnaya*, the combination of circumstances that made this particular agent's recruitment possible. Part V continues with the agent's sworn offer of service (Chapter 15), a type of record rarely missing from an Agent Personal File but looking very different when, as here, it documents a coercive recruitment, as distinct from an activist's voluntary rendering of services.

As soon as an agent was duly recruited and sworn in, records with a certain commonality invariably began to accumulate over time in the Agent Personal File. One is the kind of record that documents security concerns and the initial close monitoring of the agent: 'If the agent must be given a concrete operational task right away', the Chinese Public Security Academy's *Lectures on the Subject of Agent Work* noted in 1957, 'then he must be kept under powerful control from the outset, for example by utilising external surveillance or other agents to monitor him, in addition to which his correspondence must be subject to postal inspection so as to prevent him from colluding with the enemy to sabotage us'.[110] In the present case, the translation that illustrates this is a sample of the agent's immediate post-recruitment correspondence, as covertly monitored and studied by his handler for signs of double-dealing or betrayal (Chapter 16). After several years of loyal service, the agent often developed a good sense of what might alarm a handler and, as a result, when something unforeseen happened (such as a missed rendezvous), the agent would act swiftly to reduce concern. Once a mutually satisfactory *modus vivendi* had been developed, the agent's handler would reciprocate and might even, as in the present case (Chapter 17), lobby the superior levels for a favour on behalf of the agent.

An Agent Personal File was always very much an operational document. It included regular 'findings and results of the performance evaluations of the agent' (Chapter 18) and might also include derogatory information on him or her, including letters of denunciation from concerned citizens that were filed away with no action taken by agency officers eager to shield their covert human source from exposure. When an evaluation suggested that an agent's performance was declining, intra-bureaucratic communications discussing the pros and cons of ameliorating measures would also, in due course, be deposited in the Agent Personal File (Chapter 19).

14 Operational Brief: On the Recruitment of Yang X

When he was arrested by the Harbin Public Security Bureau in December 1949, Yang X was thirty-one years old and working as a teacher in one of the most prestigious middle schools in the city. A former member of the Guomindang intelligence and security services, the Juntong, he no longer maintained any active links to the organisation that in 1946 had become the Republic of China's Ministry of National Defence Protection of Secrets Bureau, but he remained in touch privately with some of his old colleagues. While he was in police custody, officers from the Political Protection Division developed a profile of him and, after just over half a year, they concluded that he would be amenable to an attempt to be recruited as an agent. Below is the handwritten memorandum deposited in Yang's Agent Personal File that documents the hands-on advice his rookie recruiter took from a final pre-recruitment pep talk by a senior officer on how to conduct the all-important elicitation talk with Yang. By then, a tacit understanding of sorts appears to have already been reached between Yang and his captors, and the senior officer clearly judged the risk of failure to be small. Worth noting is the attention the senior officer pays to how Yang was meant to act immediately upon release so as not to prompt suspicions among any of the men and women on whom he would henceforth be expected to inform.

Translated Text

First, when talking to him, see if you can be quite explicit. After all, he has been around and he already knows what to expect.

Key points:

1. He was a cultural collaborator under the illicit Manchukuo regime, a faithful running dog of Chiang Kai-shek and the Americans under the Guomindang, and a participant in the murder of Northeast China's youth. After Liberation, he duplicitously registered with the

Operational memorandum, 'Yang X shiyong fangfa' (How to Utilise Yang X) in the Agent Personal File maintained on Yang X by the Harbin Public Security Bureau. Closed file, weeded out from the bureau archive on an unknown date.

authorities and deceived the government. Tell him that his crimes are only too obvious, and so on and so forth. Then tell him the government is giving him a way out and wants him to atone for his crimes by meritorious service.

2. Be explicit about what we expect him to do. Tell him that in no way will it connect him to the government. It will merely let him atone for his sins. If he does not do this properly, the government will bring him to justice and send him to prison. This is *not* about 'serving the people', or any of that.

3. If he agrees [to work for us], first of all ask him to list the things he would be able to do for the government. Have him go back and put as much as possible in writing. Tell him to spell it all out now, and his sentence may be reduced. He should mention names and issues, all in detail. Should he refuse, tell him he will be imprisoned and we will no longer bother with him. Eventually, he will want to talk to us. Make him understand that it is not the government that cannot do without his services; we are merely giving him a chance to atone for his crimes by meritorious service. Unless he performs well, he *will* be brought to justice! (People like him must be made to feel real fear.)

4. Once he has agreed, make him do the following: Produce a sworn declaration. It must mention that he was a cultural collaborator who betrayed his motherland, that he carried out activities against the People after the Glorious Restoration at the end of World War II, and that his hands are stained with the blood of the youth of Northeast China whom he butchered. The declaration also must say that after Liberation, he took an anti-government stance and deceived the People's Government by duplicitously registering with the authorities and flouting the government's laws and decrees. The declaration must state that from now on he will no longer engage in activities against the People, and he will firmly oppose the American imperialists and Chiang Kai-shek and stand firmly on the side of the People and serve the People heart and soul. In his sworn declaration, he must also commit to a detailed plan of meritorious service.

Furthermore, on Yang and our plans:

(1) Will being explicit with him be effective? Given that he already did this kind of work in the past, there should be no problem. He already understands and is merely waiting for us to bring it up.

(2) We should not send him back to XXX Middle School because that is where he worked at the time of his arrest; obviously, quite a few questions might be asked, and he will be shunned by the people

14 Operational Brief: On the Recruitment of Yang X   161

around him. The best and preferable option is to send him to some other school.

(3) After we release him, he should not return to school right away, but instead he should spend maybe a month running around looking up his connections and asking friends for help. Or maybe he should go in person to the personnel section of the Bureau of Education [of the Harbin Municipal Government] and ask them to help him find a job. After a few attempts, they could finally find a job for him (as already pre-arranged by us). During this period, we could have him followed to see if he is being loyal. If not, we simply will have to haul him in again.

(4) We should develop an informant of ours in the unit where he ends up, someone who can keep a watchful eye on him and report on his circumstances.

(5) At regular intervals, he should be given an opportunity to talk to a senior officer who, depending on the circumstances, may either threaten to haul him in again or console him. In this way, if the relationship between him and any [*illegible*] officers running him were to sour, we would still command due respect.

(6) Always debrief him promptly. Use the content of his reporting to assess the quality of his work and ensure that the higher levels remain informed.

20 August 1950

15 Yang X's Offer of Service

The Agent Personal File maintained on Yang X by his handlers over the years contains two versions of the sworn declaration that his recruiter demanded he produce in order to consolidate his recruitment: a draft on plain paper, dated 23 August, and a slightly longer but otherwise identical, final version on Public Security Bureau stationery, signed and dated 31 August 1950. In the declaration below, Yang swears to 'complete the tasks assigned to me' and accept the 'most severe disciplinary sanctions and legal punishment' if he ever goes back on his word. In an attachment to the declaration (eight times its length and not translated here), Yang – who, with the agreement of the officer who would become his first handler, remained largely self-tasking for an initial period upon recruitment – also lays out his own Crime Atonement & Meritorious Service Plan. In the plan, he describes his central task as 'to inform against bandit, *tewu*, and counter-revolutionary elements'. Furthermore, he explains in detail what he calls his plan's operational Steps of Implementation, spelling out the three behavioural parameters within which he intends to work and listing the Eight Rules of Discipline that he intends to uphold.

Translated Text

I have in the past served the enemy and his illegitimate regime, and I have been a member of a total of thirteen different bandit and reactionary *tewu* organisations, including the Military Affairs Commission War Cadre Training Corps, Sanminzhuyi Youth Corps, and Guomindang. In those organisations I held positions of responsibility, including as secretariat director, instructor, head of the education administration, editorial bureau chief, and dean of students. I consistently carried out counter-revolutionary activities opposing the People, regarded the enemy as my kith and kin, betrayed my motherland, and loyally served the enemy and his illegitimate regime as a cultural collaborator, while sexually violating

Yang X, 'Xuanshishu' (Sworn Declaration). From the same Agent Personal File as Chapter 14.

15 Yang X's Offer of Service

women and cruelly harming the young by propagating opinions and words opposed to the People. I was a loyal foot soldier of the Chiang Kai-shek bandits, and my massive crimes include deceiving the [People's] Government and flouting its laws and decrees, thereby inflicting untold harm upon the People. I am guilty of crimes so truly heinous that even death would be too good for me. Under the People's Government policy of leniency and gentle education, I have come to thoroughly realise the error of my ways and I have repented my past crimes. As of now, I am resolutely, thoroughly, and cleanly abandoning my past reactionary stance, and I pin my hopes on being embraced by the People, hoping to turn over a new leaf under the leadership of the [Communist] Party and People's Government. I will honour the laws and decrees of the government, serve the People heart and soul, and expose our foes – remnants of the Chiang Kai-shek gang, reactionary elements, and American imperialists – to help eradicate the enemy at an early date. I shall complete the tasks I am given to atone for my crimes by meritorious service in order to make up for all my past crimes against the People. I swear that if I go back on my word, I will accept the People's severest disciplinary sanctions and legal punishment.

Yang XXX [fingerprint]
31 August 1950

16   Private Correspondence Monitored

Shortly after Yang's arrest, his wife and children had to leave Harbin and move in with Yang's parents in the city of Y, over 700 km to the south by train. After Yang was released and able to resume teaching in Harbin, this temporary state of affairs of having no family housing persisted for two more months, during which time the couple's private correspondence briefly provided Yang's handler with a regular source of information on Yang's state of mind and more. The two sample letters below are the earliest in a cache of transcripts of intercepted letters that, after having been perused and annotated by his handler, ended up in Yang's Agent Personal File. As one would expect from a former *tewu* who, as his recruiters put it, 'after all [has] been around and already knows what to expect' (not to mention who had as his own first rule of discipline not to jeopardise clandestinity) neither of these two letters nor any of the others contain even the slightest hint of anything untoward from a counterintelligence point of view. What they do is merely provide the historian with an intimate glimpse of the private life of the agent.

Translated Text

Letter from Yang X to His Wife

Comrade XXX,

My problems have been sorted out. At noon on 6 September [1950], I was leniently released.

I only found out that you had departed Harbin after I returned to our apartment on XXX Street. Please let me know as soon as you can what has been happening to the family since we parted. Also, try right away to find a way to mail me my blue work jacket, rubber shoes, black trousers, cap, bedsheets, and so on. I have no clothes that I can wear for work. I am

---

Correspondence intercepted and copied by Technical Services of Harbin Public Security Bureau on 13 and 19 September 1950. Six handwritten pages, registered as letter transcripts Nos. 5260 and 5332. From the same Agent Personal File as Chapter 14 above.

16 Private Correspondence Monitored

staying in the Teacher's Federation dormitory for singles where the bed is dirty and I do not have a bedspread.

I was able to get help finding work and I managed to get back my old job, teaching Chinese literature at XXX Middle School. These last few days, I have been busy teaching the first class of third-year students and the first class of first-year students.

The aid and education I have been given by the government has made me realise that I can no longer keep my head in the clouds when it comes to work. This is also why I have yet to move back to our apartment and I did not get in touch right away. (My financial situation, furthermore, does not really allow it.) Don't let your imagination run away with you. Today's new me has a clear understanding of my past crimes, and I have resolved to change and become a new man. The first gradual steps to improve myself have already been taken, and I am no longer the man I used to be. We should believe in the policies of today's government. I have suffered no losses and I nurse no grievances. Instead, I have been relieved of a heavy burden, and physically I am feeling much better than I used to.

My dormitory is on Jilin Street in Nangang district; it is the singles' dormitory of the Teacher's Federation. Meals are simple, 55 fen/day, but I can eat and sleep peacefully and comfortably. (Our old apartment has been taken over by my colleague XXX. The entire building is full of people and for now, there is no room for me.) I have borrowed some money, and other than having bought myself a pair of trousers, a pair of leather shoes, washing utensils, and so on, I still have not yet found the time to settle down. Once I know you are all OK, I will do everything I can for you from this end.

You must not worry or attempt to travel here because we will not be able to afford the train fare. By the middle of the month when I get paid, I will assess the situation and hopefully be able to wire you some money. I need time to wind down and have a chance to get into my work so that I can perform some meritorious service to the people so as to atone for my crimes!

I do not know how much progress you have made, but you must study! We all were very naïve, but now, in our work, we must temper ourselves. Whatever happens, we must unswervingly study and commit to improving ourselves. For now, do not speculate in front of the children about how I might be doing since they will only become nervous, which is no good. The people in our hometown are all staunch conservatives and hold on to the old ways, so do not talk to them about me. If mother asks, only tell her that I have gained weight. Say that I have been released and that

I am back at my old job, that's all. How is father's business doing? What do you want me to say if people ask about your brother?

Please address letters and parcels to me c/o XXX Middle School, Daowai district, Harbin. Aside from the items mentioned above, I really do not need anything else.

Your brother's two daughters should look for work, and he should not deprive society of this labour force or prevent them from making progress. Even if it means that they merely work in a factory, it is not simply a matter of earning money but a matter of studying and finding a way out. Even if they do not manage to earn a cash salary, they should still work. Your two little brothers, the apples of the old uncle's eye, may still be mere children, but they should also contribute to the workforce and in the course of their studies temper themselves. They must not hesitate!

I may well be overbearing again, and you should of course still listen to what the family has to say. Also, write and let me know what you think!

Warmest greetings, to mother and father as well!

Yang XXX
Night-time, 11 September

Letter to Yang X from His Wife

XXX:

All of us, young and old, were ever so happy to get your news. First of all, we are grateful to the government for dealing so leniently with your past. Second, from the bottom of my heart, it fills me with joy that you have found in your mind the determination to change your life and become a new person. I can truly feel the power with which the policy of today's government is capable of educating a man and changing a man. Youth understands the truth and accepts the truth. Who wants to stubbornly defend the old and, in the process, become disliked by one and all? I hope to see you become a thoroughly new Yang XXX!

Without you, I managed to hold out in Harbin for some forty days during which the school and our neighbours remained very considerate. Eventually, my older brother came and brought us all back here to XXX. At the time, I faced large outstanding power and utility bills that I was unable to pay the school, but I had a conversation with XXX about them and he very considerately offered to leave the matter and deal with it later. Now that you are back at **XXX** Middle School, once you get your first salary, make sure you settle the bills with the school, please!

The government's care for you is really meticulous. It even lets you resume your work, which I had not expected. You say that this time around, you have come to thoroughly understand your own crimes; you are so right when you say that as of now you swear to render meritorious service to the people and atone for your crimes! The only way forward is to actively and energetically devote yourself to your work; it is the only way you will be able to make up for past transgressions. XXX, while you have been introspective, I too have made a self-criticism. I bear no small responsibility for how stressful your past life was. We lived together for eight years, during which time I drained, exhausted, and took advantage of you. I have thought only about what is best for the family, while neglecting the masses. Aside from giving birth, cooking, and monopolizing my husband, what kind of contribution did I make to society? What kind of assistance did I give you? To go on: I have lost all face as a woman! I really regret it, but I am already too old. I see everyone around me is making progress, while I remain a parasite. I procrastinate and feel ashamed since, because of my own limited abilities, I amount to little more than a simple question mark! But I am still resolutely intent to move forward, to begin to study and to ask people to help me, to make a big effort at progress and to see what happens.

Upon my arrival in XXX, I procrastinated and was depressed for a time. Then on 1 June, I started to attend XXX Sewing Skills School. I assumed that once I had completed the course, I would be able to make enough to survive, and I did not think of much else (because the locals here do not know enough about me, there were few alternatives for me to pursue). Now I have already attended classes for four months, and I will graduate at the end of the month. During these four months I have already learnt how to cut and sew ordinary cadre outfits and Lenin jackets, etc. In politics, we are reading *China's Revolution: A Reader* and Ai Siqi's *History of Society's Development*, but I have not yet learnt much aside from understanding the basic principle that 'labour is the source of all wealth' and that I can no longer remain idle. Once our class has graduated, most of us will be assigned jobs by the Shenyang Bedding and Clothing Bureau. I will not be able to move far, and whether I will be able to remain and get a job with the school (to be frank, I am being well taken care of by the students and teachers in the school) is not yet certain. Furthermore, the job is one I have sought out intentionally because both my political and educational levels need to be raised; to merely develop my practical skills is not really what I would like to do (sewing is all new to me), so I have intentionally sought additional opportunities to either get a job in an elementary school, which is something I would enjoy, or to study and further raise my level relatively quickly. That is how I see it; do you have any objections? For now, I do not want to move back to Harbin, assuming you have your health and we do not have to worry on that score. If you have a chance, please take a picture of yourself and send it to us for the family to see! From now on, as long as you are able to remain completely focused on your work, we shall be relieved.

Your father is able to continue his work [as a doctor] as before, and he too goes regularly to study. His historical issues have been clarified, and he is already officially liberated. Also, there is no problem as far as money and food are concerned. Whatever else there is, is not really worth mentioning. I am able to cover my tuition and pocket money with funds wired to me by my older sister. If you have any way of helping me, I would really appreciate it since I hate to bother outsiders. But for the moment, I can still manage. Make sure, first of all, that you yourself get back on your feet! Write to me and let me know what things you need me to send to you! Your mother is really good, taking care of our children, but she has lost weight. While I am taking classes, our little third one spends all day playing on the street with his older brother and sister. When there is a meeting that goes on until late in the evening I sometimes sleep over at the school, and our little third one sleeps with granny without making a fuss, which saves me a lot of trouble. My brother runs a small shop that allows him to make a living, and my elder niece lives in the dorm of the tobacco factory, while my second niece helps the family business. But I maintain that she too should go to live in the factory dorm where she can steel herself. Uncle XXX is attending a cadre school in Anshan, and he has already been assigned a job with the municipal government, while XXX remains at home but is very eager to move out. Your older uncle's business is doing fine, and all of your other relatives are also doing fine.

That's it, warmest greetings!
XXX

[p.s.] I have sent you by post one bedcover, a blue cotton outfit, a pair of white rubber shoes, two caps, and a pair of black trousers.

17 Give and Take: Apologies and a Nanny

In the first of the two texts below, Yang apologises to his case officer in mid-January 1952 for having missed their contact meeting after becoming overburdened with end-of-term exams and additional duties in the school where he was employed. Yang's past as a writer and co-editor of a number of literary magazines during and after World War II gave him a good command of style, while his erstwhile clandestine work for the Juntong gave him a good grasp of the subtleties in navigating the potentially treacherous waters of discourse within an intelligence and security agency. He knew, in other words, just how to write a persuasive self-criticism. In the second text, from 27 October 1954, it is Yang's handler who, on behalf of his tireless agent, addresses his own superior, the head of the Political Intelligence Section, with a request for an extra monthly stipend to provide Yang with a nanny because his wife had just given birth to their sixth child. The request was granted the very same day, and it was endorsed by the head of division. This ensured that Yang would have sufficient time to manage his agent duties and, in a formal assessment of his performance two years later, it was said that some of the 'compelling reasons for his preparedness to put his operational abilities to best possible use' came about 'as a result of the care we have shown for his personal circumstances that has allowed him to lead a comfortable life'.

Translated Text

I Have 'Become Ideologically Numb and Careless'

Due to ideological numbness and carelessness on my part, I committed the error of misremembering the location where I was supposed to be on 17 January and, as a result, I failed to report on my work. The reasons for this error, for which I must criticise myself, are that subjectively I have failed to give sufficient priority to [operational] work, and I have allowed myself to become ideologically numb and careless.

Yang X, 'Jiantaoshu' (Self-Criticism). From the same Agent Personal File as Chapter 14 above.

Objectively speaking, I was quite busy that day, with exams before lunch, a meeting at the Bureau of Education during lunch, and a debate in the afternoon concerning exam grade standards. Not until 5:15 p.m. was I able to get away. The one thing on my mind all day was matters relating to the end-of-term assessment, so I thought, so as not to lose time, I would go and deliver a quick report, hurry back to complete the assessment (for which the deadline is 19 January), and submit a full [operational] report once everything was finished after 20 January. With this kind of unprofessional attitude and perfunctory attention to performance of my duties, it was inevitable that such an error would occur. On the day in question, I did what I always do. I set out for the train station at 5:25 p.m. and then waited. When no one had shown up by 6.30, I felt I was unable to wait much longer, but it was not until I was on my way back that I remembered to check the instructions that my superiors had given me, and I suddenly realised that the location where I was supposed to have made contact had been changed to the Cinema of the Northeast. By then, it was already too late to do anything about it. At 6.45, back at the school, I thought of getting in touch by telephone to arrange a new meeting to make up for the one I had missed, but when I tried to do so, the person I needed to talk to was not available. In any case, I did not have any information to bring with me to the meeting, and the whole idea was dubious from the start.

In my attempt to be self-critical, when I think back to what led to my error, I realise that by now I have become lax and ideologically deficient in my work, and I have lowered my guard, not to mention begun to show an insufficiently professional attitude. To objectively respond to a serious political struggle by adopting such an attitude indicates that I am seriously afflicted with liberalism and enemy ideology, something that, if allowed to persist, may well in due course cause irreparable damage, lead me to commit inexcusable errors, and see me deteriorate into a lazy parasite. Given that it also shows a lack of loyalty and sincerity in serving the People's cause, I take my error very seriously and am determined not to commit this kind of mishap in my work ever again. As I submit this sincere self-criticism, I also directly ask my superiors to forgive my error.

17 January [1952]

The Agent 'Should Be Given an Extra Monthly Stipend to Employ a Nanny'

[Political Intelligence] Section Chief Lu [Junjie],

Case officer's untitled handwritten note. From the same Agent Personal File as Chapter 14 above.

17 Give and Take: Apologies and a Nanny

The attitude of agent Yang XXX has all along been good, and he has a professional capacity and potential to be fostered. After having gone through training, he has already been selected for utilisation, and our aim is to direct him to 'penetrate the Muslim nationality community in greater depth and to foster him into gaining the status of a significant member of the Muslim religious community'.

In view of this, due consideration should be given to the fact that, as stated in his training plan, 'he has many children and bears a considerable financial load and hence, as a means of making him move one step further closer to us and to remain loyal to our task of protection, he deserves to be given a supplementary nanny allowance'. He was told to employ a nanny, which he did when they had their sixth child (born on 21 October). In addition to the one-off sum of 500,000 yuan that he received at the time, he should now, as of 15 October, be given an extra monthly stipend of 300,000 yuan to employ a nanny.[111]

Please issue instructions on this matter.

Shu Dajiang, [on behalf of] the Comprehensive Group,
27 October 1954.

I agree: Please have Division Chief Zhao issue instructions.

Lu Junjie, 27 October

I agree.

[Political Protection Division Deputy Chief] Zhao Chun, 27 October

18   Agent Validation: Professional and 'Leftist'

Translated below are two agent validation reports on Yang. The template for reports like these resembled be the KGB's *karakteristika agenta*, which was meant to describe, among other things, a person's 'strong points and shortcomings ... which have come to light while he was used for agent work, prospects for making further use of him, and an evaluation of his work over a particular period'.[112] The first validation report (from 1953) assesses in depth Yang's overall performance and potential as an operative, while the second report (from 1957) mainly highlights his performance during the Communist Party's Hundred Flowers Campaign. In the 1950s, China's Ministry of Public Security operated a HUMINT asset appraisal and evaluation system which, in 1953, classified Yang X as belonging in Agent Category 1 (an 'old agent backbone') and in 1957, somewhat ironically, when assessing his conduct during the Anti-Rightist Campaign, granted the former Juntong officer the status of a 'Leftist'.

Translated Text

'He Has Understood Our Intentions and the Work We Need Him to Do'

I. Yang XXX, a/k/a Yang XXX, alias Zhang XXX, male, thirty-four years of age, ancestral home Liaodong province, from Victory district, XXX municipality, family background: independent professional, personal status: teacher, university education level, currently residing at XXX XXX XXX Street, Daowai district, Harbin. Current employment as senior middle school teacher at XXX Middle School, Harbin.
II. Background: [*not translated*]
III. Method and aim of recruitment:

'Dui 147 teqing de shencha cailiao' (Agent 147: Investigation Record). From the same Agent Personal File as Chapter 14.

18 Agent Validation: Professional and 'Leftist' 173

  A. Aim of recruitment: At the time, our recruitment of him [in 1950] had no prior aim. It was only after we arrested him that, in the course of interrogation, we discovered that the individual in question had an extended reactionary background and his professional status was high, which led us to decide that he might be able to do some work for us (and that this should be tested). He was, in other words, not recruited in connection with important circumstances involving a lead in a case investigation. Later, when we had a lead in a case investigation, we purposefully transferred the running of him to the present unit, where he is being directed to work on Hu XXX, Wang XXX et al.
  B. Method of recruitment: After we arrested him, and once our interrogation allowed us to get a clear idea of the nature of all of his issues, he was given a prison sentence based on the facts surrounding his crimes. He was then offered a conditional release and given the option of atoning for his crimes by providing us with meritorious service. This is how he came to be recruited.
  C. Means of utilisation: Mainly using his past crimes to make controlled use of him. While he must be controlled, we should be bold in our use of him.

IV. His *modus operandi* and his effectiveness:

  A. *Modus operandi*: Since his recruitment, he has passed repeated tests in his work, and the way in which he operates has turned out to basically match our objectives. He is sufficiently broad in the range of options he draws upon to propose different tactics, depending on the issue and the target, and, so far, in his work he appears not to have jeopardised operational clandestinity. Mainly, however, he is someone who in his past history of participation in reactionary organisations accumulated much experience about how to handle our line of work and, as a result, as his *modus operandi* shows, he is able to handle our work very well.
  B. His effectiveness: On the whole, he is someone who, after having passed repeated tests and having been given training, turns out to be quite effective. Primary among his qualifications is his ability to get close to the enemy, identify the enemy, and infiltrate the enemy. He is also able to identify problematic issues right away and report them to us. For example, Wang XXX – an important major lead that we now control, involving contacts with Taiwan and Hong Kong – is someone whom he discovered and reported on. He has since become very close to Wang and is working on

him. The [agent] in question is someone who is able to go wherever we direct him. The reasons for his effectiveness are:

1. He is highly experienced and possesses a wide range of skills.
2. Our direction of him has been comparatively appropriate, and he has received extensive training.
3. His operational tasks have been clear-cut.
4. Our debriefing of him is given high priority.
5. Our *kompromat* is ample and [*illegible*].

Consequently, based on all of the above, one may categorise him as belonging in Agent Category 1, that of old agents and backbone elements who successfully execute the missions we assign them. Basically, he has understood our intentions and the work we need him to do.

V. Direction, and problems relating to direction:

On the whole, direction of the agent has been properly handled and, as mentioned above, it has received due priority. He has been given training specifically targeting the issues that have been on his mind, and he has also been assigned very clear tasks. His financial circumstances regularly receive consideration and, as a result, in his work he fulfils our stated aims and completes his mission. Initially, we were not sufficiently bold in our direction of him, and we did not dare to boldly [*illegible*] his work. We still have occasional problems with case officers being unable to show up on time for their meetings due to other pressing matters. Since we are unable to tell him why, we risk making him feel apprehensive about us.

VI. About the future:

All in all, here is someone able to draw on numerous operative tactics, whose professional ability is quite strong, and who has become close to us ideologically and is able to keep us informed about the enemy's circumstances. Consequently, he may be regarded as an old agent backbone and as someone to whom we can confidently give a mission and know that he will be able to execute it successfully. In the future, in order to see him become even closer to us ideologically and, being of one heart and mind, do even more work for us, the following points merit consideration:

A. Control of him needs to be intensified, with an emphasis on training in every respect and linked to the issues on his mind. Training must be clearly focused on matters of how and when (ideological and political, professional, etc.) so as to see him become even closer to us ideologically and become even better at the work he does for us.

18 Agent Validation: Professional and 'Leftist'   175

B. Our routines must be tightened up across the board and – this goes for agents as well for our own officers – instances of unreliable implementation must be identified. What is good and what is bad must be critically appraised and promptly reproved or encouraged and rewarded (which is not the same as giving praise) so that the agent, in such a case, will quickly become aware of and rectify his [*illegible*] and also understand the direction of our work as of now.
C. In the future, when it comes to his direction, one can be quite bold. But the agent's sense of being part of an organisation must be reinforced, and he must be told that he must ask for instructions and report more often (given that he has already passed the test and the tempering of [*illegible*], we already have a sufficiently good understanding of him).
D. His financial circumstances must receive our appropriate consideration.

Investigating officer: Zhang [*illegible*]
22 January 1953

'The Individual in Question Remains Loyal to Us'

The agent in question was recruited in 1950 and is an old agent who already, on two separate occasions, has been subjected to rigorous probes and training. During all these years, he has remained honest and positive in his attitude towards our work, and he has shown operational ability. Despite being a busy man professionally, he still manages to find time to carry out his agent duties, and he does not break his appointments with us.

Ideologically, he is close to the government. He is able to promptly share with us any ideological concerns that he may confront and to ask the organisation to help him resolve them. Although he was recruited with the help of *kompromat*, in the course of utilisation he has been genuinely loyal to us. Our probes indicate that he has remained honest in his work for us over the years, and we have not come across instances of any attempts by him to deceive us.

The individual in question performed positively in the Anti-Rightist Struggle when, for example, the Rightists frenziedly attacked our Party, he remained as active as he had been in the past, and he positively reported to us one example after the other of what at the time he judged to be anti-Party utterances. He did not voice any critical opinions or show any resentment in terms of how his own historical issues have been dealt with. When the Rightist elements were analysed, his stated opinions of them turned out to have been correct. Before the launch of our

'Teqing renyuan jiandingshu' (Agent Validation Report). Undated handwritten original on custom form. From the same Agent Personal File as Chapter 14.

counterattack against the Rightists, he had already suggested we should focus on Cao XXX, Liu XXX, Hu XXX, et al.

The above factors indicate that the individual in question remains loyal to us and, given his consistently positive work performance, he should be categorised as a 'Leftist'.

Validation conducted from 1 July 1957 to 22 August 1957 by:

Na Zhongwu [*signature*]

Validation examined and verified by [*blank*]

19 Declining Performance? A Two-Day Brush-Up Course

Yang's relationship with the Harbin Public Security Bureau (where, first as Agent 147, then as Agent 151, he came to enjoy a reputation as one of the bureau's 'big agents' [*da teqing*]) was simple. His own analysis of the information that he shared with his handlers enjoyed respect and was taken very seriously, albeit that by the early 1960s, some officers appear to have concluded that he was downplaying the prevailing threat level and they began to disagree with him over 'what it all means'. By early 1962, Yang was questioning their interpretation of the intelligence that he shared with them about a certain operational target. As a result, and as documented in the first two texts below, the section running Yang presented its superordinate division level with an analysis of Yang's performance, identifying 'problems' involving his 'mindset' that needed to be addressed if the case investigation he served was to stand a chance of making further progress. In the third text, the division responded positively to the section's proposal that required a training course be arranged for Yang to align his perceptions with those of his handlers and their superiors. At the same time, however, the head of the division cautioned the section against dismissing Yang's interpretation too lightly, given that, after all, he was a highly experienced agent with much to his credit. The final two texts are the training course programme and the budget for meals.

Translated Text

On a Training Course for Agent 151

Agent 151 started out being operated by the Third Section of the First Division to work on the democratic parties. In 1961, we discovered that Agent 151 and counter-revolutionary element Zhao XXX, who had been plotting to restore the old order, taught in the same middle school. In order to keep all of Zhao's ongoing activities under surveillance, on 3 July 1961 we borrowed Agent 151 for operational use. Judging from

---

Untitled operational memoranda, five items, twelve handwritten pages in total. From the same Agent Personal File as Chapter 14 above.

what has been learned in this case from our direction of Agent 151 for more than five months, and the intelligence we have been able to develop, Agent 151 has already been able to connect with the target, maintains a positive relationship with him, and is able to obtain information on his activities.

The period that Agent 151 has worked on the target may be divided into two phases:

After accepting this mission, Agent 151 step by step was able to find out more about the target's past and ongoing activities as well as to develop a sense of the target's regular movement patterns. During this period, Agent 151 made quite an effort and succeeded in obtaining some information about the target, who had begun to let him in on private matters, confiding with him about his own reactionary mindset and sharing with him some of his connections.

Since 1 October [1961], the domestic and international situations have led the target to shift from an open to a more veiled aggressive stance. Meanwhile, Agent 151 has been able (by sometimes openly, sometimes discreetly, exploiting the target's character traits) to make careful progress and to obtain additional information as well as to further deepen his own relationship with the target.

In our analysis of the agent's performance, we have identified the following problems:

Ideologically, Agent 151 has an insufficient understanding of the target. He insists that the target merely does his ordinary job and that to work on him really has nothing going for it. The target, he says, is someone who hustles others into paying for his food and drink and who is the kind of menace that can be easily exploited by the enemy, and he is nothing like a genuine *tewu*. Such is the agent's mindset that, as a result, he is no longer making progress and instead is holding back, shying away from difficulties, and he has lost interest and confidence.

Agent 151 has managed the relationship well, but the relationship has still not progressed from being close to becoming one in which the target will reveal everything on his mind to the agent. The target has revealed some things to the agent, but when it comes to substantial matters, he is still taking precautions, and the agent has not yet won the target's absolute trust. Consequently, in his work the agent has merely been able to fight some battles along the periphery without gaining the trust of the target. The agent is still quite some distance away from being able to infiltrate and carry out operational work inside the target.

The agent has admitted that he found working on the democratic parties comparatively easy, while after working on Zhao for over five months, he has still not been able to come up with anything worth mentioning. In many respects, the two personalities do not match. Getting together sometimes proves awkward, there are no settled topics of conversation, and simply nothing comes out of it. As a result, the agent has become anxious that if this goes on for much longer, he simply will not achieve what is expected of him. He has let it be known that he wants to drop this mission and he would rather be assigned a new mission.

Agent 151 is a long-standing agent with achievements to his credit, but under the present circumstances, in dealing with this kind of enemy and working single-mindedly like this, his experience and means are insufficient. To once again resort to the means of the past to acquire information on the enemy has turned out to be quite problematic. This point may be illustrated by the fact that Agent 151 is no longer making much progress and things seem to have ground to a halt.

Given all of the above, the agent's mindset must be addressed and the obstacles must be resolved in order to bring about a change in the current situation and move the case forward. The spirit of the directives we have received from Division suggests that the school winter vacation [in February] will provide an opportunity for more efficient direction of Agent 151 to serve [in operational depth] as a penetration agent, but in preparation, a training course must be organised to for Agent 151 to make him see the situation more clearly and for us to explain his mission to him – to infiltrate the enemy and conduct operational work on the inside. To serve our purposes, the following arrangements must be made:

A.   Training Content   The agent must, to begin with, be educated about the current domestic and international situations and be informed about the threat level. Our aim should be to make him attain situational awareness, elevate his mindset and improve his understanding, and rectify his current lack of vigilance.

The target's case should be subjected to detailed analysis and examination. By way of analysis and examination, our aim should be to further clarify the mission to the agent, improve his understanding, deal with the key obstacles in his mindset, and allow him to develop a better sense of the direction of future work.

Summarise the work done over the past five months, in particular with respect to the tactics called for when dealing with this kind of enemy. Determine which experiences have proven to be good and comparatively successful.

Based on all of the above, spell out and settle on what the agent's key mission is to be during the 1962 winter vacation and what tactics he should use to complete it.

B.   [The Mission]   During the winter vacation, Agent 151 should be directed to resolve the following: first of all, to clear up what goes on behind the scenes as far as the target's activities and current plans are concerned. In other words, to deal both with historical – the sleeper question (*qianfu wenti*) – and presently ongoing matters.

For more than five months now, in his work Agent 151 has employed operational tactics of direct and indirect attack, but the results have been meagre as he has not managed to get the target to reveal more than some superficial matters. During the winter vacation, the agent should go on the offensive and, at an appropriate juncture, share some carefully prepared operational disinformation (concerning his own past history and views of the present) with the target and then observe how the target reacts.

The agent should meet with the six individuals with whom the target is in fairly close and regular contact, and then somehow (eating, drinking, watching opera, etc.) get to know one or two of them and find out if what they share is merely past historical links or if they also share ongoing matters. In the process, the agent's aim is to find out if they are engaged in any organised activity.

Figure out how the target views the current situation, what his plans are, and based on that determine what his future plans may be.

Clarify the target's past history, in particular his *tewu* status and his *tewu* activities, including concrete events.

C.   Training Format   Mainly a summary of past work, discussing operations and what is on one's mind. Give the agent encouragement, most of all, and minimise criticism. On the basis of his raised awareness, get him to consciously put forward a plan for how to best exploit the opportunity presented by the winter vacation.

D.   Time and Place   From 23 January 1962 (Tuesday) to 24 January 1962 (Wednesday), two whole days, from nine in the morning until five in the afternoon. Place: Point No. 13.

E.   Participants   Ask Division Chief Ding [Wenchun] to attend and to educate Agent 151 about the domestic and international situations and about the threat level. Have Section Heads Li and Guo lay out and prepare the agent for his operational mission scheduled for the winter vacation.

Please indicate whether or not the above proposal is appropriate.

Third Section of the Fifth Division
14 January 1962

19 Declining Performance? A Two-Day Brush-Up Course

Third Section's Appraisal of Agent 151

Division Chief Ding,

As requested by Division, Comrades Guo Yutang and Wang Mingxiu and myself recently sought to assess agent work targeting operational lead Zhao XXX. We primarily assessed the value of the intelligence concerning Zhao that Agent 151 had managed to obtain and analysed some of the issues currently impacting the mindset and work of Agent 151 and our direction of him. We also further discussed and clarified the central mission of our agent's operational work targeting Zhao and, on the basis of all of the above, assessed the need for a training course for Agent 151. Comrade Wang Mingxiu has already called on the Bureau and has proposed a training course schedule: what follows below is some complementary information.

We maintain that the selection of Agent 151 to work on Zhao has been correct. He fits the profile called for, not merely in terms of social position and historical background but also in terms of operational capabilities. Agent 151 has the past and present qualifications required to remain in contact with Zhao, and therefore he also has ample qualifications for an attack on Zhao.

Agent 151 is an energetic agent of long standing, with operational skills and operational experience.

In the course of five months of work, he has obtained a considerable amount of intelligence, verifying no small number of matters and laying the groundwork for further operational progress.

At present, the key issue is the following: In his work on Zhao, Agent 151 has begun to show signs of weariness and to be shying away from difficulties. For some time now, he has largely ceased to take any initiatives. He is merely pushing the boat along with the current and adapting to the current state of affairs. He has even hinted at wanting to 'retire from the front lines'.

Our tentative assessment suggests that the main reasons for the above are as follows:

1. He prefers not to have to deal with any additional trouble. After 1953, Agent 151 worked specifically on the democratic parties and personages, and here he was able to obtain intelligence effortlessly. When he accepted the mission to work on Zhao, he did so reluctantly and in part with a financial aim in mind (he wanted to make some extra money). As time went on, we were not really all that satisfied with his performance (we did not explicitly point this out, but he is smart enough to have noticed), and as work on Zhao started to become a priority, he began to look for excuses to withdraw from the front lines, although he did not actually come out and say as much. His intelligence reporting

began to include more and more conclusions drawn far too rapidly, as in remarks to the effect that Zhao was no more than 'a historical counter-revolutionary, a political menace', who is 'politically reactionary, likes to brag and boast, and spends his days hustling others into paying for his food and drink'. In oral debriefings, Agent 151 has insisted that 'there's nothing to be had from working on Zhao; the whole thing is not worth the effort'.

2. Agent 151 has misgivings and is afraid that if Zhao's problems are blown out of proportion, he himself may suffer. In the past, he has compared Zhao to a 'pimple full of pus. If you don't squeeze it, you remain uncomfortable with it, but then again, if you do squeeze it, you worry about it becoming [*illegible*].' Of course, we also have the option of resorting to counter-operational tactics, but here Agent 151 is urging particular caution, which in itself is correct. Judging from his mindset, what he is most afraid of is that it may impact negatively on his own situation.

3. Agent 151 has an insufficient appreciation of the seriousness of current threats. A tentative analysis of his past experiences suggests that he craves greatness and success, and he shies away from difficulties. In 1951–52, we had him work on the case of the historical counter-revolutionary Wang Xiaokong (a major-general in Chiang Kai-shek's bogus army who was later executed during the Suppression of Counter-revolutionaries Campaign), and his work progressed very smoothly. In the opinion of Agent 151, Zhao now appears to be neither a sleeper *tewu* nor a worthwhile active counter-revolutionary target. Agent 151 does not understand the hallmarks of the activities conducted by sly enemies under current circumstances.

4. Agent 151 maintains the operational tactics called for are missing. This is true to a degree, but it is not a dominant factor.

Based on the above assessment, we favour continued use of Agent 151 to work on Zhao in greater depth and, should the opportunity arise, to have him operate as a penetration agent. But for now, what we need to do is to provide stronger leadership, education, and training. We maintain that, on the whole, the mission of the agent at present is to clarify one step further what goes on behind the scenes and [*illegible*] as far as Zhao's activities are concerned. In concrete terms, this means following two alternative operative assumptions at the same time: to simultaneously probe (a) the historical issue of whether or not he is a *tewu* with a sleeper mission and (b) the immediate question of whether or not he is organizing something or is engaged in a plot of some kind. It will be central to resolve whether there are any presently ongoing activities and, if

19 Declining Performance? A Two-Day Brush-Up Course 183

so, what their nature is. Are they of a sleeper *tewu* nature or are they merely an attempt to restore the old regime by a historical counter-revolutionary? What do they involve: organisation or [*illegible*]? Has an organisation already come into being, or is it all just big talk and no worthwhile action? Our task, when a suitable opportunity presents itself, will be to attempt a psychological attack or probe. Tactically, in my opinion we may direct the agent to reveal to the target his own past status (primarily that of once having served as an officer in the Sanminzhuyi Youth Corps) or, if necessary, let him, to a limited extent (in an abstruse way that would allow for deniability), share some half-truths if this would allow him to ascertain the truth about Zhao (past and present). What the agent may *not* do is imply that his own status is that of a sleeper, an idea that Agent 151 floated at one point, not as something he really intended to do but merely to test us and to see how we would respond (at his next meeting with us, he promptly rejected the idea). He should approach and come up with a way of engaging one or two of the six individuals with whom Zhao has regular conversations. Alternatively, he should use an exploratory tactic (such as, if necessary, drawing attention to some particularly controversial item published in *Reference News*) to engage Zhao in a conversation on current affairs so as to probe one step further what his views are and to see what his attitude is.

About the course: in my opinion, we should spend two days concentrating mainly on resolving the matter of his mindset but also dealing with matters of understanding and of tactics. In the main, the format of the training should be to have our leadership (including the head of our division) participate in person to talk about the current domestic and international situations, share views on certain international matters, address the threat level, and in that context bring up the Zhao case and analyse it together with him so as to arrive at a shared understanding, develop an operational tactic, and clarify his task. We should then proceed to research and deal with the operations-related activities (mission and tactics) involved, as well as ask Agent 151 to right away draw up an implementation plan. As part of training, [*illegible*] methods of research, appraise how Agent 151 intends to proceed. Assess his achievements positively (encouragement should be primary, criticism secondary), stress his untapped potential, and bring his initiative into play. At the same time, the specific problems he has when it comes to his work and his thinking must be pointed out to him. As for practical matters, see the attached plan.

The above are some of the issues that first came to mind and that I wanted to expand upon. Together with the plan for the training course, I am now sharing this with the higher levels and am requesting instructions (I have made no changes to the training course plan).

184   V From the Agent Personal File

About other matters concerning this case, such as the officers to involve, the training, and [*illegible*] issues, and so on, they also need to be resolved urgently.

Li Ke, 16 January 1962

Memorandum from the Division Chief to the Section

Comrades Mingxiu and Li Ke,

I have looked at your plan and your comments on the training of Agent 151, and I am in overall agreement. But I also want you to give the matters below some more thought. Do not alter the scheduled dates.

About the reasons why Agent 151 is now showing signs of impatience, no longer making much progress, and drawing premature conclusions: In addition to what your analysis indicates, might there not also be problems with our direction of him? I recall that this agent had more than once in the past drawn up plans for meritorious service, to which we voiced objections. Under the circumstances, is it possible that the agent thinks we are hesitating about what moves to make next and are having problems, or given that he is an agent of long standing who has many past successes to his credit (while this time around everything is dragging on and the results are meagre) that he has gotten it into his mind that we have begun to have second thoughts about him? If this is the case, you really should resolve this and give him the full credit that he deserves so that his concerns will be dispelled.

Our presentation of tactics and clarification of tasks [to the agent, during the training course] will be mainly about resolving how we may get at the essence of [the operational target] Zhao and ultimately determine what he is up to. At this point, all we have are appearances, so we need to find a solution, come up with a workable tactic, and decide how to [*illegible*] confidence. All of these things must be discussed.

Ding Wenchun
17 January 1962

Training Course Programme

For Division Chief Ding [Wenchun] to read and issue instructions.

After having researched the matter once more with Agent 151, we changed the dates of the course to 23–24 January (Tuesday and Wednesday of next week), two days in total.

Time: 23 January 1962 (Tuesday) 9 a.m.–noon.

Place: 13 Hanyang Street, Nangang district.

19 Declining Performance? A Two-Day Brush-Up Course

Content and participants: Division Chief Ding [Wenchun] on the current domestic and international situations and threat levels, and Section Chief Li [Ke] and Wang Mingxiu on analysing the issue of Zhao XXX and clarifying present and future tasks.
Time: 23 January 1962, 1:30 p.m.–5 p.m.
Place: same as the above.
Content and participants: Section Chief Li [Ke] and Wang Mingxiu on summing up, recalling, and examining work during the past phase.
Time: 24 January 1962 (Wednesday) 9 a.m.–3 p.m.
Place: same as the above.
Content and participants: Section Chief Li [Ke] on concrete clarification of tasks and exploring work methods and setting out activities and tasks during the next phase.

Li Ke, 18 January [1962]

Agreed.

Ding Wenchun, 19 January 1962

Meals

Division Chief Ding [Wenchun]:

In accordance with the spirit of the division's instructions, we are conducting a two-day training course for Agent 151 prior to the winter vacation, during which we must arrange for three meals (lunch and dinner on the first day, lunch on the second day). Below is what we are budgeting: please comment/instruct.

1. Rice. 3 *jin*.
2. Flour. 3 *jin*.
3. Cabbage. 10 *jin*.
4. Garlic bolt. 2 *jin*.
5. Eggs. 3 *jin*.
6. Sweet potato noodles. 1 *jin*.
7. Muskmelon. 6 cartons.
8. Frozen (fresh) bean curd. 20 pcs.
9. Soybean oil. 1 *jin*.

Office Director Zhang, please comment and instruct.

Ding Wenchun, 19 January 1962

Part VI

Component Chiefs: Feedback and Direction

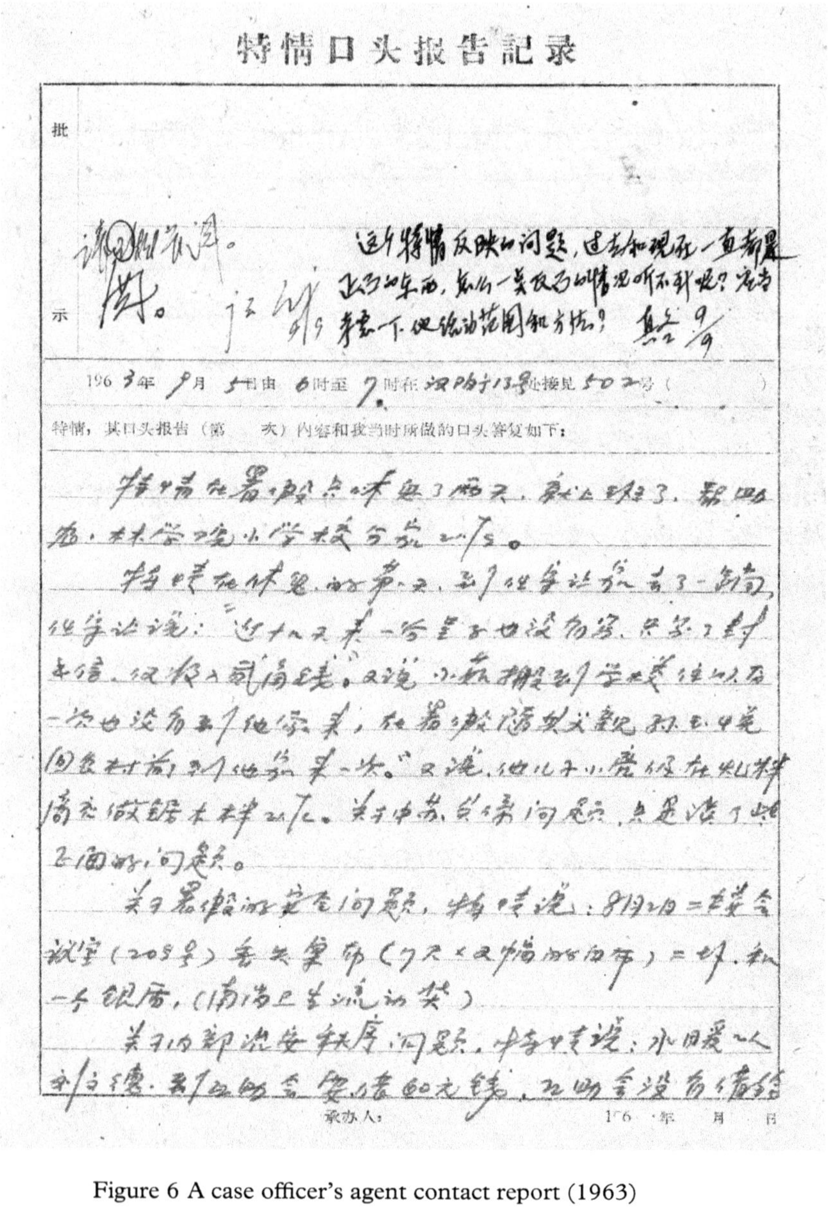

特情口头报告記录

批

示

196 3年 9月 5日由 6时至 7时在 处接见 502号（ ）

特情，其口头报告（第 次）内容和我当时所做的口头答复如下：

承办人： 196 年 月 日

Figure 6 A case officer's agent contact report (1963)

Introduction

The boundary that circumscribes the subject matter of this collection of translations traverses the desk of the head of the organisational component operating sources/agents/informers. On that desk, to cite the second half of Donald Rumsfeld's famous elaboration on how to tell intelligence from fact, 'there's judgement involved' and 'a lot of conflicting facts and information are brought together'.[113] Beyond it, HUMINT has ceased to be an intelligence *activity* and become but one of many different and competing *products* on the basis of which timely and accurate – alternatively, late or wrong – decisions will be taken by political leaderships.

In a merit-based system, HUMINT component chiefs are officers who themselves have 'been there, done that' and who, as a result, may provide specific, targeted feedback and direction to case officers. As ghost-writer authors of texts like those in Part III above, their experiences are also drawn upon for the overall development and promotion of best practices. Component chiefs may query whether a case officer's agent is being used in the best possible way, ask what can be done to improve performance, and, with respect to reporting, suggest how to 'nudge it in a more productive direction'.[114] Here, demands for political correctness often blur the distinction between the mere use of subjective words and the politicisation that ensues when case officers read into the direction they receive a desire to see the information tailored to fit the views of the political leadership. In *Exploring Intelligence Archives: Enquiries into the Secret State*, R. Gerald Hughes and Len Scott asked how far 'ideological and political factors' impinge on how case officers write up the result of their dealings with their agents.[115] Historians looking for an answer to this question will, when they are able to 'decode' its often terse wording, find the answer in the routine feedback (Chapter 20) that case officers receive from component chiefs at the very point where mediated agent reporting like that translated in Part IV above becomes a finished intelligence product.

Component chiefs must endorse the empowerment as 'agents' of persons close to and in some instances even part of the problems to be solved. They must also act on behalf of case officers to elicit approval for proposed operations from officers further up the chain of command. As emphasised by one agency, such elicitations must be expressed in terms of 'motives and the actions that flow from them, choices, strengths and weaknesses, capabilities and intentions' if they are to convince other professionals who may have additional/other intelligence at their disposal.[116] The documented elicitation that survives in Agent Work Files provides historians with a rare glimpse into how component chiefs reasoned (Chapter 21) as they outlined courses of action in just such terms, concentrating entirely on the operational and leaving aside political argumentation.

Finally, in addition to providing case officers with feedback and direction, component chiefs serve as conflict mediators when competing intelligence demands clash and prove difficult to reconcile (Chapter 22).

20 On a Case Officer's Contact Reports: 'Why Never Anything Negative?'

The routine instructions, comments, queries, and so on appearing in chronological order below are those that the leadership of the HUMINT component of the Fifth (Cultural Protection) Division of the Harbin Public Security Bureau wrote on contact reports presented to them by a case officer running an agent in Harbin's Forestry College during a three-year period ending in the spring of 1966. The agent, originally recruited in 1950 to inform on colleagues with Nationalist ties, was by the mid-1960s frustrating his case officer's superiors by his inability to develop access to newer home-grown threats presumed to exist on campus in the form of younger teachers and students afflicted by 'revisionism'. The component leadership's comments on the contact reports are addressed not only to the case officer but, now and then, they also elicit the opinions of division superiors. In 1963, the component chiefs share tradecraft-related advice with the case officer and impress on him the need for his reports to be legible and their content to foreground 'negative' things. For about a year and a half after that, they discuss how to make best use of the agent, but then eventually lose interest in him. Their extended string of comments comes to a close on the eve of the Cultural Revolution when they endorse the downgrading of the agent to quasi-dormant status.

Translated Text

Comments on Contact Report Dated 7 June 1963

Section chiefs Wang [Zhendong] and Jiang, once you have read and issued your instructions, please present this to the division chief to read and issue his instructions. I agree with the suggestion [of the case officer] to direct the agent to focus on the circumstances of problematic individuals in the Five Antis [Socialist Education] Movement.

[Section Chief] Yu Zhongmao, 7 June

Operational records in Agent Work File maintained by the Cultural Protection Division of the Harbin Public Security Bureau. Closed file, weeded out from the bureau archive after the Cultural Revolution.

[I have] read [this].

[Division Chief] Liu [Dongjiang], 7 June

Comments on Contact Report Dated 20 June 1963

[I have] already read [this]. In the future, please write more carefully in order to ensure legibility.

[Section Chief Wang] Zhendong, 24 June

[I have] read [this].

Yu Zhongmao, 24 June

[I have] read [this].

[Division Chief] Liu, 26 June

Comments on Contact Report Dated 15 July 1963

Section Chief Yu, please read. It is excellent that this agent, in addition to his oral report, has presented us with a written record based on his recollections of how the masses are reacting [to the ongoing Sino-Soviet talks in Moscow]. Tell him to be extremely careful not to lose any such written records, and that in the future he need not spell out any personal names but may simply write XXXX.

The circumstances of [the typesetter] Wang Xiangzhen, as reported [by the agent] should be looked into.

Zhendong, 15 July

Comrades [Zou] Shaoquan and Li Gui: if your agent turnover went as intended, please proceed to complete the turnover paperwork.

Yu Zhongmao, 18 July

Comments on Contact Report Dated 6 August 1963

Section Chief Yu, once you have read this, please pass it on to the division chief. Again, this time around, the circumstances reported by the agent are only positive. As of now, he should focus on collecting what people say behind other people's backs. But he should also continue to pay attention to comments on Sino-Soviet relations and, in particular, to the statements and actions by people who 'hold opinions in their minds but dare not speak openly about them'. In addition, concerning Forestry College technician Zhao Qinglin, who set off a fire [in the timber processing kiln] by violating operating procedures and refusing to heed the warnings of the old worker, we should coordinate with the Fire Fighting Division to propose what to do.

Zhendong, 6 August

[I have] read [this].

Yu Zhongmao, 6 August

[I have] read [this].

[Division Chief] Liu, 7 August

Comments on Contact Report Dated 8 September 1963

Section Chief Wang [Zhendong], please read.

Yu Zhongmao, 9 September

[I have] read [this]. Now, as in the past, the matters reported by this agent are all positive. Why does he never pick up anything negative? Do we need to give some thought to his scope of activity and how he goes about things?

Zhendong, 9 September

Comments on Contact Report Dated 28 September 1963

The circumstances of technician Han Wenguang [who is married to a woman from the Soviet Union] should, for reference, be brought to the attention of Comrade Su Yufa. I agree with your proposal to give the agent 30 yuan on the eve of the National Holiday to show our concern for his [and his large family's] wellbeing. Section Chief Wang, once you have read and commented on this, please pass it on to the division chief and ask him to issue instructions.

Yu Zhongmao, 28 September

[I have] read [this].

Wang [Zhendong]

OK.

[Division Chief] Liu, 29 September

Comments on Contact Report Dated 30 September 1963

Section Chief Wang, please read. About the stolen pushcart, ask the Protection Section and tell it to do something about [the lax implementation of] campus visitation rules.

Yu Zhongmao, 30 September

VI Component Chiefs: Feedback and Direction

Comments on Contact Report Dated 10 October 1963

[I have] read [this].

Zhendong, 15 October

[I have] read [this].

Yu Zhongmao, 15 October

Comments on Contact Report Dated 2 November 1963

Section Chief Yu, please read and issue instructions. I think we should [re-]consider our tasking of this agent, but before we do so, we should ask [his case officer] Comrade Li Gui to state an opinion.

Zhendong, 4 November

I agree with Section Chief Wang [Zhendong]. Division Chief Liu, please read and issue instructions.

Yu Zhongmao, 4 November

Consider and resolve immediately.

[Division Chief] Liu, 6 November

Comments on Contact Report Dated 21 November 1963

As quickly as you can, please come up with a considered opinion about how the agent in question should be tasked.

Zhendong, 21 November

[I have] read [this].

Yu Zhongmao, 21 November

Comments on Contact Report Dated 22 December 1963

Division chief, please read and issue instructions.

After the New Year but before the Spring Festival, show our concern for the agent by giving him 30 yuan. That should suffice. Do not entertain.

Yu Zhongmao, 23 December

20 yuan will be OK.

[Division Chief] Liu

Comments on Contact Report Dated 11 February 1964

Section Chief Wang, once you have read and issued instructions, please present this to the division chief to read and comment (*yuepi*).

20 On a Case Officer's Contact Reports

Reports on reactions to the transmission of the Centre's anti-revisionist texts should be shared with the Secretariat for reference. Comrade Su Yufa should also take a look at them.

Yu Zhongmao, 11 February

[I have] read [this].

Wang [Zhendong]

[The reports] have been read.

[Su Yufa], 19 February

Comments on Contact Report Dated 10 April 1964

Section Chief Yu, once you have read and issued instructions, please present this to Section Chief Li to read and comment.

Comrade Li Gui, please combine the safety inspection with a corroboration of the [quack doctor's] superstitious activities and an inquiry into the fire and leaking oil drums at the college. Then frame the results as our findings and share them with the departments concerned and propose that something must be done.

Zhendong, 10 April

[I have] read [this].

Yu Zhongmao, 10 April

Comments on Contact Report Dated 28 May 1964

Division chief, please read and issue instructions. Comrade Li Gui, in conjunction with the agent's validation assessment, please put forward a concrete proposal on how he should be tasked and how direction of him may be raised another notch.

Zhendong, 28 May

Whenever these problems arise, we must exchange views and state our opinions. That is the only way in which direction of the agent can be improved.

[Division Chief] Liu

Comments on Contact Report Dated 12 June 1964

Division chief, please read and issue instructions. The validation assessment of this agent must be concluded as soon as possible, and a proposal on how he is to be tasked and actually utilised must be stated.

Zhendong, 12 June

The aims and tasks of a *tewu* have to be clear-cut.

[Division Chief] Liu

Comments on Contact Report Dated 6 July 1964

[I have] read [this].

Zhendong, 5 [*sic*] July

Comments on Contact Report Dated 28 July 1964

Section Chief Yu, once you have read and issued your instructions, please present this to the division chief to read and issue instructions. Here more attention can be paid to the agent's tactics. In the past, his work for us was restricted to reporting on people's views on current affairs, but now he has been asked to broaden his scope to also cover what he hears about suspicious circumstances and incidents among the teachers, students, and staff from different social strata. In this way, the intelligence he is able to provide will increase, including on trends among the Five Kinds of [landlord, rich-peasant, reactionary, hooligan, and Rightist] Elements and including intelligence obtained indirectly that does not amount to firsthand information.

Zhendong, 29 July

[I have] read [this].

Yu Zhongmao, 30 July

Comments on Contact Report Dated 30 August 1964

Section Chief Yu, once you have read and issued your instructions, please present this to the division chief to read and issue instructions. As far as the tasks for this agent are concerned, I was present at the last meeting with him [on 27 July] and demanded that he not merely report on what was being said about the international situation but about domestic matters as well, such as the (urban and rural) Socialist Education Movement, in particular the Party's general and specific policies, its letters in reply to the Soviet Communist Party, educational reform, the Five Antis Movement, other central tasks in our schools, and so on. He should collect information on trends and political attitudes among all the different people he encounters. Comrade Li Gui, please once again outline to the agent what his tasks should be, discuss them with him, and make sure they are clear to him.

Zhendong, 3 September

[I have] read [this].

[Division Chief] Liu, 3 September

Comments on Contact Report Dated 18 September 1964

Section Chief Yu, once you have read and issued your instructions, please present this to the division chief to read and issue instructions. (1) Matters arising from the merger of Jilin Forestry Engineering College with Northeast Forestry College must first be probed from an open angle, followed by issuance of a notice to the Protection Section asking it to stay on top of how the merger is proceeding. (2) The issue raised by the person who has gone to Beijing to lodge a complaint [with the Ministry of Forestry] should either be appropriately handled by the school or she should be persuaded and educated, and the Protection Section should be informed. (3) I agree to give the agent a 20 yuan one-off subsidy and to ask Section Chief Yu and the division chief to please issue their instructions.

Zhendong, 18 September

[I have] read [this].

Yu Zhongmao, 19 September

I agree with Section Chief Wang [Zhendong]'s suggestion.

[Division Chief] Liu, 20 September

Comments on Contact Report Dated 7 October 1964

Division chief, please read and issue instructions.

Did the wife of Zhang Zhenlin lodge a complaint [with the Ministry in Beijing] because she had been transferred to the grassroots? Her name was already on our Control List of individuals lodging complaints, but now the circumstances of both Zhang Zhenlin and his wife should, for control purposes, be shared with the Protection Section. For reference, with respect to Zhang Zhenlin, his circumstances should be reported to the school's Five Antis Office.

Yu Zhongmao, 9 October

[I have] read [this].

[Division Chief] Liu

Comments on Contact Report Dated 17 November 1964

Section Chief Yu, once you have read this and issued your instructions, please pass it on to the division chief to read and issue his instructions.

Henceforth, the agent, in addition to continued collection of reactions to detonation of the atom bomb and the ouster of Khrushchev, should be tasked with gathering reactions to unfolding major domestic and international events, such as the presence of our delegations (including that of the Premier) at the Soviet Union's anniversary of the October Revolution, and so on.

Inquire at the local police station about the death [suicide] of Xiaoru mentioned by the agent.

Zhendong, 17 November

Comrade Guochen, please read.

Yu Zhongmao, 17 November

Seen.

[Division Chief] Liu

Comments on Contact Report Dated 16 December 1964

Section Chief Yu, once you have read and issued your instructions, please present this to the division chief to read and issue instructions. As far as the work safety-related issues are concerned, tell the college Protection Section to raise them at a meeting of the college administration, to launch an education drive, and to deal with them in earnest.

Zhendong, 17 December

Comments on Contact Report Dated 16 January 1965

Section Chief Yu, once you have read and issued your instructions, please present this to the division chief to read and issue instructions. It is high time that the validation assessment of this agent is completed. How he is to be tasked and utilised should be discussed specifically.

Zhendong, 16 January

There are a number of things this agent may well know that he has never voluntarily divulged. He has information on Wang X but has never shared it with us. We should thoroughly reconsider how best to utilise him.

Yu Zhongmao, 17 January

Seen.

[Division Chief] Liu, 18 January

Comments on Contact Report Dated 19 March 1965

Section Chief Wang [Zhendong], once you have read and issued your instructions, please present this to the division chief to issue instructions.

20 On a Case Officer's Contact Reports

As far as the agent's subsidy and his wife's employment are concerned, at this stage one should first have a chat with someone at their workplace to see if it can be of some assistance. For now, we should not become involved or provide a subsidy, and we should only decide what to do once the agent has been assessed and given a [reliability] grading.

Yu Zhongmao, 20 March

[I have] read [this].

Zhendong

I agree with Section Chief Yu [Zhongmao].

[Division Chief] Liu, 20 March

Comments on Contact Report Dated 31 May 1965

Section Chief Yu, once you have read this and issued your instructions, please pass it on to the division chief to read.

Zhendong, 31 May

[I have] read [this].

Yu Zhongmao, 31 May

Comments on Contact Report Dated 5 July 1965

[I have] read [this].

Yu Zhongmao, 8 July

[I have] read [this].

Zhendong, 8 July

Comments on Contact Report Dated 18 September 1965

[I have] read [this].

[Division Chief] Liu, 18 September

Comments on Contact Report Dated 18 October 1965

[I have] read [this].

Wang Zhaoxiang, 22 October

Comrade big Wang, once you have read this, please forward it to the First Section.

[Division Chief] Liu, 23 October

VI Component Chiefs: Feedback and Direction

Comments on Contact Report Dated 5 November 1965

In addition to what Zou Shaoquan has to say, one should find out what the agent's problems really are and what is prompting his odd thinking (*huo sixiang*).

Wang Zhaoxiang, 6 November

Comrade big Wang, please take a look. I agree with Comrade [Wang] Zhaoxiang's proposal.

[Division Chief] Liu, 8 November

Comments on Contact Report Dated 3 December 1965

[I have] read [this].

[Division Chief] Liu, 7 December

[I have] read [this].

Wang Zhaoxiang

Comments on Contact Report Dated 24 December 1965

Let Comrade Zou Shaoquan submit a concrete proposal and Division Chief Liu decide whether or not we should continue to utilise this agent.

Wang Zhaoxiang, 25 December

Please submit a concrete proposal.

[Division Chief] Liu, 27 December

Comments on Contact Report Dated 27 February 1966

[I have] read [this]. It seems appropriate for the [agent and his case officer] to rendezvous once every fifteen to twenty days.

[Wang Zhaoxiang], 28 February

[I have] already read [this].

Wang, 1 March

21   On Courses of Action Proposed

In the two memoranda below, HUMINT component chiefs addressing their immediate superiors request endorsement of particular courses of action proposed by their case officers. The courses of action are to further missions already known at the superordinate division level. In the first memorandum, the head of the First Section of the Political Protection Division of the Harbin Public Security Bureau is given permission to proceed with arrangements for an intimate dinner party to be hosted by a case officer's agents (one male, aged forty, and one female, aged thirty-three, married and operated by him as a pair) for two targets (a Chinese chemist and his Japanese wife) in order to proactively 'increase the intimacy of the relationship' between the two couples and, in this way, to 'create conditions for operational work in greater depth'. In the second memorandum, a course of action of dubious legality proposed by a different head of the same section is ultimately vetoed by a deputy director of the Harbin Public Security Bureau. It would, in this case, have made the case officer's husband-and-wife agents complicit in letting an operational target's daughter enter a prestigious middle school with the help of a forged letter of introduction. In the second memorandum, the section head further suggests that an operational target's recent visit to Shenyang may be exploited as *kompromat* to impose restrictions on his future movements. Neither the Political Protection Division nor the Public Security Bureau object to this proposal.

Translated Text

'No Canned Chicken Meat and One, Not Two, Bottles of Red Wine'

[Political Protection] Division Chief,

Operational memorandum, 'Guanyu zhihui 198 hao teqing liyong '10.1' fangjia de jihui shenru zhencha de baogao' (Proposal to Have Agent 198 Conduct In-Depth Surveillance During the National Holiday). From the same Case 28 File as Chapter 7 'Proposal to Recruit Yu X' above.

XXX XXX XXX XX and her husband XXX XXX, two targets under surveillance as part of Case 28, have on numerous occasions let our Agent 198 know that they would be happy to drop in on him during the 1 October National Holiday, and they have suggested that Agent 198 prepare a Mahjong table for a full day of fun. We believe that such a visit would benefit our surveillance since it would allow for emotional bonding, as well as the detection and observation of tendencies, and let us achieve the aim of controlling the movement of the targets around the time of 1 October. At the same time, their visit would also be a way to prepare the ground for further operational steps. Therefore, our concrete proposal is as follows:

To take the initiative, we should, first of all, direct the agent to extend to the pair an invitation to visit him at home. This would give XXX XXX XXX XX and XXX XXX time to prepare and avoid having them come up with an excuse and saying 'no' or putting us on the defensive by inviting the agent to come to their home. Then, we should see to it that they are invited to spend the entire day of 1 October at the agent's home. That evening, the agent and his wife may take them out for some fun and, if called for, the agent may invite them to spend the night.

It must be made very clear to Agent 198 and his wife, Agent 199, during training that to invite the couple to their home on 1 October is, on our part, an operational tactic and not an aim in itself. In this case, our aim is to further increase the intimacy in the relationship, build an emotional attachment, secure trust, and create conditions for operational work in greater depth. For this purpose, husband and wife agents (*fufu teqing*) 198 and 199 must enter the battle simultaneously, with, first of all, Agent 199 being welcoming to the friends of her husband (Agent 198) and entertaining them with all due warmth. Then, during the entire encounter and while they are all enjoying themselves, the agents are to indicate that the reason they want to become friends is because they find their guests congenial, and they enjoy their company. They should not, in the course of the conversation, dwell too much on their own problems (in particular, their historical issues). Finally, the behaviour of Agents 198 and 199 must match perfectly, and nothing must set off any alarm bells or lead the targets to believe that something is amiss.

In order to make this a success, based on what, in principle, can be obtained on the market or gotten through friendly contacts, we should prepare some non-staple food items for use by the agent. Required for this purpose are: one can of meat (pork); four *jin* of eggs; one bottle of sparkling wine; one bottle of red wine (the agents will provide beer themselves); one small chicken (already obtained and currently at the animal farm); and four *jin* of fish.[117]

Please instruct as to whether or not the above would be appropriate.

[Political Protection Division] First Section Chang Guoxing
25 September 1961

Division Chief Jiang [Changyu], please instruct.

Chang Guoxing
27 September

Agreed.

Jiang Changyu
28 September

'Could We Perhaps Do It This Way?'

According to what Agent 198 has reported, the daughter of [our operational target] XXX XXX was attending a privately-run middle school when her parents managed, through a middle school teacher by the name of Bai in Daowai city district, to get their hands on a blank letter of introduction form that, this autumn, made it possible for her to transfer to [state-run] XXX Middle School. Her parents have since become very anxious and fear being discovered. They have implored our agent to find a way of getting their daughter into a middle school that has a dormitory where she can live so as to avoid her classmates finding out.

According to our investigations, the daughter has already started to attend XXX Middle School. When we examined her school transfer letter of introduction, we discovered that the affixed official stamp is indeed a forgery. The fact that she made use of a forged official stamp and produced a bogus school transfer letter of introduction and a bogus school transcript is a very serious matter. We estimate that it is likely to have been her father who produced the forged letter of introduction and the official stamp or he had help from somebody else. The Protection Section of [her father's employer] XXXX University tells us that Secretary Li, in the university administration, had heard her children talking about how the daughter of XXX XXX had already left the privately run school without saying goodbye and was now attending XXX Middle School. They said that her father had managed to get a letter of introduction that had clinched the transfer. Secretary Li mentioned this during a meeting of trade union cadres, and

---

Operational memorandum, 'Guanyu zhihui 198 hao teqing de yijian qingshi baogao' (Request for Instructions and Opinions on Direction of Agent 198). From the same Case 28 File as Chapter 7 'Proposal to Recruit Yu X' above.

the university president also knows about it. He told the Protection Section to first seek the opinion of the municipal [Public Security] Bureau, but the university is inclined to go public about the matter.

Taking all of the above into account, in order to further increase the intimacy in the relationship between [the operational targets] XXX XXX XXX XX and XXX XXX and our agent, we are of the opinion that one may start by having XXX Middle School confront XXX XXX and having him clarify the origin of the forged letter of introduction, and then letting him know that he must involve the Bureau of Education. We then anticipate that he will ask Agent 198 for help. The agent can be instructed to respond by saying: 'I'll see what I can do', and 'I could try to have a friend in the Bureau of Culture get in touch with the Bureau of Education to resolve the matter'. Once it is resolved, the girl's parents will then feel indebted to the agent.

In practical terms, the way to proceed would be as follows:

With the assistance of the principal of XXX Middle School, approach XXX XXX and inquire about the source of the letter of introduction. When he admits that the letter of introduction is a forgery, he should be promptly told that the matter must be reported to and resolved by the Bureau of Education.

When XXX XXX XXX XX and XXX XXX turn to the agent for help, the agent may say that he will see what he can do, but as the forgery has already been discovered, he should also add that dealing with the matter may in the end be difficult. Hereupon, the agent may seek out a friend in the Bureau of Culture, invest considerable energy in the matter, and even go so far as to say [*illegible*] specifically might be able to get in touch with the municipal authorities and get the matter settled by having the Bureau of Education hush it up, thus allowing the daughter to continue with her studies.

Given the fact that many people in the university already know that XXX XXX got his daughter into [a state school] with the help of a forged letter of introduction, one should have the university leadership confront XXX XXX and subject him to criticism and education. That he forged a letter of introduction need not generally be made known to the public.

Furthermore, as concerns the operational target's visit to Shenyang. Agent 601 [of the Shenyang Public Security Bureau] has reported that XXX stayed in Shenyang for seven days during which he contacted Shenyang Medical University in professional matters and was in touch with faculty members Wang Chongxin, Su Zhongyu, and He Baoyun. During a visit to the movies together, the target was given a dozen or so pages of documents by Su Zhongu, contents unknown. During meetings

21 On Courses of Action Proposed

of the Shenyang Medical University Chemistry Teaching and Research Group, the target is alleged to have voiced reactionary opinions. The XXX University security section wants to investigate what he actually said, and once that has been determined deal with the matter in public and limit the target's future travel outside Harbin. We are of the opinion that the XXX University security section should send someone to Shenyang to investigate, given that their findings might give them *kompromat* with which to control the target's future movements.

Please comment and instruct whether or not the above proposals are appropriate.

30 October 1963

Division chief: Please, after reading and commenting, present to the bureau director for comments and instructions.

Hou Guansheng, 4 November

Agreed. Bureau Director Zhang: please examine and approve.

[Political Protection Division Deputy Chief] Liu Dedi, 5 November

We need to exploit this opportunity to [further] cultivate the agent. The problem is with the forged papers. Once they have been exposed, will the Bureau of Education actually agree to our resolving the matter in this way? Could we perhaps do it this way: the XXX Middle School orders her to quit school and the agent then, with the help of friends, manages to secure a place for her in a private school. Please look into this possibility!

[Public Security Bureau Deputy Director] Zhang Hanbin, 8 November

22 Whose Collection Requirements Should Enjoy Priority?

Like the previous item, this one (dating from late December 1963) consists of two directly related memoranda documenting operational component chiefs addressing higher echelons. In this case, two HUMINT components located in separate divisions are each asking their division superiors to mediate and resolve a dispute over who actually 'owns' the Harbin Public Security Bureau's prized Agent 151 (Yang X, whose closed Agent Personal File provided the records translated in Part V above) and whose information needs the agent was henceforth to prioritise. History is never irrelevant in disputes like this one and how far back in the past one is able, or chooses, to go in one's argumentation can often make all the difference when it comes to staking a convincing claim to something in the present. In this case, the component chief representing HUMINT in the First Division maintains that Yang X had at one point been given 'on loan' to the Fifth Division but should now be 'returned' to the First Division whose officers had in the 1950s been running him as one of their own.[118] The component chief representing HUMINT in the Fifth Division, argues on the contrary that since it had been the direct predecessor of his division that had recruited Yang X in the first place, back in 1950, he had as it were not been 'borrowed', but in 1961 simply come back to his organisational home where he should henceforth remain. In their resolution of the dispute, the division and higher echelon officers chose not to be swayed by arguments of this sort. Instead, they focused solely on what kind of operational arrangement was most likely to meet the *present* needs of all parties involved and mediated accordingly.

Translated Text

Memorandum from Section to First Division Leadership

[Deputy] Division Chief Liu Dedi,

Agent 151, Yang XXX (a member of the China Association for the Promotion of Democracy and a teacher at XXX Middle School) is one of

---

Untitled operational memoranda. From the same Agent Personal File as Chapter 14 above.

our agents among the members of the democratic parties. We use him to control Gao XXX (a member of the municipal Political Consultative Conference Standing Committee), who has been targeted by [hostile] intelligence and is a suspected *tewu* element XXX, and to monitor the states of mind and behaviour of selected democratic party members in Daowai city district. In July 1962 [*sic*], this particular agent was borrowed from us by the Fifth Division to place a suspect element in the municipal government's cadre school under operational surveillance. At the time, for the sake of adapting to a fraternal division's struggle against the enemy and after having obtained the go-ahead from [you] the division chief, we temporarily lent agent Yang XXX to the Fifth Division. In the months that have passed since July 1962 [*sic*], the Fifth Division has only forwarded nine items of intelligence to us from the agent, basically putting a stop to our work. To allow us to continue our close surveillance and control of the behaviour of the [hostile] intelligence target [Gao XXX] and the suspected *tewu* element XXX, we now ask that you consider whether you might consult Fifth Division Chief Liu [Dongjiang] and, together with him, weigh the relative priorities of the work of our two divisions. We maintain that *if* the Fifth Division were to be unable to proceed in depth with its operational surveillance of the suspect element [in the cadre school] without this particular agent, then Agent 151 should be permanently transferred to the Fifth Division. But if the Fifth Division also happens to have other agents upon whom it can rely, would it then be possible to return this agent to us, thereby allowing us to boost our work?

Please issue instructions as to the appropriateness of how to proceed.

[First Division] Third Section
25 December 1963

Memorandum from Section to Fifth Division Leadership

Division Chief Liu Dongjiang,

The agent Yang XXX (teacher at XXX Middle School), who is currently being utilised by our section, was recruited in 1950, with the help of *kompromat*, to control the activities of suspected counter-revolutionary elements on the culture and education frontlines by then Section Chief Su Deji of the First Division's Government Organ Protection Section (the predecessor of our division).

After the creation of the Fifth Division, the agent in question was operated and utilised by our division's Middle Schools Group. His successive handlers were Comrades Wang Zhaoxiang, Li Baisen, Su Deji, Li Zhansheng, and Li Shiqing. In 1955, the First Division discussed with our division the possibility of borrowing him for operational surveillance in a specific case. At the time, for the sake of adapting to a fraternal division's needs in our joint struggle and after both our section chiefs, Li Zhansheng and Li Shiqing, had asked for and obtained the go-ahead from the division chief, the agent was lent to the First Division to operate and utilise. In July 1961, because of a case calling for operational surveillance of a suspected *tewu* element, our section had Division Chief Ding Wenchun and Jiang Changyu decide, through consultation, to return this agent to the Fifth Division. At the time, the agent's work was to prioritise the needs of the Fifth Division, but at the same time the agent was to continue to provide the First Division with the information it needed. In our work, we have far from neglected directing the agent to serve the First Division, and we estimate that at least sixty items of intelligence obtained by him have been secured and swiftly shared with Comrades Dong Zhaokun (Section Chief), Chen Cheng, Ye Peichang, and Wang Zhizhong.

This agent was recruited and utilised by the Fifth Division, and we are currently directing him to control the intellectual battlefield in culture and the arts, writers and directors, and creative circles, as well as to control counter-revolutionary element Xu XXX and bad element Qiao XXX and the states of mind prevailing in Harbin's arts circles. We maintain that in order to make even more efficient use of him, and for the sake of all our operational needs, he should remain under our management while continuing, as in the past, to simultaneously provide the First Division with intelligence.

Appropriate or not, please instruct.

[Fifth Division] Third Section
27 December 1963

I have already talked to Division Chief Liu Dedi about this. The agent will continue to be operated by our division and we will, as in the past, forward to the First Division any information of relevance to them.

Liu Dongjiang

Part VII

Crisis Management

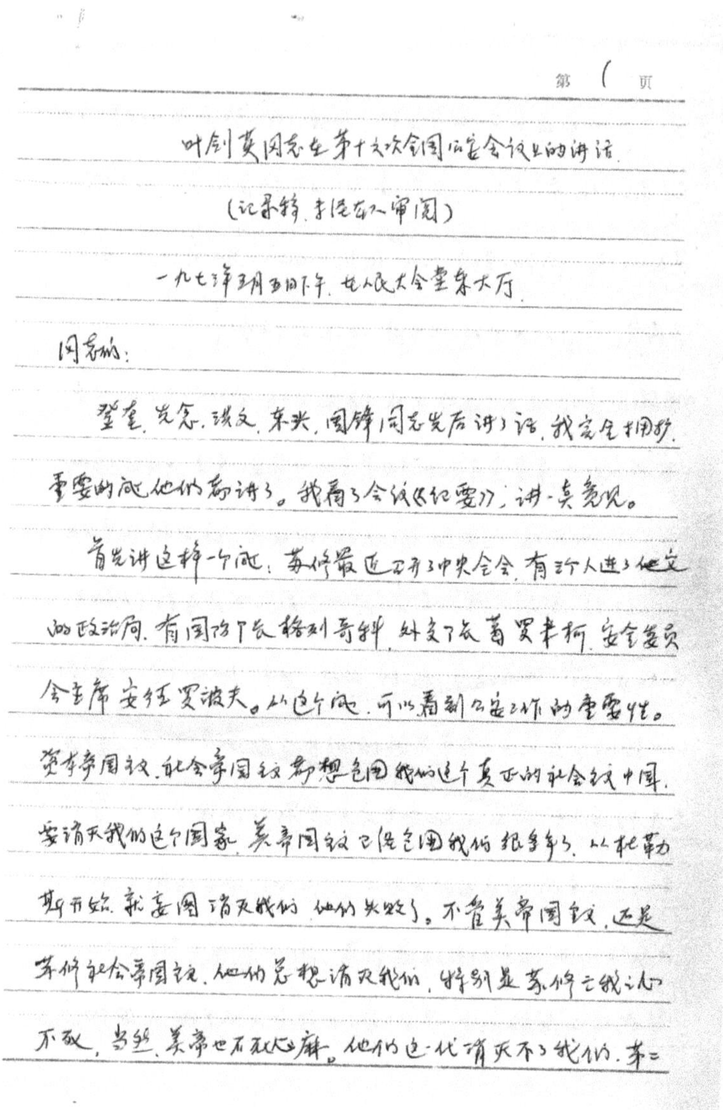

叶剑英同志在第十文次全国公安会议上的讲话

（记录稿，未经本人审阅）

一九七三年3月3日下午，在人民大会堂宴东大厅

同志们：

登奎、先念、谈文、东兴、国锋同志先后讲了话，我完全拥护。重要的向他们都讲了，我看了会议《纪要》、讲一点意见。

首先讲这样一个问题，苏修最近开了三中央全会，有三个人进了他交的政治局，有国防部长格列奇柯，外交部长葛罗米柯，安全委会主席安托罗波夫。从这个问题，可以看到公安工作的重要性。美帝国主义、社会帝国主义都想包围我们这个真正的社会主义中国。要请天我们这个国家，美帝国主义已经包围我们很多年了，从杜勒斯开始，就企图消灭我们，他们失败了。不管美帝国主义，还是苏修社会帝国主义，他们总想消灭我们，特别是苏修，要我们不敢，当然，美帝也不死心，他们还代消灭不了我们，第二

Figure 7 Marshal Ye Jianying's address to a National Public Security Conference (1973)

Introduction

The presence in society of people who secretly supply information to a domestic state security agency is seen as a necessary evil by some, while others question whether the potential benefit to society of this suspicionless investigation outweighs its cost.[119] In modern history, successfully upheld contracts between governments and silent citizen majorities have inclined the latter to accept what their national press often insists is the true state of affairs – that while such things may indeed go on *there*, they do not as a rule go on *here*. When something altogether out of the ordinary then does come to light, perceptions of it are managed meaningfully with the help of a framework of interpretation that sees uncomfortable facts merely as the exception that 'proves the rule'. Perhaps the best-known example from the Cold War Anglosphere are the extrajudicial disruptions that in 1971 became the FBI COINTELPRO scandal.[120] In Sweden, the so-called Information Bureau Affair of 1973 exposed a similar programme of covert agent infiltration of leftist, but entirely legal, NGOs and communist labour activity, on behalf of Sweden's ruling Social Democratic Party leadership and armed forces.[121]

Cold War government attempts to mitigate crises impacting HUMINT sources and methods each had their own national characteristics. The enraged public's level of tolerance differed from country to country, and some government strategies of diffusion and solution that met with acceptance in one country would have, if attempted, encountered outright rejection in another. Nonetheless, as the texts in this set suggest, transnational comparisons reveal a shared dynamic at work. In procedural scripted terms, governments took steps more alike than what any differences in their modes of governance might otherwise have led one to expect. As a first step, crisis responses involved setting up a committee to conduct an inquiry. In due course, the precise format of the committee's findings and recommendations varied, but they typically included a confidential executive summary and a longer full report, classified Top Secret or similar, depending on how delicate its findings turned out to be. The confidential executive summary outlined the findings and recommendations (Chapter 23) only to the minimum extent needed.

Potentially damaging public debate could not always be avoided, but as the next scripted step, opinions on inquiry findings and recommendations were invited from selected parties so that the government would be in a position to avoid rushing prematurely into 'possibly ill-conceived action with unforeseen repercussions'.[122] The expression of opinions here allowed lobbying: for as long as the government had yet to come down firmly in favour of any one course of action, and the findings and recommendations of inquiries continued to circulate as invitations to submit opinions, views framing domestic HUMINT in more than one way competed for attention. Ideologically driven opponents invariably insisted on framing the issue in terms of values – liberal in the case of some, revolutionary in the case of others – and accused agencies of sanctioning lawbreakers (Chapter 24). However, proponents of HUMINT as an invaluable component of a domestically oriented intelligence enterprise, on the other hand, favoured a different reading of the recommendations and maintained that any curtailment of proven collection techniques (Chapter 25) was likely to result in information deficiencies potentially playing into the hands of adversarial forces capable of endangering national security.

Meanwhile, working to the advantage of all those eager to see the crisis simply go away is what George Orwell called 'the magical properties of names. Nearly all human beings feel that a thing becomes different if you call it by a different name.'[123] The past shows that those who object to a return to the *status quo ante*, accompanied by skilful management of perceptions, have yet to find a potion able to counteract in the present what Harvard biologist Edward O. Wilson called 'a form of sympathetic magic, an expression of the near-universal belief among prescientific peoples that the manipulation of symbols and images can influence the objects they represent'.[124] Therefore, as a final step in their crisis responses, governments that master how to do things with words in politics will put just this kind of magic to good use when a decision at the highest level is finally taken.[125] Once the authority with the necessary symbolic power (Chapter 26) has issued the performative utterance that crisis resolution calls for, rescinded key doctrinal terms, and 'deconflicted' policy and public opinion, agencies are in a position to confidently announce that their offending, now former, praxis is safely history and something better (Chapter 27) has taken its place.

23 Agent Work: Findings and Recommendations of an Inquiry

This is a summary of the findings and recommendations of a 1968 inquiry into the operation of agents and 'undercover cadres' in one of China's most populous provinces. In the nationwide mass movement of the Cultural Revolution, popular resentment towards informers – branded 'despicable perfidious turncoats', 'sinister tentacles of their counter-revolutionary masters', and the like – had surfaced and refused to go away as an incendiary issue. Mao's base came to regard with animosity their very existence as a signature instrument of governance endorsed by the 'revisionist' officialdom that the Cultural Revolution targeted – persons 'within the Communist Party who are in authority and are taking the capitalist road'.[126] With much of the country under martial law, in a remarkable act of populism, at the end of 1967 Mao empowered military officers aligned with his own values to conduct determinations – province by province – of the facts surrounding the extent/severity of any illegal, improper, or unethical acts carried out specifically by agents of China's public security organs.[127] In the province of Yunnan, bordering on Burma, Laos, and Vietnam, more than 80 per cent of the agents came to be identified as bad guys 'from very dubious backgrounds, including former puppet regime military and political officers, police, gendarmerie, and intelligence operatives'.[128] In the landlocked southeastern province of Jiangxi (with a population of 25 million) an estimated 4,070 former Public Security Bureau agents were outed and subjected to public humiliation and denunciation, arrest, and imprisonment.[129] In the executive summary below, the recommendations merit careful reading; although, in principle, they favour dispensing with all further recruitment and use of agents as well as making the identities of all past and present public security agents public, they also refrain from pre-empting the results of investigations on a case-by-case basis by making a distinction between agents in general and any 'counter-revolutionary elements who have committed major crimes' that might be 'lurking among them'.

People's Liberation Army Provincial Public Security Organs Military Control Committee 'Guanyu yin'gan teqing chuli yijian' (Opinion Concerning Disposal of Undercover Cadres and Agents). Mimeographed typescript from the weeded holdings of a county-level archive.

Translated Text

'Undercover cadres' and 'agents' are the products of the Liu [Shaoqi], Deng [Xiaoping], Peng [Zhen], and Luo [Ruiqing] counter-revolutionary revisionist line and its aggressive promotion of 'isolationism' and 'mysticism' in the public security, procuracy, and legal sectors. So-called undercover cadres and agents are, for the most part, landlord, rich peasant, counter-revolutionary, bad, Rightist elements, renegades, *tewu*, Catholic priests, monks, imams, senior officers in Chiang Kai-shek's bandit army, core elements in reactionary political parties and organisations, or degenerate [Communist Party] elements. They form a counter-revolutionary fifth column created to prepare in organisational terms for the restoration of capitalism. From what the masses have brought to light, when utilisation of 'agents' peaked in our province, their number in the province as a whole exceeded 28,000. According to the original Public Security Bureau statistics for the second half of 1965, the total number of 'agents' in the province that year totalled 2,581. Although meant to discharge its 'undercover cadres' in 1965, the provincial Public Security Bureau continued to draw on nine of them.

After the founding of the People's Republic of China, most of these people were provided with entirely new identities and biographical legends. Protected by the Party Group of the provincial Public Security Bureau, they were able to survive successive political campaigns unscathed, do colossal damage and cut counter-revolutionary deals on a massive scale.

Take, for example, the big renegade and big counter-revolutionary XXX XXX who had joined the Communist Party in 1936 and then, upon his arrest in 1941, withdrew from the Party. In 1944, with the help of a Japanese *tewu*, he revived his Communist Party links and eventually managed to sneak [the *tewu*] into the Party as well. In 1948, while working on the railway, he joined the [ROC Ministry of National Defence] *tewu* organisation known as the 'Serve the People Team'. Since Liberation, he has served all along as an 'undercover cadre'. In 1964, the sinister Party Group of the provincial Public Security Bureau positioned him at the head of a Political Consultative Conference Division and had him promoted from rank 14 to rank 12. Meanwhile, the Japanese *tewu* continues to serve as a rank 17 'undercover cadre'.

Another example is XXX XXX who joined the Communist Party in 1930 and defected to the enemy and turned renegade in 1931. He served in numerous reactionary positions [before Liberation], including as a major-general heading the offices of the bandit Sun Lianzhong and as the phoney mayor of the city of Shijiazhuang. An 'agent', he now holds rank 15.

And then there is XXX XXX, a Catholic Father in the parish cathedral of XXXX municipality who, even though he organised a reactionary Legion of Mary and continued proselytising underground after Liberation, was recruited as an 'agent' and protected accordingly. He was also a physician, and when people came to him for medical help, he sexually exploited and abused the women, and even raped a sick young girl after sedating her. When this was brought to the attention of the sinister Party Group of the provincial Public Security Bureau, the Party Group did no more than admonish him.

These elements, given their massive crimes and seriously problematic pasts, must not be allowed to remain at large. In our opinion:

The Cleansing of the Class Ranks Campaign is to be employed to shed further light on the state of the contingent of 'undercover cadres' and 'agents'.[130] The true faces of these people must be unmasked, and more light must be shed on the criminal activities of the counter-revolutionary revisionist line in the public security, procuracy, and legal sectors prior to the Cultural Revolution. Powerful blows must be delivered at counter-revolutionary elements who have committed major crimes and who are lurking among the 'agents' and 'undercover cadres'.

1. The true identities of the 'agents' and 'undercover cadres' are to be disclosed to the revolutionary masses in their respective workplace units. The individuals in question should join the Cleansing of the Class Ranks Campaign and submit to investigation by the masses. All their public security files and other records are to be transferred to their respective workplace units. All payment of secret salaries to 'agents' and 'undercover cadres' are to end.
2. 'Agents' and 'undercover cadres' who have maintained illicit contacts with foreign countries and have provided them with intelligence or who actively engage in counter-revolutionary activity are major criminal elements who are to be detained and investigated by the Military Control Committees (Groups). All of their criminal activities are to be thoroughly investigated and they themselves are to be punished according to law. The disposal in the fields of religion and united front work of 'agents' and 'undercover cadres' who, for a variety of reasons, cannot be made to join the Cleansing of the Class Ranks Campaign in their respective workplace units is to be suitably managed by the Military Control Committees (Groups) in charge.
3. Based on the spirit of the Centre's relevant texts as well as their own command of the concrete circumstances, the Military Control Committees (Groups) are to share what they know with the workplace units home to 'agents' and 'undercover cadres'. Those units are to be

briefed on the relevant policies and told to responsibly conduct serious investigations of the politics, pasts, and all criminal activities of the concerned individuals. The latter are to be handled differently depending on the nature of their problems and crimes. A strict distinction is to be made between antagonistic contradictions and non-antagonistic contradictions and policy in this respect must be adhered to. Attempts are to be made to win them over by explaining Party policy to them and by showing them a way out. They are to be encouraged to come clean about all of their criminal activities, to turn against those with whom they had wrongly sided, to expose the evildoers and the damage done, and, in this way, to atone for their own crimes. Strict precautions are to be taken to prevent suicides, acts of violence, escapes, and so on.

4. If discovered in the course of the investigation of these people, matters touching on state secrets or incidents seriously implicating members of the public security, procuracy, and legal sectors prior to the Cultural Revolution are to be promptly reported to the higher levels.

PLA Military Control Committee
of the Public Security Organs in XXX Province
December 1968

24 Opponents: 'Shitting and Pissing on the Heads of the People'

In this exposé, officers in a police academy in the coastal province of Zhejiang (population thirty-three million) provide feedback on recommendations, such as those in the above inquiry. They use a miscarriage of justice to pick apart and invalidate the argumentation in favour of using agents that had prevailed in China's public security sector up to 1967. Exploiting societal grievances in their narrative, they describe agents in the harshest possible terms as having 'capitalised on their legalised agent status to bully and ride roughshod over the masses' and they lobby for a complete dismantling of all remnants of what they insist had been nothing less than a 'dictatorship of agents' enforced by 'the handful who held power in the old public security organs'. The authors are insiders with firsthand knowledge of operational details and the practice of absolving agents involved in activities of dubious legality from criminal responsibility on the recommendation of the public security organs. Although many of their demands for reform were accepted and implemented locally, their pithy formulation 'dictatorship of agents' never gained much traction outside of Zhejiang, and it was called into question by senior officers from the Ministry of Public Security in Beijing who visited the province on a fact-finding mission in the autumn of 1970.[131]

Translated Text

The unjust court sentencing and execution of poor peasant Dong Changbao and his son, Dong Renhuo, in Yongkang county in 1958 was yet another heinous crime committed by the handful who held power in the old public security, procuracy, and legal sectors and who relied on agents to subject the labouring people to blood-stained oppression. It is

---

'Bokai "teqing zhuanzheng lun" de san zhang huapi' (Strip Off the Three Disguises of the 'Agent Dictatorship' Thesis), in *Geming da pipan xuanbian* (Selected Revolutionary Great Criticisms) (N.P.: Struggle-Criticism-Transformation Cadre School of the Public Security Organs in Zhejiang Province, January 1970), pp. 75–79. Photocopy in Maoist Legacy Collection, University of Freiburg.

also ironclad evidence of the old public security, procuracy, and legal sectors enforcing a bourgeois dictatorship.

What must be pointed out is that this massive injustice is but one of countless examples typical of the damage done by agents in our province. The crimes committed by agents as a whole are too many to mention. For seventeen years prior to the Cultural Revolution, the agent contingent provided for by the old public security organs committed every conceivable evil, making one's blood boil with anger. Agents were able to exploit their status to get away with things like counter-revolutionary networking on a massive scale, the organisation of counter-revolutionary groups, development of counter-revolutionary 'underground armed forces', and the stealthy pursuit of counter-revolutionary activity. Claiming to be acting on behalf of the Communist Party, they gulled, hoaxed, and bamboozled, extorted and racketeered, engaged in speculation and profiteering, and took their share of the spoils of robbery – while ensuring that they were not personally implicated – and they did massive damage to social order. They capitalised on their legalised agent status to bully and ride roughshod over the masses, and in so doing they acted as a special task force of the old public security, procuracy, and legal sectors to oppress the labouring people. In addition, they took advantage of their extraordinary relationship with the public security organs to offer bribes and to buy off people, offer and provide sex, and corrupt the public security officer contingent as a whole by dragging its members into the mire. In short, there is no evil that the agents did not do, and they are guilty of countless crimes. They are little Chiang Kai-sheks who, having crawled on top of them, were shitting and pissing on the heads of the people.

To cover up their criminal plot of enforcing a bourgeois dictatorship with the help of agents, the handful who held power in the old public security organs concocted a complete assortment of counter-revolutionary nonsense that boasted preposterously of the miraculous utility of agents. They spouted rubbish, such as: 'Agents are an indispensable operational resource'; 'Agents can play special roles that members of the ordinary masses cannot'; and 'Agents make up an important component of public security capacity building'. This is all truly absurd to the extreme and reactionary through and through! It must be thoroughly exposed and bitterly denounced.

First, the thesis that 'agents are an indispensable operational resource': To begin with, let us have a look at what sort of people the agents are. Everyone knows that a majority of the altogether 7,000 agents in Zhejiang province are landlord, rich peasant, counter-revolutionary or bad elem-

24 Opponents: 'Shitting and Pissing on the Heads of the People' 219

ents, hardened robbers and thieves, and local riffraff and loafers, hooligans, or dregs of society idling around and doing no decent work. The four agents utilised by the public security organs in the Yongkang county unjust case were an ex-captain in the army of the puppet regime, a member of the local riffraff and active counter-revolutionary element who had organised a counter-revolutionary group, a former public security officer in custody for manslaughter, and a criminal on death row. Can bad people like this really be relied upon as operational resources? No, they cannot, absolutely not! Our great leader Chairman Mao teaches us: 'Whether in socialist revolution or in socialist construction, it is necessary to solve the question of whom to rely on, whom to win over, and whom to oppose.' In operational work, what fundamentally distinguishes a proletarian dictatorship from a bourgeois dictatorship is the proletarian dictatorship's reliance on the broad popular masses and not on the ox-monsters and snake-demons. If we sum up our experience and 'concentrate it into one point', we find that the dictatorship of the proletariat is 'a people's democratic dictatorship under the leadership of the working class (through the Communist Party) and based upon the alliance of workers and peasants'. A dictatorship of the bourgeoisie, in contrast, to condense it into one point as well, relies on counter-revolutionaries to exercise dictatorship over the broad popular masses. An absolute majority of agents are no more than reactionary bad elements, even including some counter-revolutionary fanatics. The classes they represent are the landlord class and the reactionary bourgeoisie, and, as such, they are targets of the people's democratic dictatorship. The outcome of relying on these agents to crack cases can only be the shielding of the real enemies and letting them off the hook, while attacking and falsely incriminating the good guys. It can only be to make it as convenient as possible for the agents to attempt a counter-revolutionary coup and restoration of the old order, to engage in wanton counter-revolutionary persecution, and to impose a bourgeois dictatorship over the proletariat. The performance of the agents in Yongkang county proves this perfectly. The nonsense that 'agents are an indispensable operational resource' concocted by the old public security organs serves no purpose other than to organise the counter-revolutionary class ranks and turn them into a resource to be relied upon in a counter-revolutionary coup. In both ancient and present times, in both China and abroad, this is how the reactionary classes behaved. To safeguard their reactionary rule and to buttress their own counter-revolutionary class ranks, they remain constantly on the lookout for all kinds of ox-monsters and snake-demons that can be recruited. Didn't the Soviet revisionist renegade clique, in order to meet its own anti-China, anti-Communist, and anti-People needs, collude, join forces with, and enter into a counter-revolutionary 'Holy Alliance' with American imperialism and the reactionaries of all countries? Didn't the big renegade Liu Shaoqi, as he sought to usurp the leadership of our Party and government with the aim of restoring capitalism, also do everything in his power to gather around him vast numbers of renegades, *tewu*, landlord, rich peasant, counter-revolutionary, bad, and Rightist elements to build a bourgeois headquarters? By providing for large numbers of agents and organising counter-revolutionary 'underground armed forces', weren't the old public security organs also taking orders from their sinister boss Liu Shaoqi and preparing an 'indispensable resource' to be relied upon to restore capitalism?

Second, the thesis that 'agents can play special roles that members of the ordinary masses cannot': What are these special roles? In the words of the handful who held power in the old public security organs, 'it is easier for agents to gain access to the criminal underworld and to develop contacts there. Their use facilitates infiltration of the enemy ranks and penetration operations.' This is all pure deceit. Our great leader Chairman Mao teaches us: 'The counter-revolutionary elements are not so slow-witted; those tactics of theirs are very cunning and ruthless.' 'How do they succeed in deceiving us by their false appearances while furtively doing the things we least expect? All this is blank to thousands upon thousands of well-intentioned people.' In the Yongkang county unjust case, agent XXX XXX had since 1950 exploited his agent status to organise six different counter-revolutionary groups, one after the other, and to recruit well over a hundred 'little agents' of his. With his henchmen and underlings in every corner, he assumed the role of a commander, issued orders, and ran countywide counter-revolutionary operations. *That* was the counter-revolutionary essence and truth behind the claim, held by the handful in the old public security organs, that 'it is easier for agents to gain access to the criminal underworld and to develop contacts there'.

In addition, the so-called 'special roles' of agents also find expression in the special ability these people possess to cruelly injure the working people. In order to frame Dong Chenbao and his son, the two agents conducting 'in-prison surveillance' in the Yongkang county unjust case came up with one venomous scheme after the other, which they presented to the handful in the old public security organs. They set trap after trap starting [unsuccessfully] with the ruse of inflicting injuries on themselves to win the confidence of their victims, then [successfully] managing to trick and, by fabricating false confessions of their own, deceive Dong and his son into admitting to bogus charges. They even went so far as to concoct a prison escape plan that they said would allow them all to head

24 Opponents: 'Shitting and Pissing on the Heads of the People' 221

for the mountains and become bandits. The two agents played out a full repertoire of sinister and ruthless counter-revolutionary tricks and in so doing they were indeed able to 'play special roles that members of the ordinary masses cannot'.

Here we can see ever so clearly that the claim, made by the handful who held power in the old public security organs, that agents can 'play special roles that members of the ordinary masses cannot' has nothing to do with special roles in the cracking of cases; it is all about serving a counter-revolutionary coup. A host of facts from the seventeen years prior to the Cultural Revolution prove this beyond a doubt. It was the agents in their special roles upon whom the handful in the old public security organs relied when they recruited deserters and traitors, enlisted the services of ox-monsters and snake-demons, organised counter-revolutionary 'underground armed forces', and set about to extend their claws overseas to collude with imperialism, revisionism, and the reactionaries of all countries in acts of subversion and sabotage. It was also the agents – now in the special roles of hatchet men – that the handful in the old public security organs made use of to repress the working people and to operate a bourgeois dictatorship. In a nutshell, in every instance it was upon the special role of agents that the handful in the old public security organs relied as they maintained illicit relations with the enemy, provided the enemy with supplies, sustained the enemy, and repressed the working people. To strip off the camouflage, the so-called 'special roles' of the agents are special because they draw on years of accumulated past counter-revolutionary experiences, on capacity for counter-revolutionary action, and a full repertoire of fascist dictatorship skills. These were precisely the 'special roles' that the handful in the old public security organs needed most of all to restore capitalism.

Third, the thesis that 'agents make up an important component of public security capacity building': This would suggest that the public security organs should develop agents on a massive scale, recruit agents in large numbers, and devote extensive resources to cultivate agents, and it was, indeed, precisely what the handful in the old public security organs did for seventeen years. They sweated blood, and, at a cost of millions of yuan, set up and painstakingly operated an enormous counter-revolutionary agent contingent of more than 7,000 members. They not only utilised agents in political operational work but in targeting ordinary crime as well. They not only ran case agents but also what they referred to as control agents and investigation agents. Agents were 'all over the place' and could be found in every corner of society. They had penetrated all sectors, including politics, economics, culture, and science. In order to further cultivate their agent contingent, the handful in the old public security organs used every means at their disposal to impose a complete array of protection measures. The bigger the counter-revolutionary, the better the protection he would be accorded; the more evil his crimes, the more all-encompassing the care he would be provided. Under the pretext of needing to ensure that operations would not be compromised, they had agents positioned in all departments, with their true identities concealed, entrusted with heavy responsibilities, given high salaries, and all along being shielded and made useful. They let agents set up clandestine premises or they permitted them to operate their own small businesses or to manage their own private stalls, allowing them to do as they please without any state interference. They even went so far as to have the public security organs provide the capital for the establishment of counter-revolutionary entities, like the Four Big Corporations, to serve as 'sanctuaries' and 'air raid shelters' for ox-monsters and snake-demons and as 'liaison stations' and 'base camps' of counter-revolutionary activity.[132] Claiming they had to give full play to the initiative of their agents, they showed care and concern for them politically as well as economically in every possible way. In successive political campaigns, the handful in the old public security organs protected their agents and ensured their survival, shielding them from being attacked by the people. During holidays and celebrations, the handful in the old public security organs always made a special point of presenting their agents with gifts and treating them to banquets, thus greatly boosting enemy morale. Finally, when it came to caring for their agents in economic terms, they were even more ready to do their utmost, granting whatever they requested and even going so far as to making sure that the sons and daughters of their agents were able to enter higher-grade schools, or join the military, or find the jobs they coveted, and so on. All of this shows that what the handful in the old public security organs did as they engaged in public security capacity building was to organise counter-revolutionary 'underground armed forces' and to turn the dictatorship of the proletariat into a dictatorship of the bourgeoisie.

Chairman Mao pointed out that 'what is false is false; disguises must be stripped away'. Stripping away the above three disguises, the counter-revolutionary features of the handful in the old public security organs are completely laid bare. They did not run agents on a massive scale in order to operationally crack cases; their real criminal aim was to stage a counter-revolutionary coup to restore the old order.

25 Proponents: 'An Indispensable Operational Resource'

Given their disruptive impact on the public security *modus operandi*, the kind of recommendations made in Chapter 24 were quietly resisted in many quarters where public security officers dragged their feet or otherwise declined to endorse what Mao's base was calling for. In Shenyang, the officers now in charge of the Public Security Bureau that He Xia, the author of Text No. 2 above, had once headed, continued to operate agents in all but name. Spoken of locally as 'monitoring and control resources', they were positioned where they could 'effectively control the activities of enemy operatives and in real-time monitor the movements and attitudes of operational targets'.[133] Elsewhere, including in the Ministry of Public Security, as the excerpts from two classified texts (from 1971) below illustrate, those who favoured the retention of agents also stressed the importance of retaining the crucial informational advantage provided by HUMINT. In the first excerpt, military officers on a peacekeeping mission in one fractious central China prefecture are lobbying for expanded use of agents ('henceforth to be uniformly referred to as informants rather than as agents'). In the second excerpt, a vice-minister of Public Security in Beijing reminds senior colleagues nationwide that a much-needed revival of the system of agents ('that is to say, what we now call "informants"') that he himself favours, does, in order to generate due results, call for the reinstatement and promotion of competent older case officers.

Translated Text

'Reinforce in Accordance with Chairman Mao's Policy'

In accordance with our great leader Chairman Mao's teaching that 'public security organs must conduct more systematic operational work' and on the basis of stronger Party Committee leadership and implementation

---

Excerpt from People's Liberation Army Prefectural Public Security Organs Military Control Committee, 'Guanyu zhengzhi baowei gongzuo yijian' (Opinion Concerning Political Protection Work). Mimeographed typescript, from the weeded holdings of a county-level archive.

of the mass line, covert assets (henceforth to be uniformly referred to as informants rather than as agents) capacity building and utilisation of necessary technical operational instruments are to be reinforced so as to allow us to engage in covert struggle energetically as well as shrewdly and to effectively mitigate and strike at acts of sabotage by *tewu*, spies, and hidden counter-revolutionary elements. ...

Reinforce covert asset capacity building in accordance with Chairman Mao's policy of having 'well-selected cadres working underground':

(1) Targets selected for recruitment [to serve as informants] should primarily be politically reliable individuals in positions that allow them to observe the enemy's circumstances. Also permissible is the exploitation, for specific purposes, of elements who have split off from the enemy camp and surrendered completely. One must, however, use Mao Zedong Thought to strengthen the education of such people and, when utilising them, heighten one's vigilance, draw clear demarcation lines, and guard against being duped by them.

(2) In accordance with the spirit of the directives issued by the Military Control Committee of the provincial Public Security organs, informants are to operate mainly in decent-sized municipalities in or around places and sites where the threat level merits concern; in important mountain regions and regional peripheries where the threat level merits concern; in proximity of prominent and fairly prominent reactionary elements in the community of united front personages; and among spies and suspected spy elements in the foreign expatriate community. Informants may also be recruited and utilised for specific major cases, but as soon as their mission is over, their utilisation should be suspended. When the circumstances of a counter-revolutionary group or a reactionary secret society can be clarified by relying on the masses and by [overt] investigative work, as a norm one should not opt for the use of covert means. When the utilisation of informants proves indispensable, it must be strictly controlled, and it must cease as soon as the case in question has been cracked. Erroneous practices, such as 'using a long line to catch a big fish' or 'incitement to commit a crime', are to be firmly opposed.

(3) In so far as the individual informants are concerned, they are not to complete any formalities or be given any titles. The leadership is to exercise direct management, and it shall assign a specific officer to the running and utilisation of each informant. In the process of their utilisation, the political and ideological education of the informants is to be strengthened and their ideological orientation subjected to timely monitoring and periodic assessment. Informants who serve no

function are to be cleansed out as the occasion demands. Informants who do bad things are to be dealt with swiftly and sternly.

(4) Endorsement and limits of authority to recruit: the recruitment of informants must, without exception, be examined at the prefectural level and may proceed only once endorsement has been granted at the provincial level.

August 1971

'Chairman Mao Always Paid Great Attention to Intelligence Obtained in This Way'

Unless we are able to make really good use of our old public security officers, it will be very difficult for us to accomplish the public security mission that the Party has given us. It will also be very difficult for us to actually enforce the minutes of the Fifteenth Public Security Conference. Beijing recently uncovered a very important lead, but the comrade who had managed the case in question [before 1967] had been sent down to the countryside, and there was no one else around who was on top of the matter. Within two days of his return, after having been briefed on the lead, this comrade was able to link it to past intelligence, which clarified what was going and settled the entire case. Without our old officers, this case would have remained pending. This is one example.

Also, here and there we still have democratic personages who used to be operational surveillance targets. In the past, as a means of keeping them under surveillance, we operated agents (that is to say, what we now call 'informants') in their proximity who regularly updated us on their circumstances. Chairman Mao always paid great attention to the intelligence we obtained in this way. During the Great Cultural Revolution, as part of our attack on mysticism and closed door-ism, without due analysis we suspended all use of agents and we saw our links being severed in our operational surveillance of those democratic personages. We severed our links, but our enemy did not sever his. During these past two years, the enemy has sought, in every possible way imaginable, to keep his links active. We have been idle, but the enemy has been 'at work'. His links may have been reactivated, but we may not have been aware of it. Therefore, in operational work it just will not do to rely solely on new hands. Without the old hands, if everyone is a rookie when this line of work is reactivated,

Excerpt from 'Li Zhen tongzhi zai shengshi zizhiqu gongan jiguan fuzeren zuotanhuishang de jianghua' (Comrade Li Zhen's Speech at a Meeting of Senior Officers in the Public Security Organs of Provinces, Municipalities, and Autonomous Regions), 24 December 1971. Printed document marked 'Stenographic record not checked by speaker. Solely for reference'. In Maoist Legacy Collection, University of Freiburg.

its successful implementation will be very difficult. It is just not possible to strengthen public security work by relying solely on new hands and not relying on any of the old officers; unless the new and the old join forces, it will be impossible to strengthen public security work.

Recently, we have again faced the same problem. There is a major case, and our old comrades have been able to very quickly get their contacts up and running and very quickly get a grip on what is going on. If we are going to engage the enemy in a covert struggle, we have to know his circumstances because, otherwise, we will not be able to go on the offensive. Right now, to be honest, we are very much on the defensive. The enemy is operating in the shadows, whereas we are out there in the open. The enemy can see us very clearly, but as we watch him, we cannot see him clearly. Now the only things we know about the enemy's movements come via Guangdong province, but it is very little.

As long as we remain incapable of infiltrating the enemy and, in that way, get a handle on the enemy's situation, we will always remain on the defensive. In this line of work, it is very important to reactivate some of our past agent (i.e., 'informant') contacts; this is very important. But our new hands are not yet up to it. I do not mean to say that our new hands are never going to be up to it, but they need to study and learn so that our work can be resumed more quickly. For our work to expand quickly, we cannot proceed in a roundabout way; instead, we have to rely on the old comrades. This is why I maintain that having the young and the old join forces is a big thing. Joining forces, with the old leading along the young, is very important, and it is the only way forward. On numerous occasions, the Premier has said that without the old officers serving as core elements in our contingent as a whole, we shall not be successful.

26 The Government Advocates a Return to the *Status Quo Ante*

In January 1973, after four long years, China's Ministry of Public Security was finally able to share with public security officers performative utterances by Premier Zhou Enlai that brought the crisis in domestic HUMINT work to a long overdue close. The proposed resolution, already hinted at during a national conference of public security officers convened by the Ministry in the winter of 1970–1971, had up to this point remained pending. In Zhou's remarks circulated by the Ministry, the doctrinal term 'agent' was officially rescinded and in its stead the Premier gave the officers closest to the problem a policy mandate to unequivocally reactivate the term 'informants'. The immediate task of the now rebranded agents differed little from what it had been prior to the Cultural Revolution, again including long-term monitoring of the views of a cross-section of communities believed to be hostile to the government and detection of changes in attitudes, trends, and undercurrents in society. As part of this rebranding and capacity *re*-building exercise, the Ministry drew attention to modified best-practice solutions by the municipal Public Security Bureau in the capital that were to be held up for study and emulation nationwide.

Translated Text

In November 1972, in the course of talking about public security and protection work, Premier Zhou issued important directives on reactivating and developing informants.[134] Below are his key points (wording not checked by the Premier):

The Premier said the Great Proletarian Cultural Revolution resulted in an ideological mobilisation and a mobilisation of the masses. The major weakness in our work now is that we are no longer sufficiently in touch with what is happening in society. The first issue that must be resolved is in the public security sector, where informants must be reactivated and

---

Ministry of Public Security, 'Guanyu chuanda Zhou zongli dui huifu he jianshe ermu gongzuo zhishi' (On the Transmission of Premier Zhou's Directives Concerning Reactivation and Development of Informants). OCR transcript in Chinese library database, accessed in 2012.

results must be achieved before the end of this year. Our contacts among foreign expatriates, for example, were in some respects quite useful. If you do not use them, there really are no other people who can play the same role.

The Premier said that in society and in people's daily lives the neighbourhood residents' organisations play a role, and in 90 per cent of our work we rely on them and on their ability to promote justice among the masses. But the [community] informants we used to have are no longer functioning. We no longer receive timely reports and, as a result, we cannot promptly resolve matters.

The Premier's directives are very important, and we expect you to study and discuss them conscientiously, see them in the context of your own actual circumstances, and draw up a plan for the reactivation and development of informants. You are to solicit the opinions of the Party committee of your province, municipality, or autonomous region, and once they have endorsed it, your plan should be implemented under leadership and in a systematic fashion. A copy of the plan should be forwarded to the Ministry of Public Security for the record.

For your research and reference, we now share with you a document on the positive reactivation and recruitment of informants carried out by the Beijing Municipal Public Security Bureau:

Beijing Municipal Public Security Bureau Positively Expands Reactivation and Recruitment of Informants

In accordance with the important directives issued by Premier Zhou on 5 November 1972 on reactivating informants, the Military Control Committee of the Beijing Municipal Public Security Bureau took the denunciation of Lin Biao and rectification of work styles as the key link and, after determining right and wrong on the basis of political lines, began to positively expand the recruitment of informants.[135] By the end of 1972, some *nnnn* informants had already either been reactivated or recruited. Including those recruited in the preceding two years, the municipal Public Security Bureau now operates a total of *nnnn* informants. These may be divided into two categories: one is that of the political operational informants, *nnn* in total; the other is that of the confidential guardians, *nnn* in total, who are utilised in the fight against common criminals and in safeguarding key factories, mines, and enterprises. The reactivation and recruitment of informants not only contribute positively to our surveillance and control of the intelligence activities of the missions in China of the imperialist, Western, and revisionist nations, and of the *tewu* of the Chiang Kai-shek gang, but also to the monitoring of threats and trends in society in general and our understanding of the prevailing political ideological state of upper-strata reactionary elements. However, since the time devoted to the reactivation and recruitment of informants has been relatively brief, the Beijing informant contingent as a whole remains small in terms of numbers and weak in terms of quality. Since the contingent is still far from able to meet the real needs of the struggle, the reactivation and recruitment of informants has to continue and be intensified.

3 January 1973

The contents of this document may be shared orally with the public security organs in prefectures and large and medium-sized cities.

19 January 1973

27 Deconfliction: *Provisional Guidelines on Informant Capacity Building*

These guidelines regarding the recruitment and use of agents (here referred to as the development of informants) show how, after years of uncertainty, one operational component responsible for the security of critical infrastructure responded to the demands of China's central government for a revival of agent work. Subjects covered in the guidelines include the principles and demands to guide recruitment, the scope and qualifications of targets, deactivation, authority to recruit, running, record keeping, and more. Some minor modifications aside, there is no alternative paradigm at work here, and what the guidelines propose differs little from what had been the case prior to 1967. As far as HUMINT is concerned, the Cultural Revolution (1966–1969) had now become something more akin to an aberration than, as originally intended, 'a new stage in the development of the socialist revolution in our country, a deeper and more extensive stage'.[136] The characterisation of capacity building, in the opening sentence of the *Provisional Guidelines*, as an 'extremely urgent matter', is not solely in local compliance with Zhou Enlai's November 1972 'important directives' (as conveyed in Chapter 26 above) but is likely in part to have been prompted by the presence of ever-more foreigners in Beijing due to the full or partial normalisation of relations with countries like Japan, West Germany, the United States, and so on, in the winter of 1972–1973.

Translated Text

Given the present state of affairs, informant capacity building (*ermu jianshe*) has become an extremely urgent matter. It concerns an instrument we cannot dispense with as we seek to boost our capacity to fight hidden enemies. Its utilisation is a serious public security and protection task. Therefore, in accordance with Chairman Mao's teaching that 'the

---

Beijing Railway Sub-Bureau Public Security Sub-Division Military Control Group *Circular* No. A-11 (1973), 'Guanyu ermu jianshe gongzuo de shixing yijian' (Provisional Guidelines on Informant Capacity Building). Mimeographed typescript in a file of documents from 1973 in the archive of the Nankou railway police station. Archive weeded on an unknown date.

public security organs must conduct more systematic operational work', the spirit of the Fifteenth National Public Security Conference, and the opinions of the Beijing Public Security Bureau and the Public Security Division [of the regional Beijing Railway Bureau] concerning the development of informants (*jianshe ermu gongzuo*), and while taking the concrete situation in our own [Beijing Railway Sub-Bureau Public Security] Sub-Division into account, we have drawn up the following provisional guidelines:

Principles and Demands to Guide the Recruitment of Informants

1. The recruitment of informants (*jianli ermu*) must proceed from Chairman Mao's principle of having 'well-selected cadres working underground'. In accordance with necessity and capability, cautious recruitment efforts are to be initiated immediately, in response to leads in case-related operational activity and in locations where the threat level merits concern, to allow us to identify the enemy, monitor his movements, and control and strike at him. In this context, one must 'proceed with energy and caution', carefully pick targets for recruitment, emphasise quality, and stress practical results. Informant recruitment should, in a planned fashion, aim at meeting the actually prevailing needs in the concerned unit. Once conditions are ripe, the target should be recruited, and once its utilisation is endorsed, it should be put to use. There should be no recruitment in batches, but our aspiration is to see effective results by the end of the first half of the year [1973]. Refrain from blind and chaotic recruitment in pursuit of quantity and do not go down the old disastrous road of 'the agent is the single most important tool'. At the same time, guard against letting recruitment efforts be guided by an overcautious ideology that ties one's hands and feet.
2. The general policy of combining reliance on the broad masses of the People with specialised work must, by necessity, be correctly interpreted and applied. Where an issue or a situation or a case-related operational activity or lead and so on can be handled with the help of Communist Party and Youth League members, Public Order Protection Committees, and activists among the masses, there is, in principle, no need for informants to be recruited. Operative use of informants inside the Communist Party or among the People is strictly prohibited. Informants are only to be used where ordinary overt work cannot proceed and in order to deal with enemies.
3. In informant capacity building, Party committee leadership must, by necessity, prevail from beginning to end. Informant capacity

building calls for particularly strong Party leadership. To keep it secret, under some pretext, from the Party committee or to maintain less stringent Party leadership by citing its special nature as an excuse is wrong. Consequently, when profiling potential informants as well as when selecting, developing, utilising, or writing them off, one must always report to the leading comrades on the Party committee of one's unit. One must inform the Party committee of the aim and purpose of the recruitment and one must obtain and follow the instructions of the Party committee; an informant that the Party committee rejects may under no circumstances be recruited. During utilisation, one should, at regular intervals, report to the Party committee how work is progressing and actively draw on the committee for leadership and monitoring. When an informant is to be written off, the Party committee should be given a summary of what has been achieved. Post-termination arrangements require careful and skilful handling, and they must be endorsed by the Party committee.

Scope of Recruitment and Qualifications of Prospective Informants

Circumstances in our Sub-Division suggest that recruitment of informants should take place mainly in the proximity of the targets of case-related operational activity and in locations where the threat level merits concern. Targets of case-related operational activity refers to targets that, with superior level public security organ endorsement, have been identified as those of either [predicated] case investigations or leads motivating operational work. Locations where the threat level merits concern include train carriages, scheduled runs, or crews where there is a relatively strong presence of staff belonging to the social bases of imperialism, revisionism, and reaction.

The qualifications of prospective informants must satisfy the Ministry of Public Security's *Notification Concerning the Strengthening of Secret Operational Assets and Utilisation of Operational Instruments* [of 19 March 1971]. First of all, the prospective informants must be politically reliable and in a position to get close to the operational target and to do work for us. Alternatively, they may be elements formerly within the enemy camp who, after having unconditionally surrendered to us, can be used to execute a specific mission.

As a qualification, politically reliable means that issues in the prospective informants' political histories have already been examined and clarified, or in the case of major historical issues, a formal conclusion has been reached after investigation. The prospective informants' current behaviour should indicate an ability to close ranks with us, genuine support for our Party and the socialist order, and support for Chairman Mao's revolutionary line.

Cleanse the Original Agent Contingent and Reactivate Individuals with Utility Value

With respect to the agents utilised prior to the Great Cultural Revolution, units are to re-examine them from the principled point of view of 'energy and caution, necessity and capability'. On no account are they to reactivate those former agents whose political past has not yet been conclusively clarified, or who have already been compromised and are known to the masses, or who are no longer in a position to serve, or who themselves are no longer willing to work for us, or, in the opinion of the Party committee, are unsuited to the task. Those who meet the following criteria may, however, be reactivated:

1. Their political pasts have already been conclusively clarified and they are genuinely supportive of our Party and socialism.
2. In the Great Cultural Revolution, they only reported to the Army Propaganda Team and their unit leadership that they had been doing work for us, or admitted as much to the masses, but only to a limited few, and they are now needed and able to work for us and in a position to do so.
3. Those who were shaken up in the course of the Cultural Revolution but are able to deal with the issue correctly, not displaying any hostility and willing to resume working for us.

[Assuming they meet the above criteria] prospective recruits who originally served as protection agents may become confidential guardians (a document on the criteria for confidential guardians has already been issued), while those who had operational targets may now become informants.[137] In each instance, however, as a matter of procedure, their altered status must receive higher-level endorsement.

Endorsement and Limits of Authority to Recruit

1. The recruitment of an informant linked to a case-related operational activity must be endorsed by the unit endorsing the operational investigation of the case or the lead. Such an informant is to have as his case officer the senior comrade leading the investigation.
2. Informants positioned in sites where the threat level merits concern may be recruited with the agreement of the Party committee of the

Beijing Railway Sub-Bureau and with examination and endorsement by the head of its Public Security Sub-Division. Their recruitment is to be reported for the record to the [regional] Railway Public Security Division.
3. The informants themselves are not to complete any formalities. It is the unit recruiting them that is to fill out the *Informant Recruitment Permission Form* and present it to higher levels for approval and instructions. When informants are to be written off, the same authority limits apply.

The Running and Utilisation of Informants

1. In the course of running and utilising informants, one must abide by Chairman Mao's teaching that 'The [political] line is the key link; once it is grasped, everything falls into place.' The key link should be line education; one should regularly educate informants about the overall situation, threat levels, and the need to safeguard clandestinity. One should aspire to see them acquire immunity [from malign influences]. One should seek to develop in them a correct recognition of the excellent domestic and international situations, raise their class- and line-struggle awareness, promote in them a readiness to be loyal to the dictatorship of the proletariat, help them denounce and resist [malign] influences emanating from hostile classes and degenerate forces, boost their political immunity, and repeatedly drive home the imperative of safeguarding operational clandestinity. When seeking to obtain information, one must not resort to counter-operational tactics, engage in 'incitement to commit a crime', or slip into subjectivism. Reporting should be timely, accurate, truthful, and reliable. Informants should be given opportunities to develop covert combat skills, agility, and flexibility in order to be able to fight the enemy even more effectively.
2. One should persist in sharing missions, policies, and tactics with the informants, and monitor their performance. Their activity and reporting should be assessed and analysed at regular intervals, primarily with respect to intelligence sources and the means used to elicit intelligence, whether the content has substance, whether its key points are clear, whether it contains contradictions, and whether it matches the overall threat level and the regular behaviour of the operational targets, and so on. When called for, steps should be taken to investigate and assess the informants' work, in particular in the case of informants who come from the hostile classes. In the process of utilising such informants, one must heighten one's vigilance and not be deceived.

3. The running of informants must abide by the principle of 'common soldiers matched against other common soldiers; generals matched against other generals'. This is in order to ensure that the running of the informant is efficient and that the informant's motivation is fully mobilised. Officers are to regularly monitor the thinking and attitudes of their informants, put politics in command, and employ Mao Zedong Thought to educate them. Two officers are to be present at each rendezvous with an informant. Older officers should be encouraged to mentor younger officers, and the young and the old should join forces. In principle, male comrades are not to run female informants nor are female comrades to run male informants.
4. When it comes to how the informants are to be run, there should be clear contact routines and each rendezvous must be preceded by thorough research and ample preparation, while in the aftermath, the relevant leadership must be given a briefing, and a concise contact report must be written and filed for reference. Informant work is to be examined and assessed once a quarter, and lessons are to be learnt and experiences are to be summed up, all in order to gradually raise work efficacy.

Informant Files Must Be Created

On the day the recruitment of the informant is endorsed, an informant file must be created. To be deposited in it are records endorsing recruitment of the informant, his autobiography and background information, copies of conclusive investigations of him by his [workplace] unit, documentation of his performance during successive political campaigns, his work records and relevant reports, assessments and [performance] evaluations of the informant, work plans, and receipts and records relating to informant activity expenses and allowances, and so on. The informant's case officer is responsible for creating the file, while a specially designated desk officer remains in charge of the uniform safekeeping of all such files.

People's Liberation Army
Beijing Railway Sub-Bureau
Public Security Sub-Division
Military Control Group
26 February 1973

Glossary

This glossary is designed as a simple reference tool for use by readers of Chinese HUMINT records. The meanings of the terms and expressions are illustrated by quotations translated from original Cold War-era sources.

babing (把柄): *kompromat*, compromising material that leaves the victim vulnerable to blackmail.
'Stains on a person's private life should not be exploited as *kompromat*'

baomi (保密): safeguard clandestinity, keep secret.
'Agents must always pay attention to *safeguarding clandestinity*'

baomi (暴密): compromise clandestinity/secrecy.
'Blank agent forms should not be left lying about and should not be produced in an excessive number, as this may *compromise secrecy*'

'bixu yu keneng' de yuanze ("必须与可能"的原则): [ministerial doctrine] principles of necessity and capability.
'The 1952 National Conference on Operational Work favoured cultivation of agents in accordance with the *principles of necessity and capability* in a steady, planned, targeted, bold, and all-out way'

cailiao (材料): information.
'Agent work is by no means simply a matter of locating people who are capable of providing *information*'
'Just about anything that is concrete and real and that has a definite value in the context of intelligence analysis may constitute *information*'

da (打): 'sticks'.
'In the context of agent recruitment, the balance between 'carrots' and '*sticks*' must be handled properly' (See also ***la***)

dajinqu (打进去): infiltrate.
'Operational use of penetration agents normally involves either *infiltration* or the recruitment and development of an agent in place'

daihao (代号): code number.
'Each agent will be assigned a *code number* by the Division'
'Agents are to be referred to by their *code number* or by their alias'

danxian lingdao (单线领导): one-to-one contact and autonomous leadership [of agent].
'Agents must be *directed individually* by operational line departments'
'The *running* of an agent must involve direct one-to-one interaction'

diqing (敌情): enemy circumstances, threats, threat level.
'Our agents provided updates on the *enemy's circumstances*'
'A card catalogue of documented *threats*' 'Operational work must be strengthened where the *threat level* is elevated'

dite (敌特): enemy operatives.
'One may exploit Protestant elements to conduct surveillance on *enemy operatives* inside the Catholic church'

dite (帝特): imperialist operatives.
'We have already conducted a broad investigation of their social basis, but we have been unable to identify any clandestine activity by British *imperialist operatives*'

duixiang (对象): target.
'Nothing must lead the *target* to believe that something is amiss'
'The informant must be in a position to closely approach the operational *target*'

ermu (耳目): informant, eyes and ears.
'At best, he would be able to serve as a common *informant*'
'We should have our *informant* keep a watchful eye on him'

fanying (反映): inform, report, update.
'What has been *reported* concerning issues involving specific individuals is confidential'
'We operated an agent who regularly *updated* us on the target's circumstances'

fan zhencha (反侦察): counter-operational tactics.
'What do we mean by adopting *counter-operational tactics*? It is when an operational unit directs the operational officer to assume an outwardly reactionary appearance and then proceeds to incite the operational target to commit a crime. Such *counter-operational tactics* [of entrapment] may not be used by People's Public Security units' **arch**.

fazhan (发展): develop, cultivate [an agent].
'Our new and recently *developed* agents have been vetted based on information already in our bureau files'

fuxian (复线): duplicate line agent.
'Utilise physical surveillance or *duplicate line agents* to monitor the behaviour of newly recruited agents'

guanmenzhuyi (关门主义): closed-doorism.
'We must overcome *closed-doorism* and break with the practice of working behind closed doors and operating in secrecy'
'*Closed-doorism* and mysticism are in essence attempts to evade party leadership and mass supervision'

gulizhuyi (孤立主义): isolationism, seclusion.
'He openly resisted the general policy of Chairman Mao's mass line in public security work by engaging aggressively in the kind of cryptic *isolationist* operational activity touted by the State Political Directorate of the Soviet revisionists'
'Huang Chibo borrowed extensively from Sherlock Holmes' mysticist way of operating in *seclusion*'

jiandie (间谍): spy.
'Informants are to operate among *spies* and suspected spy elements in the foreign expatriate community'

jianli (建立): recruitment.
'An agent *recruitment* operation involves both preparation for recruitment and the actual recruitment process'

jianshe (建设): capacity building, construction.
'We intensified agent work *capacity building* while also stepping up efforts to root out enemy operatives'
'The magazine *Public Security Construction* is the official organ of the Ministry of Public Security'

jietou (接头): operational rendezvous, agent contact.
'During each *rendezvous* with the agent, the case officer should take careful debriefing notes and thereafter immediately edit the notes'

jietou judian (接头据点): secret rendezvous premise or site used by special arrangement for meetings with agents.
'For a limited time, his residence was used as a *secret rendezvous premise*'

jingji baowei (经济保卫): economic protection.

'The Ministry of Public Security tasked its *Economic Protection* Bureau with coordinating operations to protect China's economic infrastructure'

jingying (经营): operate [an agent].
'When it comes to the utilisation of agents, case officers must be prepared to make long-term calculations and to expect painstaking *operation*'

kongzhi (控制): control.
'It often proved difficult to *make controlled use* of individuals who had close relations with enemy operatives'

la (拉): 'carrots'.
'In the context of agent recruitment, whether one should begin with *'carrots'* or with 'sticks' depends on the circumstances' (See also ***da***)

lachulai (拉出来): develop an agent in place.
'Once we are in the possession of sufficient *kompromat* we may be able by way of persuasion and education to *turn an element* inside the enemy's organisation *into an agent in place* who goes on to serve us wittingly'

liliang (力量): intelligence asset or operational resource.
'We initiated a validation review of our existing *assets*'
'Reinforce *covert asset* capacity building in accordance with Chairman Mao's policy' 'They spouted such rubbish as 'Agents are an indispensable *operational resource*''

mimi baoweiyuan (秘密保卫员): confidential guardian.
'The economic protection sector in our province currently operates a large number of agents, *confidential guardians*, and informants'
'Many *confidential guardians* are utilised in the fight against common criminals and in safeguarding key factories, mines, and enterprises'

mimi diaocha teqing (秘密调查特情): secret investigation agent.
'The plan is to selectively assign permanent roles to the *secret investigation agents* among the senior technicians who are in a position to control a particular sphere'

mimi judian (秘密据点): a clandestine premise used for meetings with agents.
'A *clandestine premise* is a permanent site located in a building that belongs to the public security organs'

neibu baowei (内部保卫): internal protection.
'Immediately after the founding of the People's Republic, the security of important party and government organs, state-run factories, cadre schools,

etc. was safeguarded by the *internal protection* components of the public security bureaus'

neixian (内线): penetration agent/asset, 'someone on the inside'.
'What made it possible to crack the case was the recruitment of a *penetration agent* who could perform operational tasks on the inside'
'Activists are reliable and expedient, but they are not really suitable to serve as *penetration agents*'

niyong (逆用): turning [an adversary into an intelligence asset].
'There are two kinds of penetration operations, one by inserting someone from the outside, the other by *turning* someone already on the inside'
'In the past, we used to think of the term 'agent' as designating only (or mainly) *turned* elements from the antagonistic classes'

peiyang (培养): nurture, foster.
'Our aim is to *nurture* the capabilities of the agent and to see him become proficient in his craft'
'The attitude of the agent is good, and he has professional potential that can be *fostered*'

qingbao (情报): intelligence, intelligence product.
'The division has only forwarded to us nine items of *intelligence* from the agent'
'Some foreign visitors from capitalist countries want to study China's political system from a comparative angle, while others come to engage in *intelligence* activity'
'Agents who have maintained illicit contacts with foreign countries and have provided them with *intelligence* are to be detained and investigated'
'Chairman Mao always paid great attention to *intelligence* obtained in this way'

qingkuang (情况): intelligence information, circumstances.
'Our own investigations corroborate the *information* provided by the agent'
'I met with the agent who reported the following *circumstances*'

shenmizhuyi (神秘主义): mysticism.
'Luo Ruiqing allowed himself to be influenced by the *mysticist stuff* from the Soviet Union'
'Closed-doorism and *mysticism* are in essence attempts to evade party leadership and mass supervision'

sheqing (社情): social intelligence.
'*Social intelligence* investigation is to focus on the attitudes of specific social strata to major party and government policies and measures'

'*Social intelligence* reporting has to be detailed, truthful, lively, and timely'
'*Social intelligence* must not become a hodgepodge of everything imaginable that nobody is able to make heads or tails of' *arch*.

tefei (特费): special expenditures.
'Agents are not formally members of our staff and the cost of running them is covered by funds from the state's *special expenditures* budget'

tegong renyuan (特工): [enemy] intelligence officer, 'spook'.
'The spook, an element from their Second Office, suspected we were on to him' *colloq*.

teqing (特情): agent.
'An absolute majority of our *agents* consist of patriotic elements who have been recruited on the basis of their ideological awareness'
'They capitalised on their legalised *agent* status and acted as a special task force of the old public security, procuracy, and legal sectors to oppress the labouring people'
'The psychology of the ordinary *agent* invariably involves the attainment of financial security'
'Means used to deal with antagonistic class elements may not be used to handle *agents* who belong to our Party or Youth League or who are members of the ordinary masses'

teqing duixiang (特情对象): prospective agent, recruitment candidate.
'Consider whether among our *prospective agents* there are people who are willing to serve us and who are up to the task'
'Operational officers must be able to spot *prospective agent* targets that have true potential'

teqing gongzuo (特情工作): agent work, HUMINT.
'Our *agent work* must proceed in accordance with 'necessity and capability''
'In capitalist countries, *HUMINT* involves the use of provocation, slander, intimidation, etc.'

teqing renyuan (特情人员): See *teqing*.

waixian (外线): physical surveillance.
'It is part of our mission to subject each and every one of the foreign officials to prolonged and careful study, using *physical surveillance*, agents, and other operational instruments'

wuse (物色): profiling [candidates for agent recruitment].
'Protection units in factories and mines are to assist in agent *profiling*'

'When *profiling* potential informants as well as when selecting, developing, utilising, or writing them off, one must always report to the leading comrades on the party committee of one's unit'

yanhu (掩护): operational cover/protection.
'The organisation of the democratic party is his *cover*'

yaohai baowei teqing (要害保卫特情): agent tasked with guarding critical assets.
'*Agents* from the ranks of senior technicians *tasked with guarding critical assets* are to be controlled by the relevant operational line department of the public security organ'

zhencha (侦察): operational activity.
'Public security bureau *operational activity* involves the use of instruments such as agents, physical surveillance, covert postal inspection, technical operations, etc.'

zhencha renyuan (侦察人员): operational officer, case officer [of an agent].
'It is not good for *operations* to switch the *officer* directing the agent too often'

zhengzhi baowei (政治保卫): political protection.
'*Political protection* departments maintain control over our overseas sources of intelligence and have additional operational means at their disposal'
'When determining where to place the priority in operational work, *political protection* should come first and economic protection should come second'
'The *political protection* divisions should avail themselves of the opportunity represented by the proselytising activities of religious organisations to recruit and train believers and they should task them with operating on the inside of the organisations in question'

zhiye judian (职业据点): dedicated operational premise/base.
'Liaison with agents should be conducted on *premises set up specifically for that purpose*'
'We set up separate *dedicated premises* in suitable locations to rendezvous with our agents'

zhuan'an zhencha (专案侦察): predicated case investigation, operational investigation/work.
'In order to achieve clarity with respect to her status as a possible enemy operative, we launched a *predicated investigation* of her *case*'
'You may close Case 5004, suspend further *operational work*, and henceforth limit yourselves to long-term observation and monitoring of the target'

Notes

Preface

1. Steve Hewitt, *Snitch! A History of the Modern Intelligence Informer* (New York: Continuum, 2010), back cover.
2. Philip H. J. Davies and Kristian C. Gustafson, eds., *Intelligence Elsewhere: Spies and Espionage Outside the Anglosphere* (Washington, DC: Georgetown University Press, 2013).
3. Christopher Moran, *Classified: Secrecy and the State in Modern Britain* (Cambridge: Cambridge University Press, 2013), p. 326; Richard J. Aldrich and Rory Cormac, *The Black Door: Spies, Secret Intelligence and British Prime Ministers* (London: William Collins, 2016), p. 7.
4. Moran, *Classified*, pp. 329–349. See also Connor Woodman, *Spycops in Context: A Brief History of Political Policing in Britain* (London: Centre for Crime and Justice Studies, 2018), pp. 5–6.
5. Peter Jackson, 'Introduction: Enquiries into the "Secret State"', in R. Gerald Hughes, Peter Jackson, and Len Scott, eds., *Exploring Intelligence Archives: Enquiries into the Secret State* (London: Routledge, 2008), pp. 1–11.
6. For an introduction to the institutional development and policy priorities of agent work (HUMINT) in the early PRC, see Michael Schoenhals, *Spying for the People: Mao's Secret Agents, 1949–1967* (Cambridge: Cambridge University Press, 2013), pp. 15–50.
7. Christopher Andrew and Vasili Mitrokhin, *The Mitrokhin Archive: The KGB in Europe and the West* (London: Penguin Books, 2000), p. xxxix.
8. Umberto Eco, *How to Write a Thesis* (Cambridge MA: The MIT Press, 2015), p. 50.
9. See Chapter 5.
10. John Edgar Hoover, 'Communist "New Look": A Study in Duplicity', *The Elks Magazine*, Vol. 35, No. 3 (August 1956), p. 47.
11. *'Teqing gongzuo' jiangyi* (Lectures on the Subject of Agent Work) (Beijing: Zhongyang renmin gongan xueyuan, 1957), p. 3.
12. In a critical retrospective on the field of intelligence history, Rüdiger Bergien observes that 'academic research on intelligence services, especially in the Anglo-Saxon world, has largely been carried out by former (and active) members of these organizations'. See 'Intelligence History', Version: 1.0 in *Docupedia-Zeitgeschichte* (3 August 2021), p. 2. http://docupedia.de/zg/Bergien_intelligence_history_v1_en_2021.

13. See Christopher Andrew, 'Intelligence, International Relations, and "Under-theorization"', in L. V. Scott and Peter Jackson, eds., *Understanding Intelligence in the Twenty-First Century: Journeys in Shadows* (London: Routledge, 2004), pp. 29–41.
14. Philip Davies, 'Ideas of Intelligence: Divergent National Concepts and Institutions', in Christopher Andrew, Richard J. Aldrich, and Wesley K. Wark, eds., *Secret Intelligence: A Reader* (London: Routledge, 2009), p. 16; Philip H. J. Davies and Kristian C. Gustafson, 'An Agenda for the Comparative Study of Intelligence: Yet Another Missing Dimension', in Davies and Gustafson, eds., *Intelligence Elsewhere*, p. 8; Philip H. J. Davies, *MI6 and the Machinery of Spying* (London: Frank Cass, 2004), p. 2.
15. Davies, 'Ideas of Intelligence', p. 16; Davies, *MI6*, p. 19; Davies and Gustafson, 'An Agenda for the Comparative Study of Intelligence', p. 8.
16. Peter Hennessy, 'Foreword', in Scott and Jackson, eds., *Understanding Intelligence*, p. x.
17. Andrew, 'Intelligence, International Relations, and "Under-theorization"', pp. 34–35.
18. Andrew, Aldrich, and Wark, *Secret Intelligence*, pp. xv–xviii; F. R. Ankersmit, *History and Tropology: The Rise and Fall of Metaphor* (Berkeley: University of California Press, 1994), p. 89.
19. Hayden White, 'Interpretation in History', *New Literary History*, Vol. 4, No. 2 (Winter 1973), p. 281.
20. Ian S. Lustick, 'History, Historiography, and Political Science: Multiple Historical Records and the Problem of Selection Bias', *American Political Science Review*, Vol. 90, No. 3 (September 1996), pp. 605–618.
21. Davies, 'Ideas of Intelligence', p. 17.
22. Eric Hobsbawm, *On History* (New York: The New Press, 1997), p. 275.
23. Directorate of Intelligence, *Style Manual & Writers Guide for Intelligence Publications*, 8th ed. (Washington, DC: Central Intelligence Agency, 2011), p. 30.
24. Hobsbawm, *On History*, p. 238.
25. Peter Gill, 'Theories of Intelligence', p. 2. PDF document: doi.org/10.1093/oxfordhb/9780195375886.003.0003.
26. G. R. Elton, *The Practice of History* (London: Fontana, 1984), p. 120.
27. Directorate of Intelligence, *Style Manual & Writers Guide*, p. 157.

Part I: Agent Recruitment

28. *Webster's New Dictionary of Synonyms* (Springfield: G. & C. Merriam, 1978), p. 529.
29. John le Carré, *The Looking Glass War* (London: Penguin, 2011). p. 137.
30. Manfred Hempel, *Die Wirksamkeit moralischer Faktoren in Verhalten der Bürger der Deutschen Demokratischen Republik zu inoffiziellen Zusammenarbeit mit den Organen des Ministeriums für Staatssicherheit*, PhD thesis, Institut für Psychologie, Juristische Hochschule Potsdam, 1967, quotes on p. 56, 60, 68, 63, and 68.

31. Christopher R. Moran, 'The Pursuit of Intelligence History: Methods, Sources, and Trajectories in the United Kingdom', *Studies in Intelligence*, Vol. 55, No. 2 (2011), pp. 676–700; Hempel, *Die Wirksamkeit moralischer Faktoren*, p. 104.
32. Nikita Shah, *Secret Towns': British Intelligence in Asia during the Cold War*, PhD thesis, Department of Political Science, University of Warwick, 2016, p. 41.
33. Robert W. Winks, ed., *The Historian as Detective: Essays on Evidence* (New York: Harper Torchbooks, 1969), p. 346.
34. Allan Nevins, *The Gateway to History* (Boston: D. C. Heath, 1938), p. 144.

Chapter 1: The Target's Own Story

35. Xiu Lairong, *Chen Long zhuan* (Biography of Chen Long) (Beijing: Qunzhong chubanshe, 2011), p. 182.
36. *Haerbin shi gongan shi changbian 1945–1949* (Extended History of Public Security in Harbin 1945–1949) (Harbin: Haerbin shi ganganju, 1986), p. 50.
37. 'Mr Ma' was Ma Jingzheng (1920–1978), a CCP Social Affairs Department cadre and former Eighth Route Army soldier, who, in 1947, headed the Public Order Section of Harbin Special Municipality Public Security Bureau.
38. Wang received assurances after having signed, before dawn on 21 May, a so-called Voluntary Offer of Meritorious Service to Atone for Crimes Committed. Cf. Schoenhals, *Spying for the People*, p. 161.
39. Liu Xingya's identity is not known. Zhao Minqiang was the Guomindang intelligence officer who had been sent from Changchun to Harbin by the ROC Ministry of National Defence Protection of Secrets Bureau in May 1947 to serve as acting head of the Songjiang Group.
40. Wu Guodong was an undercover Guomindang intelligence officer whose home on Sevastopolskaya Street served as the clandestine headquarters of the Songjiang Group.
41. The Songjiang Group maintained two separate and different radio communications cipher/code books; Zhao Minqiang controlled the one known as the Group Transmission Cipher (*zubaomi*). Incoming messages encrypted with its cipher/code were handled directly by the receiving communications officer Zhao who, in turn, entrusted decryption to his personal aide Zhang Peirun. When the encryption of outgoing messages with the help of the Group Cipher book was called for, this procedure was reversed.
42. The Desk Cipher here refers to the Songjiang Group's second radio communications cipher/code book, known as the Desk Transmission Cipher (*taibaomi*). The book, and its use, were controlled by Wang Yaoguang in his capacity as chief radio communications officer (*taizhang*).
43. Zhou Yunting's identity is not known.
44. Wang would never be told the truth, namely that by then 'Zhao Minqiang and the others' had already been rounded up and arrested. As noted in an official history of public security in Harbin (*Haerbin shi gongan shi changbian*, p. 51): 'The Songjiang Group was uncovered; its acting head Zhao Minqiang, its chief radio communications officer Wang Guangyao, and its other members

were arrested, and their equipment and identification papers were all captured *in May 1947*' (emphasis added).
45. 'Yue Guang' was Wang Guangyao's *zi* or 'fancy name'.

Part II: Capacity Building

46. Hoover, 'Communist "New Look"', p. 47. See also Joshua Reeves, *Citizen Spies: The Long Rise of America's Surveillance Society* (New York: New York University Press, 2017), pp. 1–15.
47. Bengt Nylander, *Det som inte har berättats: 25 år vid Säpos kontraspionage* (Stockholm: Hjalmarsson & Högberg, 2016), pp. 75, 79 (emphasis added).
48. R. Gerald Hughes and Len Scott, '"Knowledge Is Never Too Dear": Exploring Intelligence Archives', in Hughes, Jackson, and Scott, eds., *Exploring Intelligence Archives*, p. 23.
49. Sherman Kent, quoted in the introduction to H. Bradford Westerfield, ed., *Inside CIA's Private World: Declassified Articles from the Agency's Internal Journal, 1955–1992* (New Haven: Yale University Press, 1995), p. xiii. The characterisation of Kent is from John Ranelagh, *The Agency: The Rise and Decline of the CIA* (London: Weidenfeld and Nicolson, 1986), p. 197.
50. Murray Edelman, *The Politics of Misinformation* (Cambridge: Cambridge University Press, 2001), p. 113.
51. See, for example, Bettina Bock, *'Blindes' Schreiben im Dienste der DDR-Staatssicherheit: Eine text- und diskurslinguistische Untersuchung von Texten der inoffiziellen Mitarbeiter* (Bremen: Hempen Verlag, 2013); Thomas Großbölting and Sabine Kittel, eds., *Welche 'Wirklichkeit' und wessen 'Wahrheit'? Das Geheimdienstarchiv als Quelle und Medium der Wissensproduktion* (Göttingen: Vandenhoeck & Ruprecht, 2019); and Steffen Pappert, 'Verdecken under Verschlüsseln durch Fachsprache? Zur Transformation von Alltagssprache in die Sprache des MfS', in Steffen Pappert, Melani Schröter, and Ulla Fix, eds., *Verschlüsseln, Verbergen, Verdecken in öffentlicher und instituioneller Kommunikation* (Berlin: Erich Schmidt Verlag, 2008), pp. 291–313.
52. Peter Mattis and Matthew Brazil, *Chinese Communist Espionage: An Intelligence Primer* (Annapolis: Naval Institute Press, 2019), p. 26.
53. Kevin C. Ruffner, ed., *Forging an Intelligence Partnership: CIA and the Origins of the BND, 1946–56* (Washington DC: CIA National Clandestine Service Europe Division, 2006), Vol. 2, p. 437.

Chapter 2: A Director of Public Security Remembers

54. On the term '*tewu*', see Schoenhals, *Spying for the People*, p. 2.
55. The Central Statistics Bureau (Zhongtong) was Republican China's FBI and its civilian secret policemen 'thought of themselves as the equivalent of clean-cut FBI agents'. Frederic Wakeman, Jr., 'American Police Advisers and the Nationalist Chinese Secret Service, 1930–1937', *Modern China*, Vol. 18, No. 2 (April 1992), p. 131.
56. See Schoenhals, *Spying for the People*, pp. 148–152.

Chapter 3: Developing Doctrinal Terminology

57. Beijing shi renmin zhengfu gonganju guanxunchu, 'Guanyu tongji gongzuo de jiancha baogao' (Self-Critical Report on Statistical Work) [23 October 1951], *Renmin gongan zengkan* (People's Public Security: Supplement) No. 32 (31 December 1951), p. 16.

Chapter 4: Trial and Error

58. This note occurs in the original Chinese text.
59. On the Military Statistics Bureau (Juntong), see Frederic Wakeman, Jr., *Spymaster: Dai Li and the Chinese Secret Service* (Berkeley: University of California Press, 2003).
60. On the Yiguandao, see S. A. Smith, 'Redemptive Religious Societies and the Communist State, 1949 to the 1980s', in Jeremy Brown and Matthew D. Johnson, eds., *Maoism at the Grassroots: Everyday Life in China's Era of High Socialism* (Cambridge, MA: Harvard University Press, 2015), pp. 340–364.
61. On social intelligence, see Michael Schoenhals, ed., 'Public Security in the People's Republic of China: A Selection of Mood Assessment Reports (1951–1962)', *Contemporary Chinese Thought: Translations and Studies*, Vol. 38, No. 3 (Spring 2007), pp. 48–53.
62. See Schoenhals, *Spying for the People*, pp. 39–40.
63. Compare Chapter 5 below.

Chapter 5: Big Brother Dispenses *Operativnyy* Experience

64. Schoenhals, *Spying for the People*, p. 24.
65. Ibid., pp. 176–179.
66. Harvey Matusow, *False Witness* (New York: Cameron & Kahn, 1955), pp. 7–16.
67. See Robert M. Lichtman and Ronald D. Cohen, *Deadly Farce: Harvey Matusow and the Informer System in the McCarthy Era* (Urbana: University of Illinois Press, 2004), pp. 9, 59, 78.
68. See Schoenhals, *Spying for the People*, pp. 145–148.
69. Ibid., pp. 154–156.
70. On the *Agent Manual*, see ibid., pp. 32–33.
71. The three terms in Russian elaborated upon by the speaker (translated as *lianluo teqing, luxian teqing*, and *zhenji teqing* by his Chinese interpreter) are likely to have been *agent marshrutnyy, agent-svyaznik*, and *agent opoznavatel*. Compare Vasiliy Mitrokhin, ed., *KGB Lexicon: The Soviet Intelligence Officer's Handbook*, with a foreword by Peter Hennessy (London: Frank Cass, 2002), pp. 150–151, 154.
72. This note occurs in the original Chinese text.

Part III: Best Practice

73. John Le Carré, *The Spy Who Came in from the Cold* (London: Penguin, 2010) p. 127.
74. Darren E. Tromblay, *The U.S. Domestic Intelligence Enterprise: History, Development, and Operations* (Boca Raton: CRC Press, 2016), pp. 192–193.
75. On one such pilot programme, see Michael Schoenhals, 'Recruiting Agents in Industry and Trade: Lifting the Veil on Early People's Republic of China Operational Work', *Modern Asian Studies*, Vol. 46, No. 5 (September 2012), pp. 1345–1369.
76. Westerfield, *Inside CIA's Private World*, p. xxii.
77. Ibid., p. xiii.
78. 'Tongzhi' (Notification), *Xi'nan gongan tongxun* (Southwest Public Security Newsletter), No. 1 (31 May 1950), p. i; 'Qianyan' (Introduction), *Hashi gongan zengkan* (Harbin Public Security: Supplement), No. 1 (6 October 1954), p. i.

Chapter 6: Agent Files: *Management and Utilisation Regulations*

79. *Dang'an gongzuo ke jiangshou tigang* (Classes on Archival Work: Lecture Outline) (Beijing: Renmin gongan xueyuan, 1954), p. 12.

Chapter 7: Recruitment: One Template and Two Profiles

80. Here and elsewhere, my translation has been anonymised in compliance with what I understand to be the essence of EU privacy law, Sweden's Ethical Review Act (SFS 2003:460), and the US court ruling in *Irons* v. *Bell* which in 1979 called the disclosure of an informer's identity as 'unwarranted invasion of personal privacy'. I have also in some instances edited out unverifiable derogatory information not already in the public domain.
81. On the Sanminzhuyi (Three People's Principles) Youth Corps, see ch. 2, in Jennifer Liu, *Indoctrinating the Youth: Secondary Education in Wartime China and Postwar Taiwan, 1937–1960* (Honolulu: University of Hawai'i Press, 2024).
82. On the organised suppression of Nationalist counter-revolutionary activity in urban China at the time, see Fredrick Wakeman, Jr., '"Cleanup": The New Order in Shanghai', in Brown and Pickowicz, eds., *Dilemmas of Victory*, pp. 21–58.

Chapter 8: Agent Termination

83. '*Gongye baowei xitong dangqian zhencha gongzuo de jiben qingkuang he jinhou gongzuo yijian*' (The Basic State of Operational Work in the Industry Protection Sector at Present and Opinions Concerning Future Work) (Beijing: Gonganbu shisiju, 5 November 1956), p. 1.

Notes to Pages 84–104

84. The documents in question appeared in *Gongan jianshe*, No. 184, 5 March 1957, pp. 1–23.
85. For a case study on the involvement of public security organs in the three-year-long government and state employee security risk assessment known as the *Sufan* (internal 'elimination of counter-revolutionaries'), see Michael Schoenhals, 'The Intelligence Sleeper Who Never Was: Han Fuying and Case 5004', in Daniel Leese and Puck Engman, eds., *Victims, Perpetrators, and the Role of Law in Maoist China: A Case-Study Approach* (Berlin: DeGruyter, 2018), pp. 52–74.
86. As used rather loosely by Chinese public security officers in the 1950s, the expression 'grey agent' meant an agent recruited from the so-called 'grey masses', a fuzzy intermediate social category of people who appeared in public to be neither backward nor progressive. See Schoenhals, *Spying for the People*, pp. 93–97.

Part IV: From the Agent Work File

87. Gerald K. Haines and David A. Langbart, *Unlocking the Files of the FBI: A Guide to Its Records and Classification System* (Wilmington, DE: Scholarly Resources, 1993), p. 130.
88. *KGB Lexicon*, p. 332.
89. Haines and Langbart, *Unlocking*, p. 133.
90. *Wirklichkeit*, pp. 25, 28. and 32–34.
91. Harry Ferguson, *Spy: A Handbook* (London: Bloomsbury, 2004), p. 91.
92. Ibid., p. 76.
93. Ward Churchill and Jim Vander Wall, *The COINTELPRO Papers: Documents from the FBI's Secret Wars Against Domestic Dissent* (Boston: South End Press, 1990), pp. 205–207.
94. Timothy Garton Ash, *The File: A Personal History* (New York: Vintage, 1998), pp. 230–231.
95. Hewitt, *Snitch!* p. 57.

Chapter 10: Raw Intelligence: All Quiet in the Northeast Linen Mill

96. The mill was renamed Harbin Linen Mill when it became fully operational in 1952; at the time, it was the biggest factory of its kind in all of Asia. It was constructed with Soviet assistance on the basis of a Soviet blueprint. Compare the declassified CIA *Information Report* 'New Textile Factory, Harbin' (29 December 1952), www.cia.gov/readingroom/docs/CIA-RDP82-00457R015600380004-8.pdf.
97. At the conversion rate (of 9.5=1), applied by the authorities when the regional currency circulating in Harbin in 1950 was withdrawn from circulation in 1951, this amount corresponded to roughly 31,600 yuan in the national People's Currency (RMB). After the currency reform of February 1955, it would have equalled 3.16 yuan.

Chapter 11: Welfaring Agent 107: 'She Now Has Misgivings ...'

98. Ronald Suleski, 'Manchukuo and Beyond: The Life and Times of Zhang Mengshi', *International Journal of Asian Studies*, Vol. 14, No. 1 (2017), p. 80.
99. An amount corresponding to roughly 2.11 yuan in today's People's Currency.
100. The Kingly Way Academy was a school established in Changchun in 1937 to promote an ideology that conservatives asserted would confer spiritual legitimacy on Manchukuo.

Chapter 12: Tasking Agent 371: Active Measures

101. *Zhuan'an zhencha* (Predicated Case Investigation) (Beijing: Zhongguo renmin gongan daxue chubanshe, 1987), p. 69.
102. The term *niyah* in Islam refers to one's intention and is connected to the Islamic ideals of supporting our fellow human beings and taking care of our own bodies and souls.

Chapter 13: Debriefing Agent 594: Monitoring Campus Unrest

103. The 'attachments' (agent reports, copies of big-character posters, etc.) mentioned in some contact reports have been left untranslated.
104. Section Chief Chen Xianqing was the senior officer to whom Agent 594's handler, Li Jingui, regularly reported. On occasion, the two men debriefed their agent together.
105. On the two writers mentioned here by name, one a Canadian physician, the other a co-founder of the Chinese Communist Party, see https://en.wikipedia.org/wiki/Norman_Bethune and https://en.wikipedia.org/wiki/Li_Dazhao.
106. On Jiao Yulu, see https://en.wikipedia.org/wiki/Jiao_Yulu.
107. On the Socialist Education Movement, see Roderick MacFarquhar, *The Origins of the Cultural Revolution III: The Coming of the Cataclysm 1961–1966* (New York: Columbia University Press, 1997), pp. 334–348.

Part V: From the Agent Personal File

108. Nylander, *Det som inte har berättats*, p. 76.
109. *KGB Lexicon*, p. 246.
110. '*Teqing gongzuo*', p. 40.

Chapter 17: Give and Take: Apologies and a Nanny

111. The two amounts equal 50 yuan and 30 yuan, respectively, in today's People's Currency.

Chapter 18: Agent Validation: Professional and 'Leftist'

112. *KGB Lexicon*, pp. 404–405.

Part VI: Component Chiefs: Feedback and Direction

113. D. H. Rumsfeld interviewed by Charlie Rose on 26 January 2016. www.youtube.com/watch?v=GlAYzQaAOvo.
114. Joseph W. Wippl and Donna D'Andrea, 'The Qualities That Make a Great Collection Management Officer', *International Journal of Intelligence and Counterintelligence*, Vol. 27, No. 4 (2014), p. 809.
115. Hughes and Scott, 'Knowledge Is Never Too Dear', pp. 14–15.
116. Directorate of Intelligence, *Style Manual & Writers Guide*, p. 171.

Chapter 21: On Courses of Action Proposed

117. On the handwritten draft translated here, a senior officer has crossed out the words canned chicken meat and changed two bottles to one bottle of red wine.

Chapter 22: Whose Collection Requirements Should Enjoy Priority?

118. Yang's operational work subsequent to his move from the First to the Fifth Division on 3 July 1961 is discussed in Chapter 19 above.

Part VII: Crisis Management

119. Robert M. Bloom, *Ratting: The Use and Abuse of Informants in the American Justice System* (London: Praeger, 2002), p. 158; *Unleashed and Unaccountable: The FBI's Unchecked Abuse of Authority* (American Civil Liberties Union, September 2013). www.aclu.org/documents/unleashed-and-unaccountable-fbis-unchecked-abuse-authority.
120. See Churchill and Vander Wall, *The COINTELPRO Papers*.
121. Anna-Lena Lodenius, *Spionjakt i Folkhemmet: Ett halvsekel med IB-affären* (Lund: Historiska Media, 2023).
122. Sir Humphrey Appleby, quoted on BBC2, 2 March 1981.
123. In 'As I Please 27' (2 June 1944). *George Orwell: Essays, Selected and Introduced by John Carey* (New York: Alfred A. Knopf, 2002), p. 664.
124. Edward O. Wilson, *Consilience: The Unity of Knowledge* (New York: Alfred A. Knopf, 1998), p. 227.
125. J. L. Austin, *How to Do Things with Words* (Cambridge, MA: Harvard University Press, 1975), pp. 25–38.

Chapter 23: Agent Work: Findings and Recommendations of an Inquiry

126. Michael Schoenhals, ed., *China's Cultural Revolution, 1966–1969: Not a Dinner Party* (Armonk, NY: M. E. Sharpe, 1996), p. 37.
127. Schoenhals, *Spying for the People*, pp. 1–3.
128. Zhang Jiuchun, 'Dapo guanmenzhuyi he shenmizhuyi' (Break Down Closed-Doorism and Mysticism) in *Quanguo gongan huiyi geming dapipan cailiao xuanbian* (Selected Revolutionary Great Criticism Materials from the National Public Security Conference) (Kunming: Quansheng gongan huiyi mishuzu, 1971), p. 38.
129. 'Shanghai, Hebei, Jiangxi, Shanxi deng shengshi daibiao fayan jiepi "sirenbang"' (Speeches by Delegates from Shanghai, Hebei, Jiangxi, and Shanxi Exposing and Denouncing the 'Gang of Four') in *Di shiqici quanguo gongan huiyi jianbao* (Seventeenth National Public Security Conference Bulletins), No. 89 (28 December 1977), pp. 5–6.
130. On the Cleansing of the Class Ranks Campaign, see Roderick MacFarquhar and Michael Schoenhals, *Mao's Last Revolution* (Cambridge, MA: The Belknap Press of Harvard University Press, 2006), pp. 253–262.

Chapter 24: Opponents: 'Shitting and Pissing on the Heads of the People'

131. Shi Yizhi, *Wo zai gonganbu shinian* (My Ten Years in the Ministry of Public Security) (Beijing: Privately printed, 2002), pp. 30–32.
132. I have been unable to identify the 'Four Big Corporations'.

Chapter 25: Proponents: 'An Indispensable Operational Resource'

133. Shenyang shi geming weiyuanhui renmin baoweizu, 'Guanyu zuohao guoqingjie anquan baowei gongzuo de fang'an' (Work Plan for Successful Security Protection Work During National Holiday Celebrations) (9 September 1972) (Shenyang, 1972), p. 4.

Chapter 26: The Government Advocates a Return to the *Status Quo Ante*

134. Zhou Enlai's 'important directives' were sanitised snippets from a one and a half-hour long lecture (delivered in the evening of 5 November 1972) by an angry Premier to a gathering of senior civilian and military officers responsible for security in the Chinese capital. For context, see MacFarquhar and Schoenhals, *Mao's Last Revolution*, pp. 376–377. A longer informative extract from Zhou's lecture can be found in Mu Yumin, *Beijing jingcha bainian* (One

Hundred Years of the Beijing Police) (Beijing: Zhongguo renmin gongan daxue chubanshe, 2004), pp. 561–563.
135. On the denunciation of PRC Defence Minister Lin Biao and rectification of work styles, see MacFarquhar and Schoenhals, *Mao's Last Revolution*, pp. 345–347.

Chapter 27: Deconfliction: *Provisional Guidelines on Informant Capacity Building*

136. Schoenhals, ed., *China's Cultural Revolution*, p. 33.
137. The document referred to here, dated 8 February 1973, bears the title 'Guanyu jianli mimi baoweiyuan de yijian' (Guidelines on the Recruitment of Confidential Guardians) and was circulated by the Military Control Group, Public Security Sub-Division, of the PLA Beijing Railway Sub-Bureau as an attachment to its '1973 gongzuo yijian' (Guidelines on Work in 1973).

Index

Agent Work Manual, 52, 67
Ai Siqi, 167
Anda, 143
Andrew, Christopher, x, xii
Ankersmit, F. R., xii
Anti-Rightist Campaign, 87, 172

Baichengzi, 146
Beijing, 56, 76, 120, 121, 127, 145, 146, 197, 230, 233–235
Beijing Public Security Bureau (PSB), 31, 228–229, 231
Bethune, Norman, 140
Budenz, Louis, 43

Canada, ix, 99
Changchun, 6, 8, 76–77, 78, 110, 111, 115, 127, 245
Chiang Kai-shek, 35, 159, 182, 218, 228
Chinese Ministry of Public Security, 34, 42, 67, 74, 83, 90, 91, 172, 217, 223, 227, 228, 232
Chinese People's Liberation Army (PLA), 76, 214–216, 223–225, 228, 233–235
Cleansing of the Class Ranks Campaign, 215
Communist Party of the Soviet Union (CPSU), 135, 138, 145, 196, 219
Cultural Revolution, 213, 215, 216, 218, 221, 227, 230, 233

Dajishan, 38
Dalian, 20, 80
Dandong, 131
Deng Tuo, 133
Deng Xiaoping, 214

Eco, Umberto, x, xiv
Edelman, Murray, 16
Elimination of Counter-revolutionaries (*Sufan*), 85, 86, 120, 123

Ganzhou, 38
Germany, 15, 16, 230
  Ministerium für Staatssicherheit (MfS), 3–4, 63, 98
Guangdong, 226
Guomindang Central Statistics Bureau (Zhongtong), 21, 35, 75, 77
Guomindang Military Statistics Bureau (Juntong), 35, 159, 169, 172
Guomindang Sanminzhuyi Youth Corps, 77, 102, 109, 115, 162, 183

Harbin, 5, 80–82, 156, 164, 166
Harbin Forestry College, 191–200
Harbin No. 1 Medical School, 130–151
Harbin Public Security Bureau (PSB), 106, 159, 162, 177, 201, 206
  Cultural Protection Division, 130–151, 177–185, 191–200, 207–208
  Economic Protection Division, 74, 101–107
  Political Protection Division, 108–118, 119–129, 159–161, 169–171, 172–175, 177, 201–205, 206–207, 208
He Xia, 19–30, 155
Hebei, 39–41
Heilongjiang, 74, 83, 92–94
Hejiang, 76
Hennessy, Peter, xii
Hobsbawm, Eric, xiii, xiv
Hong Kong, 74, 75, 77, 81, 82, 173
Hoover, J. Edgar, xi, 15, 64, 98
Hughes, R. Gerald, 189
Hundred Flowers Campaign, 172

Indonesia, 46
Inner Mongolia, 58, 83–89
Italy, 102

Japan, 5, 28, 80, 115, 214, 230
Jiang Qing, 137
Jiangxi, 37–38, 213

Jiao Yulu, 142
Jilin, 115
Jinggangshan, 149

Kalinin, Mikhail, 43
Kent, Sherman, 16
Keshan, 111
Khrushchev, Nikita, 135, 141, 198
Kingly Way Academy, 110
Korea, 28, 102, 107, 118

le Carré, John, 3, 63
Lectures on the Subject of Agent Work, xi, 42
Legion of Mary, 215
Li Dazhao, 140
Liaoning, 74, 75–80, 83, 172
Lin Biao, 228
Liu Shaoqi, 214, 220
Luo Ruiqing, 31–33, 35, 36, 44, 91, 214

Ma Jingzheng, 5–12
Malaya, 46
Manchukuo, 110, 115, 141, 159
Mao Zedong, 135, 138, 140, 225
Mao Zedong Thought, 50, 133, 134, 141, 149, 223, 224, 230, 235
Matusow, Harvey, 43
Mitrokhin, Vasiliy, ix
Moran, Christopher, 4
Mudanjiang, 6

Orwell, George, 212

Pakistan, 36
Pan Fusheng, 133
Peng Zhen, 214
People's Daily, 134
Pingxiang, 38

Qiqihar, 11

Reference News, 183
Rumsfeld, Donald, 189

Scott, Len, 189
Shandong, 76
Shaoshan, 149
Shenyang, 6, 80, 167, 201, 204–205
Shenyang Public Security Bureau (PSB), 19–30, 34–36, 67–73, 90–91, 223

Shijiazhuang, 214
Socialist Education (Five Antis) Movement, 143, 191, 196
Songjiang, 5, 76
Soviet Union, 15, 16, 106, 137, 141
  KGB (Komitet Gosudarstvennoi Bezopastnosti), xi, 42–59, 97, 98, 155, 156, 172
  Red Army, 5, 111
Sun Lianzhong, 214
Suppression of Counter-revolutionaries Campaign, 77, 78, 79, 182
Sweden, 15, 63, 155, 211

Taiwan, 57, 115, 173
Thailand, 46
Tianhe, 38
Tianjin, 76, 78, 119–125, 126, 127
Tibet, 58
Tonghe, 146

Ukraine, 57
United Kingdom, ix, xii, 4, 98
  Secret Intelligence Service (SIS), x
  Security Service (MI5), x, xii
United States, ix, xi, 107, 107, 111, 118, 159, 220, 230
  Central Intelligence Agency (CIA), x, xiii, xiv, 16, 64
  Communist Party (CPUSA), 43
  Federal Bureau of Investigation (FBI), xi, 43, 63, 64, 97, 98, 155, 211

Wang Yaoguang, 5–12
White, Hayden, xiii
Wilson, Edward O., 212
Winks, Robert W., 4
Wu Shuyun, 47

Xinjiang, 36–37
Xinyang, 110

Yan'an, 149
Yiguandao, 35
Yunnan, 213

Zhao Minqiang, 7–10
Zhejiang, 217–222
Zhou Enlai, 198, 226, 227–228, 230

For EU product safety concerns, contact us at Calle de José Abascal, 56–1°, 28003 Madrid, Spain or eugpsr@cambridge.org.

www.ingramcontent.com/pod-product-compliance
Ingram Content Group UK Ltd.
Pitfield, Milton Keynes, MK11 3LW, UK
UKHW022139240226
468380UK00018B/386